BE

GW00579058

Feargal Cochrane is Professor Emeritus and Senior Research Fellow at the Conflict Analysis Research Centre, University of Kent. He was born and grew up in Belfast, and is the author of twelve books including *Northern Ireland: The Fragile Peace*.

Further praise for *Belfast*:

'Tells the rich and complex history of the city, the qualities of which are often overlooked amid a focus on sectarianism and violence.'
John Manley, *Irish News*

'Commendable ... Shows that Belfast is interesting and beautiful.'
Malachi O'Doherty, *Literary Review*

'In this book there is more than a vague hope that Belfast can be an intellectual and cultural powerhouse that drives respectful, democratic debate and guide a love-filled future.'
Mary McAleese, President of Ireland 1997–2011

'This work is a heartfelt and thorough testament to the fact that Belfast is more than the violence which has taken place within it. An exciting and inspirational read which made me fall in love again with my home city.'
Marisa McGlinchey, author of *Unfinished Business*

'A fine piece of work. This book reaches back to a personal, social and political history of Belfast but also looks around and ahead to encapsulate the rich cultural heritage and the hopes and dreams of the city.'
Joanne Murphy, author of *Management and War*

BELFAST

THE STORY OF A CITY AND ITS PEOPLE

FEARGAL COCHRANE

YALE UNIVERSITY PRESS
NEW HAVEN AND LONDON

First published in paperback in 2024

For information about this and other Yale University Press publications, please contact:
U.S. Office: sales.press@yale.edu   yalebooks.com
Europe Office: sales@yaleup.co.uk   yalebooks.co.uk

Set in Adobe Garamond Pro by IDSUK (DataConnection) Ltd
Printed in Great Britain by Clays Ltd, Elcograf S.p.A

Library of Congress Control Number: 2024932149

ISBN 978-0-300-26444-9 (hbk)
ISBN 978-0-300-27867-5 (pbk)

A catalogue record for this book is available from the British Library.

10 9 8 7 6 5 4 3 2 1

To Belfast – and its people

CONTENTS

LIST OF ILLUSTRATIONS

the Records, the Public Record Office of Northern Ireland and the National Museums of Northern Ireland, D1403_2/059/A.

11. Ulster Day: covenants ready for signing in Belfast City Hall, R. Welch, 1912. The Deputy Keeper of the Records, the Public Record Office of Northern Ireland and the National Museums of Northern Ireland, D1403_2/060/A.

12. Workers by the RMS *Titanic* shortly before its launch, 1911. Photo 12 / Getty Images.

13. RMS *Titanic*, R. Welch, 1912. The Deputy Keeper of the Records, the Public Record Office of Northern Ireland and the National Museums of Northern Ireland, D1403_2/029/A.

14. Army observation post, Bridge End, Belfast, 27 September 1969. The Deputy Keeper of the Records, the Public Record Office of Northern Ireland and the National Museums of Northern Ireland, A/7/1515.

15. Extensive bomb damage, Royal Avenue, Belfast, 1974. The Deputy Keeper of the Records, the Public Record Office of Northern Ireland, INF/7/A/7/53.

16. Royal Avenue from the City Hall, 1971. Northern Ireland Government Information Service. The Deputy Keeper of the Records, the Public Record Office of Northern Ireland, INF/7/A/17/87.

17. River Lagan, Belfast, 1971. Northern Ireland Government Information Service. The Deputy Keeper of the Records, the Public Record Office of Northern Ireland, INF/7/A/17/87.

18. Belfast City Hall, 13 August 2017. Giorgio Galeotti / CC-BY-SA 4.0.

19. Parliament Buildings. maddock1238 from Pixabay.

20. *Belfast Romances* mural, Leo Boyd. Author's own.

21. Samson and Goliath cranes, Harland and Wolff shipyard. Angela from Pixabay.

22. Titanic Belfast. Author's own.

23. King Charles III meeting Michelle O'Neill and Alex Maskey during the events around Queen Elizabeth II's funeral, September 2022. Niall Carson / Getty Images.

24. The Assembly Rooms. Author's own.

ACKNOWLEDGEMENTS

This has been a very personal book to write. Like all good ideas it began as a conversation, about how Belfast has changed over time from being internationally notorious as a location for violent political conflict reaching a point where its reputation has become much more positive. The peace process of the 1990s and the establishment of political institutions has certainly helped the city to rebrand itself as being a great place to visit, though obviously this remains something of a work in progress. However, the fact that Belfast was able to make a credible bid in 2017 (along with Derry and Strabane) to become the European Capital of Culture in 2023 showed how far it had come since the Troubles era. While the UK's departure from the European Union led to the abandonment of this application, it convinced me that it was time to take a fresh look at the history of Belfast and the way in which its unique past has shaped the region and those who live there.

The book has taken over two years to complete, and I owe a debt of gratitude to a number of people who have helped me along the way – first and foremost my wonderful editor at Yale, Jo Godfrey, who convinced me to take the project on and guided it skilfully through to completion. Rachael Lonsdale, Lucy Buchan and Katie Urquhart at Yale provided clarity and guidance throughout the production process, while copyeditor Rachel Bridgewater brought a fine eye for detail to the text.

I would especially like to thank those who spoke to me about some of the core themes within the book and who allowed me to participate in some of the political and historical tours of the city. In particular I want to thank Dr Paul Mullan, Northern Ireland Director of the National Lottery Heritage Fund, Paul Donnelly and Mark Wylie from DC Tours in Belfast and Seán

Napier from the 1798 Walking Tour. I learned a huge amount from everyone I talked to during the writing process and can certainly say that I know a lot more about Belfast now than when I began writing the book.

I would also like to thank poet and songwriter Steafán Hanvey for permission to use a quotation from his wonderful poem 'Carson-Parson' and his publisher Merrion Press-Irish Academic Press for extending the copyright permission for the use of the quotation. I am also indebted to Steafán for jogging my memory about a particular incident that occurred in a Canterbury pub, recalling it more accurately than I could, and for reassuring me that it wasn't a figment of my overactive imagination.

I am blessed to have some great academic friends and colleagues, many of whom have helped to shape my thinking about the main arguments in the book. I wrote most of the manuscript after taking early retirement from the University of Kent, and had I not done so I certainly would not have had the time to take on this project. While I have joined the ranks of Professors Emeriti I retain valuable research and social connections with colleagues in the Conflict Analysis Research Centre (CARC) and the School of Politics and International Relations as a Senior Research Fellow of CARC. The school and CARC provided me with very generous financial assistance to help undertake research fieldwork in Belfast in February 2022, and I would like to express my thanks for the support that was provided. The invitation to take part in the school's research seminar series in December 2022 to discuss the main themes in the book was also greatly appreciated and helped me to refine some of the arguments before final submission of the manuscript.

I would like to thank the Head of the School of Politics and International Relations, Dr Nadine Ansorg, Professor Neophytos Loizides, my successor as Director of CARC, and Dr Edward Morgan-Jones for their friendship and collegiality during the writing process. During the last four years I have been fortunate to have worked in CARC with Professor Neo Loizides, Dr Edward Morgan-Jones and Dr Laura Sudulich (University of Essex) on a project funded by the United States Institute for Peace (USIP) that focuses on citizen preferences in the design of effective peace settlements. This project developed a pioneering conjoint methodology, applied to political opinions, that helped to shape my thinking about Belfast's possible political future. This has been an amazingly rich research collaboration, and several of the themes and arguments at the centre of this book emanate directly from that project. I would like to thank my three collaborators for their patience when discussing the complex methodology with me, and I am grateful to the USIP also for funding the research of which this is in part a product. This has led to another hugely beneficial research collaboration, *Citizen Inclusion in Power-Sharing Settlements* INCLUSIVEPEACE, funded by the Seventh Round of Open Research Area (ORA) for the Social Sciences along with other funding agencies and led by Professor Neophytos Loizides at Kent and Professor Allison McCulloch at Brandon University in Canada. I would like to thank Neo, Allison and ORA7 for their generosity in including me in this project as a co-investigator and for the support provided in the publication of this book.

I would also like to thank my family, who lived through many of the experiences related in the book and who helped me to dredge some memories back to the surface. My parents, Roisin and Gerry Cochrane, have always provided a sounding board when I went 'home', and they showed great stoicism in the face of my constant attempts to interview them at family gatherings about experiences from the 1970s. My brother Niall, who is two years older than me, was also a ready supplier of recollections from childhood, and I would like to thank him and my sister-in-law Geraldine Cochrane for all the conversations about the book and growing up in Belfast. My friends Greg and Kathie Irwin, Donald and Deborah McWhirter and Dr Alison Montgomery have also been a great support and sounding board during the writing process, and I am indebted to them for the advice they have provided. My partner Professor Rosaleen Duffy and my son Oisín have shown heroic patience and forbearance as this book has gestated over the last two years, and they have my undying love and gratitude.

Finally – though less romantically – I would like to thank the two anonymous reviewers who provided feedback on both the initial proposal and the finished manuscript and who helped me to think about the structure,

ACKNOWLEDGEMENTS

accuracy and cohesion of the narrative. These reports went beyond the call of duty in terms of the eye for detail and expertise provided, so I am immensely grateful for the work that was put into them. Obviously, despite all of the help that I have received, the usual caveat applies, and all errors of fact and interpretation lie solely with myself.

PREFACE

One of my earliest memories is of playing with a Tommy gun in the back garden. At the age of four, it was my favourite toy by some distance. Ironically, given that I would end up becoming a professor of international conflict analysis and spending a thirty-year academic career based in the peace studies discipline, I was very keen on guns as a child. As ever, context is everything, and it wasn't just any gun, it wasn't just any garden and it wasn't just any time. The gun in question was a pretty convincing piece of kit – at least I thought so – and I can still picture it to this day. One of its best features was a circular bullet chamber with a red light underneath that flashed when you pulled the trigger and a rasping rapid fire setting that could be heard right down to the bottom of my family's long back garden. Later in life I saw old cine film footage of me doing military-style manoeuvres, jumping off the patio and rolling into a sniper position while letting off a few rounds at some unsuspecting wood pigeons.

My garden was in East Belfast off the Holywood Road, and it would have been the summer of 1969. It was a beautiful garden – enclosed and mature, with an incredible lawn that led to a 1960s-built bungalow. My father, an architect and all-round engineering genius, had built the house with his own hands six months before he got married, on land that had been rented from the estate of Gustav Wolff (the Wolff of Harland and Wolff), whose former mansion was next door over a massive laurel hedge. The owners when we lived there kept the little red wolf on the roof of their summer house in the garden as a reminder of the previous famous resident.

One day back in the summer of 1969 my mum and dad sat me down and told me that my beloved gun would have to go back to the shop to get fixed because the light was malfunctioning. This seemed odd to my four-year-old brain, as I could see no dip in its performance that required attention – but I trusted them, as any young child would.

It never fired again – at least not by my hand. This was the summer that the British Army arrived on the streets of Belfast, with armed patrols looking for paramilitaries and quickly transforming from peacekeepers to law enforcers. There were real Thompson sub-machine guns in Belfast that year as the Official Irish Republican Army (IRA) and what would become the Provisional IRA tooled up for war with loyalist paramilitaries and the British state. Unionist law, including curfews and internment without trial, was enforced in large part against the Catholic population by the British Army during these years, until the murder[1] of fourteen unarmed civilians by the Parachute Regiment at a civil rights march in Derry in January 1972 on 'Bloody Sunday' forced the UK government to take back political responsibility for the region. Shooting stopped being child's play when the adults in Belfast started firing live bullets at real people.

Years later, while researching this book, I brought up the story of the missing gun with my parents and asked why it had never come back from the workshop – had it really been badly damaged? They confirmed that there had been nothing wrong with it but they had taken it off me because people outside the protective bubble of my own home were being shot dead by real guns and the last thing they or anyone else needed was the sight or sound of another gun – even a toy one brandished by a pint-sized wannabe sniper.

From 1969 onwards real guns became part of everyday life in Belfast as the police became increasingly militarised and the army were on the streets patrolling, with rifles poking out of their armoured vehicles, or on foot, with their hands on their weapons ready for action.

I lived in East Belfast for the first sixteen years of my life, before the family relocated to Loughinisland in County Down as life became more difficult in the late 1970s. I then returned to Belfast as a student and lived and socialised in the university area as my academic career progressed, before leaving for a job at Lancaster University in 1998 in my early thirties. This personal context is important because how you experience violent conflict in a divided society is highly dependent on your position within it, your age, your class, your gender and, in the case of Belfast in the 1970s, your religion and your location in the city.

Being a Catholic living in a predominantly Protestant part of the city afforded me a different experience to that of a Catholic living in a mainly Catholic part of the city. By the early 1970s, after their initial efforts at peacekeeping had disintegrated into coercive enforcement, the British Army had effectively decided that Catholics were the enemy and that Protestants were the lesser of two evils. The majority of engagements between soldiers, police and armed republicans were in other parts of the city such as North and West Belfast, where the Catholic nationalist community was much larger than it was in the east of the city. There were, of course, loyalist paramilitaries in East Belfast, but the army and police were less concerned about their activities (and in some cases they turned a blind eye or colluded with them). To put it in simple terms, the army thought my area was Protestant and loyalist, and they were trying to round up Catholics and republicans. Also, for the average squaddie I did encounter who was not *au fait* with the sectarian patchwork quilt of school uniforms that cast us all as being one religion or another, I looked just like any other Protestant kid in the area.

As a result, my relationship with the army during my childhood was standoffish rather than overtly antagonistic, and while it was scary to see a soldier pointing a rifle at you out of an army Saracen while you walked down the street, there were also more positive interactions. On one occasion, when my bike broke down on my way home from playing football at Stormont and my friends continued on home leaving me to my fate, I was stopped by the military police 'red caps'.[2] I would have been around nine years old at the time and was probably feeling very sorry for myself and uttering whatever few swear words I knew. However, after I explained my plight to the soldiers, the two 'Brits' put my bike in the boot of their car and drove me home. The astonishment of my mates who saw me being chauffeured to my front door was only surpassed by the look on my mother's face when she opened it to the sight of me and my broken-down bike flanked by the two red caps, who explained their rescue mission.

The way in which you experience a violent conflict does not just depend on who you are and where you live, it is also contingent on how you are perceived by those around you, not least your neighbours. In 1970s Belfast, there was a world of difference between playing in your street and playing in someone else's street. As a child living through an emerging low-level armed conflict, the difference became most palpable when you got a bicycle. That might sound unlikely to readers who have only lived in relatively peaceful societies – but getting your first bike as a child allows you to range more widely and more quickly across your physical geography. Streets that would have been beyond your reach on foot become attainable (and sometimes desirable) once you have 'wheels'. This also takes you further away from the protective bubble of your home and the network of neighbours who know you.

The street I lived on growing up was mainly Protestant, but there were other Catholics living there as well as us, and it was safe and friendly. We knew our neighbours and they knew us, though as we got older, bigger and louder, sometimes those relations became a little strained – such as when our football smashed through our neighbour's hedge for the millionth time. My gang of friends was either out on the street playing or in and out of one another's houses. In the summer holidays as primary school kids, our mates knocked on our door for us to come out to play and we knocked on theirs. There was no such thing as arranged playdates, as everyone knew that lunch was at 1 pm, dinner was at 5 pm and bedtime was (depending on the time of year) 8 pm or 9 pm, and woe betide you if you were not home before dark. Other than that, we were given free rein, and the street was our playground for football, kerbsy, riding our bikes or just hanging around the 'Boulie' (the Boulevard, our local newsagent). It was a cocoon, of course, beyond which bombs were going off and people were being killed on a daily basis, and once you left the street, a starker experience awaited.

One of my first memories of political conflict came in the early summer of 1974, when I was nine years old. I was cycling around my street when I went off-piste, presumably because I had heard the noise or my neighbours talking about trouble down the road. Off I went on my bicycle, out of my street, onto the 'Mainie' (as we imaginatively referred to the main road) and about half a mile down the Holywood Road, where I was surprised to see a home-made barricade of old furniture being erected and gruff-looking men with impressive facial hair and flared trousers standing around it. I don't remember any police or army being there, but if they were they were keeping a low profile. Curious to know more, I pedalled my way closer and asked one of the men what they were doing. 'What does it look like we're doing, wee lad,' came the response, 'clear off if you don't want yer bike put on our barricade'. My curiosity satisfied, and concerned that my wheels would be impounded, I left them to it, pedalled home and wondered what was going on 'out there'.

What was going on politically at the time was that a devolved 'power-sharing executive' had been established between moderate unionists and nationalists after months of negotiation between the main political parties and the British government. The more radical unionist politicians, along with militant trade unionists and loyalist paramilitaries such as the Ulster Defence Association (UDA), had combined as the Ulster Workers' Council (UWC) to bring it down. They announced a 'constitutional stoppage', a show of force at street level, with local UDA units and their wider support bases erecting street barricades to enforce the strike and symbolically demonstrate that they, rather than the power-sharing executive at Stormont, were in political control.

Barricades and roadblocks were part of everyday life in the 1970s, while army checkpoints became a semi-permanent reality as they attempted to prevent bomb attacks in the centre of the city. As I got older I got used to being stopped by the army and the police and asked for personal information: where did I live, why was I in the area, where was I going, why was I going there? The adults spoke of little else than the emergent violence taking place outside the house, while the media provided a daily blow-by-blow account of deaths, injuries, explosions and bomb scares in the city. New phrases became clichéd or contested in a daily diet of menace in the early 1970s as politics failed and local politicians could not agree to disagree. The phrase 'suspect device' became so ever-present that Belfast punk band Stiff Little Fingers wrote a song of the same name in 1978.

While this might sound a bit downbeat – depressing even – I had a wonderfully happy childhood, and while Belfast in the early 1970s might have looked grotesque from the outside, it was my normality and I adapted to it. I had both Protestant and Catholic friends as a child and thought nothing of it. However, that changed once I went to secondary school, as, due to the nearly complete religious segregation of schooling, our school uniform effectively branded us as either Catholics or Protestants and thus as potential targets for sectarian attack. Once, when my brother Niall and I were standing waiting for the school bus on the Holywood Road, he was punched in the face by another teenager who was riding down the road in a milk float. Our school uniform was sufficient incitement for this unprovoked act of violence, and seeing it they stopped the float, got out, smashed my brother in the face and then continued with their milk deliveries.

Such was the day-to-day reality for teenagers everywhere in Belfast during the 1970s – assuming the daily bomb scares allowed you to travel to school in the first place. Certainly, as you got older it became less possible to avoid being caught up in the sectarian vortex. For me this led to an incremental but inexorable slide into a more uncertain physical environment, because while religion and politics were never a barrier with my friends in our street, it was a different matter when I met their friends in their streets. They had bikes, too, and when they visited our street or I was drawn onto theirs, an invisible charade would commence. We knew enough by the time we were ten or eleven to understand that our names and our school uniforms were dead giveaways of our religion. So I was always Fergie, never Feargal (an Irish Gaelic name that is transparently Catholic, while the former could be short for Fergus as a first name, and potentially Protestant or Catholic). This is a banal example of the everyday precautions you took living where I did in the early 1970s, and I thought little of it. Fergie became a convenient nickname and in any case was preferable to any of the other more graphic options that I was offered by my school friends.

We all learned to follow a series of unwritten rules in order not to give too much away about who we were or where we lived. It convinced me at an early age that politics was not confined to the formal sphere of institutions or elected politicians but was being played out on the streets of Belfast along with discussions about democratic legitimacy, self-determination, freedom, justice and 'law and order'. These debates were much more interesting and relevant to me as a child than learning how to multiply fractions, do simultaneous equations or work out how to conjugate verbs in Latin – and my education took place as much outside school as it did within it. I developed a critical perspective towards the world around me long before I found out that universities liked that sort of thing. I questioned the notion of 'security forces' that seemed more interested in securing other people than me or people like me. I learned to question issues of authority and legitimacy up to and including the state itself. I learned that the law was not neutral; it was political and took sides.

In truth, we are all moulded by our environments in terms of our cultural and political identities, and Belfast certainly left an indelible imprint on me and most of those around me. Politics, history and culture were absorbed rather than learned, and sectarian violence was a relatively normal part of life rather than an abstract concept learned at school. A conflict mindset was branded into me in my formative years, which bred a sense of scepticism, and without it I doubt that I would have developed such an interest in politics or in conflict research in my adulthood. I am certain that had I not grown up in Belfast during the 1970s I would not have become an academic with a fascination about the politics of divided societies and that I would not be writing this book now about my home city. The other catalyst for writing the book was that I felt the time was right to do so. Having spent most of my childhood growing up in a city that was defined by violence, I felt that Belfast deserved a closer look, both to contextualise its divisions and to show that there is now a much more positive side to the story.

So the book is a love letter of sorts – but written from the perspective of someone who is repeatedly vexed by the relationship, aware of the shortcomings of the city, yet simultaneously welded emotionally to the place that will always be home.

The book is dedicated to Belfast and everyone who lives there – or used to. It's a warts-and-all story, but our warts are smaller now than they used to be, and on closer inspection there is a beauty there to be appreciated. The city can face the twenty-first century in hope rather than trepidation, with a sense of collective pride about where it has come from and confidence about where it is going.

INTRODUCTION

This book reveals the history of Belfast, a village that became a town that became a city. The story about why and how it made this journey is one of dazzling achievement perforated by heart-breaking failure, a combination of triumph and tragedy that has produced a unique and radical identity. Belfast is a city of stunning beauty and cultural vitality which has been disfigured by generations of division, hatred and conflict. It is also the place I still call home despite having left it a quarter of a century ago. My aim here is not to provide a comprehensive 'neutral' history of the city, stripped of overt judgements or conclusions. No histories are neutral – especially those that claim they are – as what we deem worthy of recording, and the interpretation we put on that, is just as much a political and cultural act as what we do not select or include. In this sense it is *my* story of the city, my personal reflection and assessment of the place where I was born and spent the first three decades of my life at a point when the city literally exploded into violence.

It is a rags-to-riches-and-back-again tale of a town that became a city on the back of textile manufacturing and the industrial revolution. Nestled on the north-eastern edge of the island of Ireland, Belfast presents a jumble of contradictions, with a generosity of spirit sitting alongside more squalid religious, political and cultural divisions. It is a city that was divided and at war with itself but simultaneously energised those who lived there into producing a vibrant intellectual, architectural and cultural inheritance for those who came after. It is a city that in the later twentieth century became internationally recognised as a site of sectarian hatred and religious intolerance, but transitioned into a model for peacebuilding in the twenty-first, as swords were clumsily hammered into ploughshares.

1

Two interrelated arguments lie at the centre of the book. The first is that while Belfast has a reputation for political instability and violence, the roots of this go much further back than the period in the late twentieth century known as the Troubles. The argument here is that these traits have structural causes that go back multiple generations and have shaped the economy, culture and political character of the city.

One of the main purposes of the book is to dispel the idea that political instability and violence in Belfast were simply the result of unreasonable people doing unreasonable things to each other, or that they consumed the entire existence of those who lived there. From an early age I resented how Belfast was stereotyped as a place apart, an aberration even, whose residents were stuck in a seventeenth-century religious time warp and doing their level best to fight their way further into it. It was *normal to me* and there was so much more to the city than the one-dimensional focus on sectarian conflict portrayed by the British and international media.

Certainly, some people did unreasonable things – unspeakable things, even – but that was not because of some geographically specific psychosis, theological intolerance or primordial defect; rather, it was in large part because of the political, economic and cultural circumstances that surrounded them. This does not diminish the fact that some people chose to be violent and others did not, or seek to evade the personal responsibility that everyone in Belfast had for their actions. It is simply to argue that Belfast was a normal city warped out of shape by events and structures within which political ideologies and behaviours developed. Some of these were relatively sudden, such as the arrival of partition in 1921, the deployment of the British Army in 1969 and arrival of policies such as internment without trial in 1971, the prorogation of the Stormont parliament in 1972 or the Brexit referendum in 2016. Others were more incremental, such as the cumulative rise of nationalist grievances between 1921 and 1972 over electoral malpractice and discrimination.

While they are often seen as a post-1968 phenomenon, in reality Belfast has had Troubles since partition in 1921, and arguably well before the twentieth century. It is a barely one-dimensional outlook that views Belfast as exploding into sectarian violence in the late 1960s, as this phase was a continuation of divisions and tensions that had existed over many previous generations. I have spent my thirty-year professional career as a university academic attempting to add the other two dimensions to the perception of Belfast as a city of 'intractable violence', where conflict was regarded as a sad inevitability.

The second argument in the book is that, partly in response to the previous point, Belfast has always had a radical edge which has both driven it forwards and, paradoxically, held it back. There is a direct bluntness, an iconoclastic stoicism – some might see it as a type of bloody-mindedness that can be traced over generations and centuries, from the Belfast Presbyterian liberal radicals in the eighteenth century to less liberal political perspectives in the twenty-first century. Having a radical edge does not always lead to progressive urges or a quiet life, but it does lend itself to a colourful political history, and Belfast certainly possesses that.

Geographically, Belfast sits in a bowl between the Irish Sea on one side and Cave Hill on the other, like a crucible, which partly explains why it rains a lot, as cloud can hang stubbornly over the city. For anyone who took chemistry in secondary school, a crucible is a good way of picturing Belfast, because periodically, over several centuries, Bunsen burners have been lit underneath it in a way that has caused its contents to heat up, become unstable and boil over. The point here is that external forces over the generations – such as the Protestant Reformation in the sixteenth century, the plantation of Ulster in the seventeenth century, the French Revolution and American War of Independence in the eighteenth century, the Home Rule crisis in the nineteenth century, the partition of Ireland by Britain in the twentieth century, and Brexit in the twenty-first century – have all helped to shape attitudes and behaviour in the city.

The argument here does not deny that Belfast was and remains a deeply divided city, violently so between 1969 and 1994, or that those who lived there still had a choice about whether they contributed to violence and instability regardless of their political and economic circumstances. Instead, it seeks to explain that these endemic divisions are one dimension of a much more complex set of political, economic and cultural forces that have shaped the region over several centuries.

The Troubles era that provided Belfast with a degree of global notoriety did not emerge from the ether like a political version of the Higgs boson particle, unilaterally sparking off violent events and providing mass for the emergence of sectarian hostility. The Troubles was the symptom of a broken political system, not the cause of it. When the question is posed about why people in Belfast are so politically stubborn, or so insecure about their political identity, or so mistrustful of one another or of political initiatives coming from Britain, Ireland or the European Union, the answer is often because experience has driven them into those positions.

Fascinating, infuriating, exhilarating, Belfast has seen the best of times as well as the worst since it was formally inaugurated as a town in 1613, but in order to understand both its accomplishments and its misfortunes, we first need to understand its history.

A brief historical overview provides an indication of the radical changes that took place as Belfast grew from a village into a town and eventually a city and the scale of human triumph and tragedy that accompanied that journey. It is known that people have lived in the area since Neolithic times, as the Giant's Ring on the outskirts of Belfast and McArt's Fort on Cave Hill which overlooks it provide archaeological evidence that people have been living there for at least 5,000 years. Sir Arthur Chichester's development of Belfast as a strategic base for English control after he was appointed Lord Deputy in 1605 led to the granting of borough status in 1613. This was crucial for establishing the growing town as a hub for administrative development, which led to further investment and growth. Borough status also entitled Belfast to return two MPs to the Dublin parliament (appointed of course by the Lord Deputy to do his bidding) but further emphasised Belfast as an important centre of power. By 1700 the population of Belfast was around 5,000, the majority of whom were Presbyterians and Episcopalian Church of Ireland Protestants. In 1737 the *Belfast News Letter* was established by Francis Joy, and it is still published to the present day, making it the oldest English-language newspaper still in production in the world.

The mid-1770s witnessed the peak of Presbyterian emigration to America, as a result of their political discrimination at the hands of the Church of Ireland, which dominated the Dublin parliament. By the end of the 1700s more than 200,000 Presbyterians had departed for the New World from Ulster in search of better fortunes, and many of them fought in the American War of Independence against the English Crown. During the 1780s the Presbyterians became increasingly economically successful but remained excluded from political influence by Anglicans in the Church of Ireland. As a result, this highly educated, increasingly wealthy but politically discriminated-against community in Belfast began to discuss their situation and look for alternatives. They became increasingly radical during the 1780s in their commitment to self-government from England, and while there were inevitable splits in the movement, a core group of Belfast radicals linked up with allies in Dublin including Wolfe Tone to pursue militant revolutionary separatism. The *Northern Star* newspaper was established in 1792 and became one of the leading publications in Belfast, promoting the ideals of the newly formed Society of United Irishmen.

This group were inspired by the French Revolution and the philosophical ideas of John Locke and Thomas Paine, along with a commitment to liberal democratic principles. This culminated in the 1798 Rebellion, an insurrection against the English Crown in Ireland that was doomed before it had begun, as the rebels were by that point hopelessly split. Before the 1798 Rebellion took place, the British government had brought in some reforms, including raising the level of the grant given to the Presbyterian clergy. This thinly veiled bribe convinced some Presbyterians to move away from the radical agenda of the United Irishmen and those who could not be bought off were repressed before and after the insurrection took place. As a result, the radical sentiment had waned in Belfast by 1798 as many Presbyterians shied away from violence and accepted the limited reforms introduced by the government. They were also chastened by the realities of armed Catholic rebellion and sectarian attacks against Protestants who got in their way.

Following the Act of Union in 1801 and other legal and political reforms, the Presbyterians and Anglicans in the Church of Ireland became more politically, economically and socially aligned, and energy went into commerce and industry, rather than insurrection. The cotton industry had taken off in Belfast by 1805, and a number of cotton mills were built over the next twenty years as production peaked and fortunes were made.

In 1823 the Belfast Gas Works was opened, signifying another major advance, with light being brought into the centre of the town, bringing more money, people and infrastructure with it. As the population expanded, so did social problems linked to poor quality housing, unemployment and disease. There were major typhus and cholera epidemics in Belfast in 1832 and between 1839 and 1841, which led to new workhouses, hospitals and graveyards being established. In 1845 Crumlin Road Gaol was opened, another indication of population expansion and the emergence of a more systematic criminal justice system. There were further outbreaks of typhus in 1847 and cholera in 1848 due to increased population density and poor sanitation.

By this point, linen had replaced cotton as the main focus of manufacturing, and from 1860 until the end of the nineteenth century Belfast became the linen capital of the world, earning the nickname of Linenopolis. In 1849 Queen Victoria and Prince Albert visited Belfast and Queen's University was opened, while in 1888 the town was finally granted city status by Queen Victoria in recognition of its importance and commercial success.

By the time Belfast had become a city, its political, economic and cultural divisions were well established and mapped easily onto the religious distinction between Protestants and Catholics. As a result, religious affiliation became an easy proxy for political and cultural identity and the establishment of a binary mentality within the city. As the nineteenth century ended and the twentieth began, the wider political debate over Home Rule for Ireland (limited self-government within the British Empire) was demarcated by Protestant/British/unionists who opposed it and Catholic/Irish/nationalists who supported it. The issue of Home Rule dominated political divisions in the city from the 1880s until the eventual partition of Ireland in 1921. Belfast then emerged as the centre of a new and contested political region known as Northern Ireland, which further enhanced its city status.

From 1921 until 1972 Northern Ireland was a devolved region within the UK with its own parliament in Belfast, where the majority Protestant/unionist community was able to dominate the minority Catholic/nationalist one. The political boundaries of Northern Ireland were deliberately drawn to ensure that unionists comfortably outnumbered nationalists and to guarantee political stability. However, while unionists were politically and economically dominant, nationalists' grievances surrounding their discrimination eventually boiled over with the emergence of a civil rights movement in the 1960s and the Troubles era from 1969 to 1994. Nationalists were treated as second-class citizens in what they saw as an illegitimate political regime and unionists oscillated between apathy and arrogance for the next half-century, while the British government was glad to be able to ignore the place entirely.

Like every other city, of course, Belfast has evolved and changed, its multiple stories turning history into heritage, terror into tourism, hatred into hope and back again. It is a city of complexity, of passionate intensity and often of depressing parochialism.

The starting point is that the city and those who live there have been moulded by their divided past, a fractured experience that has shaped the history, politics, geography and culture of the place and its people. Belfast is a city nested within a conflicted society, but with a more complex, radical and culturally rich heritage than the popular media caricature would suggest.[1] From the perspective of the external media, the focus on sectarian violence and political instability is understandable, as it finds symptoms of conflict such as violence much easier to cover than causes, such as generational discrimination or latent resentment. In this sense, Belfast is treated like everywhere else, where journalists will be mobilised to cover riots rather than reconciliation. However, the fact that Belfast is geographically and politically distant from the British 'mainland' has led to it being thought of as 'a place apart' by many of those who live in Great Britain.

Over the last century this became more pronounced, as Northern Ireland was created in 1921 and Belfast was designated as the capital city of this new 'country'. Northern Ireland is not a country in the formal sense, but it has suited many on both sides of the Irish Sea to think of it in such terms. We tend to use language loosely or in a colloquial manner which easily leads to the sort of imprecision that seems relatively minor but can have a major existential impact. To call Belfast the 'capital' of a 'country' is to legitimise the partition of Ireland and post-1921 arrangements that led to the creation of Northern Ireland, which some still regard as a 'bastard' statelet with no political legitimacy. This is certainly less the case in the twenty-first century than it was in the twentieth, but promotion of the idea that Belfast was the capital of a country helped to encourage the notion that it was less of a responsibility for politicians in London to govern those who lived there.

The establishment of a system of devolved government in 1921 with a distinct (if short-lived) proportional representation electoral system further set the region up as being politically distinct from the rest of the UK. The creation of its own bespoke criminal justice system with new emergency legislation such as the Special Powers Act, as well as the creation of the Royal Ulster Constabulary (RUC) and B Specials in the early 1920s, all set Northern Ireland and its capital Belfast at the exotic and slightly alarming fringe of the British 'imagined community'. The convention after 1921 that issues pertaining to the region were to be dealt with by the devolved government at Stormont and not raised in London in the House of Commons contributed to a cumulative ignorance in Britain (especially in the corridors of power) about what was happening in Belfast or Northern Ireland more generally. Out of sight was out of mind, and over several generations throughout the twentieth century, Belfast was pushed so far to the back of the consciousness in Britain that it seeped into the unconscious. Belfast was still considered British, of course – but perhaps more like the way that Gibraltar was than in the way that Guildford in England or even Glasgow in Scotland were. This collective ignorance was not especially malicious, but it was corrosive, as when violence exploded onto the streets of Belfast, Derry and other parts of Northern Ireland in the late 1960s and 1970s, little was known about the structural drivers that had led to it or even the physical geography of the region. This frustration concerning how little political engagement there was in London with events in Northern Ireland blew up in the House of Commons in 1972 when nationalist MP Bernadette Devlin crossed over to the government front bench and slapped then Home Secretary Reginald Maudling across the face. Devlin was incensed at her inability to speak in parliament about the Bloody Sunday massacre by the Parachute Regiment the previous day. It was a devolved matter that Stormont was responsible for and thus not for the attention of Westminster. Devlin spoke to the media afterwards and claimed that Maudling had made a derisory three-minute statement about the shootings in the House of Commons. Despite the fact that she was the only MP who had been in Derry the day before and had even been fired upon herself by the British Army, she was not allowed to speak about it in parliament. When asked by an English reporter if she intended to apologise to the Home Secretary for hitting him, her response suggested a disinclination: 'I'm just sorry I didn't get him by the throat.'[2] Maudling played the part of disdainful colonial governor with some aplomb, demanding of his underlings, 'bring me a large scotch, what a bloody awful country', as he left Belfast following his first visit as Home Secretary in 1970.

This arms-length unfamiliarity was summed up by English journalist Ed Pearce in the early 1990s when trying to communicate why English people were perplexed by the region.

> Do the British care about Northern Ireland? Are we alert to her nuances? Do we knowingly allude to Derry and the Six Counties or Londonderry and Ulster? Not so as you would notice . . . And, religion apart, we find Ireland one long piece of perplexity. . . . The feeling about the North is that it is like Yorkshire but less use and more trouble. . . . We can't cope with the hatred or the memories, or the art of making a life out of ever-lasting rage. It isn't quite sane.[3]

While it would be easy to write this off as a typical example of lofty English condescension towards the political and cultural periphery, or embellishment for effect of a less pronounced drifting apart, it is undeniable that this feeling exists at some level. As a city, Belfast is not viewed in Great Britain in the same way Birmingham is, and Northern Ireland is not synonymous with Norfolk or Northumbria. It is a place apart, and the violence and instability that has dominated media coverage of the region over the last half-century has only served to widen the existential distance between Belfast and Great Britain over the period. The same could also be said of the relationship between Dublin and Belfast after partition, and certainly during the Troubles era, when it felt like a lot more than 100 miles between the two cities.

At an anecdotal level, some years ago when I discussed conducting some research fieldwork in Belfast with a university I worked at in England (well after the 1994 ceasefires and the conclusion of the Good Friday Agreement in 1998), I was given a detailed risk assessment form by the institution.[4] They were worried about the legal and insurance implications of me going over to Belfast in a way that they were not for other UK cities. This was the result of a pervasive view within Great Britain (an opinion shared internationally) that Belfast was a wild frontier, a dangerous outpost of the Union where different rules applied than in the rest of the UK.[5] Belfast had obviously earned this reputation due to a generation of political violence from the late 1960s to the late 1990s – and there is no shying away from the destruction, brutality and pain that took place during this period. During the 1970s and 1980s, in particular, shootings, bombings and security alerts were an everyday reality for people living in the city, and it is not surprising that external observers have viewed Belfast through that lens. But ferocious though it undoubtedly was, it is important to contextualise and understand this violence. For the most part (with some notable exceptions such as Lenny Murphy's Shankill Butchers)[6] violence on all sides was rational, targeted and politically motivated. This is important for people from outside Northern Ireland to understand – such as journalists like Ed Pearce, who respond to their own exasperation by diagnosing insanity as an explanation for political disagreements over policies designed as much in London as they are in Belfast.

There was always the chance that 'outsiders' would get caught up in the violence, and scores of them (including many children) did, but for the most part they were not the targets of it and were at much less risk than those who lived in the city. The late Professor Frank Wright has written convincingly about the self-sustaining dynamics of politically motivated or ethnic violence and its creation of negative intercommunal spirals, as opposed to individualised acts of violence that have less connection at the community level.[7] To put this more simply, in intercommunal violence we are all linked to it in some way as either perpetrators or victims. It is either an attack by our community on another ethnic or religious group, or an attack by that section of the population on us, and it is understood in those terms by everyone who lives there. Thus, we are connected to it, either feeling some form of collective guilt over what our community has done to the other, or fearing reprisals on our own group due to the violence that our side has perpetrated. This type of violence is much more prone to self-sustaining spirals of tit-for-tat violence that maintains conflict in a closed sectarian loop than individualised acts of violence in more stable societies.

The violence of the 1970s and 1980s was undeniably awful in Belfast and is not shied away from in this book – nor, for that matter, are similar violent episodes from earlier in the twentieth century or the centuries before that avoided. However, reputations are notoriously slow to change, and the fact that Belfast today is no more dangerous in terms of violent crime than any other mid-sized city in Ireland or the UK has yet to penetrate public opinion as broadly as it perhaps should. One of the aims of this book, therefore, is to provide a more realistic understanding of Belfast today and how it has developed over time. The intention is to restore the city's reputation as a crucible of radicalism, democratic liberalism, industry, architectural innovation and cultural achievement.

One of the broader ideas at the core of the book is the belief that we can only understand events and people's behaviour by connecting them to their wider historical, political, economic and cultural context. This is based within an approach that emphasises the interconnections between the triggers of violence within deeply divided societies and the underlying political, economic and structural conditions that can help to produce it.[8]

In different ways, the chapters that follow explore how history, religion, conflict, violence, politics and culture bleed into one another and help to explain why people think the way they think and act the way they act. This includes examining the economic, political and cultural development of Belfast from its early foundation to the present day. It is worth reflecting on the fact that cities are where they are for a reason, and Belfast is no different to many others in having some strategic advantages over other areas. Its proximity to the sea on the one hand and a vigorous river system on the other, with major freshwater tributaries such as the Lagan, the Blackstaff and the Farset, were crucial for Belfast's early development and its expansion during the industrial revolution.

The Lagan and other rivers that run through Belfast provided its lifeblood and facilitated the growth of a mercantile class, as the cotton trade in the eighteenth century gave way to the linen industry in the nineteenth. The history of the Lagan itself shaped the political ecology[9] of Belfast, the port and the river facilitating the growth of the city and allowing raw materials to be easily transported, fuelling the expansion of commerce and industrial development.

The growth of trade and industry led inexorably to population expansion and competition for space and resources, and unsurprisingly some groups benefited more than others as the economy grew. As the town evolved and became a city, relationships within it crystallised around religion, class and rival economic interests. One of the most interesting and dynamic groups at the end of the eighteenth century that drove Belfast forward was the mercantile Presbyterian community, who embraced the liberal enlightenment and brought a radical social and political activism to the city that has left an indelible imprint to the present day.

The activities of radical campaigners led to the emergence of the Society of United Irishmen and the *Northern Star* newspaper, the main mouthpiece of the movement. In eighteenth-century Belfast, religious affiliation was intimately connected to political and economic interests as well as social background, rather than being simply an abstract or private theological practice. This was an exciting and tumultuous period, when Belfast became a crucible for European liberalism and social reform in the spirit of Thomas Paine. The formation of the United Irishmen in a Belfast pub and their commitment to political reform of the Irish parliament based on liberal principles of civil rights and religious liberty marked a dynamic period of political and cultural activity in Belfast. This was led, for the most part, by Presbyterians like Rev. William Drennan,[10] his sister Martha McTier, her husband Samuel McTier, Samuel Neilson, Henry Joy McCracken and his sister Mary Ann McCracken.[11] Mary Ann was a pioneering Presbyterian who wanted Irish independence and a social reformer who campaigned against Belfast's role in the slave trade.[12]

This was a formative era in the political and economic history of Belfast that remains relevant today, and several of the institutions established during this period (such as the Linen Hall Library and the *News Letter*) are still thriving more than 200 years later.

The development of the River Lagan to enhance commerce together with the expansion of the city into a global centre for the linen industry in the nineteenth century positioned Belfast to take advantage of the industrial revolution. Cotton and linen were in turn superseded by engineering and shipbuilding as key drivers of the city's economic success. The story of Belfast is inextricably linked to the evolution of Harland and Wolff shipyard – bloating the economy during war years, while being a site of friction during periods of economic decline. The boom-and-bust story of the shipyard, established in 1861, was emblematic of broader political, economic and religious tensions in Belfast that continue to plague the city to the present day. The shipyard presents a good metaphor for the connection between politics and religion and the way that these stretched the fabric of the city to breaking point in times of economic hardship.

During the 1850s and 1860s conservative clerics such as Henry Cooke preached a gospel of religious fundamentalism and intolerance in outdoor sermons that enraged the Catholic community and incited Protestant mobs. The shipyard workers found themselves on opposite sides of these inflammatory events, and having fought one another in the streets on Sundays, they had to go and work together on Mondays, which resulted in predictable friction and violence.

The Harland and Wolff shipyard has become synonymous with the city of Belfast, its two huge banana-yellow cranes an indispensable part of the urban landscape. The cranes have become part of the essential physical fabric and identity of the city and its iconic architecture. Unsurprisingly, in Belfast, as in many divided cities, the civic architecture goes beyond the bricks, mortar, glass and steel of the structures themselves. They are sites of cultural, political and historical significance, a point captured well by cultural commentators such as poet Tom Paulin. His poem 'A Partial State' reflects the feeling that the architecture itself seemed to be buckling and warping under the political pressure of the times. Parliament Buildings, for example, known more popularly as Stormont, is dripping with historical political and cultural significance. Opened in 1932 by Edward, Prince of Wales, the huge white building on top of a hill can be seen for miles across the city – which was in many ways the whole point. It was a physical marker that Northern Ireland was here and was here to stay. The devolved government ushered in nervously after partition in 1921 was making a public declaration through this enormous building that it was confident and (it thought) permanent. From its opening in 1932 the building became the embodiment of unionist political and cultural domination, with the magnificent statue of former leader of the Unionist Party Sir Edward Carson gesticulating defiantly at its foot. The building became the public manifestation of a divided community, with protest demonstrations by unionists (and occasionally nationalists) taking place there from the 1960s to the 1990s. In recent years Parliament Buildings has been the site of a power-sharing government between the two main communities, led by the Democratic Unionist Party and Sinn Féin and including the five largest parties in the region. While this has experienced some difficult moments and has collapsed on numerous occasions, it reflects the building's enduring relevance to the political, economic and cultural life of Belfast. The physical fabric of the city reflects the waves of economic development, political radicalism and liberal enlightenment of the eighteenth century, the rise of the linen industry and shipbuilding of the nineteenth century and the political polarisation of the twentieth century.

During the latter half of the twentieth century these buildings and the fabric of the city became engulfed in political instability and violent conflict during the period that is popularly known as the Troubles. From 1969 until 1999 Belfast metastasised into a heavily militarised city with steel gates and turnstiles protecting the centre of town and wire mesh cages encasing police stations, courthouses and even public houses. Army lookout posts were commonplace, wrapped in camouflage and sandbags, with military vehicles on the streets and army helicopters hovering semi-permanently overhead.

It is impossible to write about Belfast without confronting the Troubles themselves, their causes and consequences, but in doing so it is important to place the post-1969 period in its political, historical, economic and social context and consider why and how violence emerged. This locates the violent conflict that erupted in Belfast in the late 1960s as a continuance of, rather than a departure from, the city's divided past. We cannot understand the outbreak of violence in the late 1960s and the instability that endured for another generation without placing it within this wider context. The emergence of paramilitary organisations on both republican and loyalist sides was a direct consequence of a complex set of structural circumstances that preceded their arrival. The devolved government at Stormont had proved itself incapable of governing a divided community effectively, and the relationship between the Catholic nationalist minority and the Protestant unionist majority had calcified over several generations to the point that Belfast and the rest of the region was politically, economically, culturally and socially segmented into two communities rather than one. An arrogant but periodically insecure unionist majority governed a sullen and excluded nationalist minority, with the former confident they would win every election and the latter equally resigned to losing. The nationalist community had been excluded from political power since Northern Ireland was created in 1921, discriminated against in employment, denied public housing on the basis of their religion and harassed by the legal system.

The unionist administration at Stormont had no answer to nationalist complaints, either ignoring or repressing dissent, while the British government in London was barely even aware that nationalists were complaining about discrimination and maltreatment. However, nationalist grievances over political, religious and cultural discrimination and fair employment *were* legitimate. These festered for decades, but those in Belfast and London who were in a position to redress them preferred to muddle through and keep a lid on protests. Eventually, in the 1960s a civil rights movement emerged in Derry and in Belfast that sought to achieve political reforms based on peaceful direct action, modelled on the American civil rights movement that was seeking political change in the US. Unionist insecurity, denial and overreaction to these demands for reform led eventually to street rioting between nationalists, unionists and the security forces, the implosion of law and order and the deployment of the British Army onto the streets of Belfast and Derry in an attempt to restore stability. However, British security policies failed to make people feel secure and were frequently counter-productive, swelling the ranks of paramilitary organisations and increasing international support from Libya, the US and elsewhere for the aims and objectives of the IRA's 'armed struggle'. This brings us back to the fact that the army and politicians in London knew very little about Belfast or the rest of Northern Ireland when the Troubles erupted. They had remained wilfully ignorant and were therefore ill-prepared to reduce or mitigate the violence that was tearing Belfast and the rest of Northern Ireland apart.

From the late 1960s until the late 1990s Belfast became notorious as a city engulfed in political violence and sectarian hatred. Its undeclared war between militant republican and loyalist paramilitary groups, with the British Army and armed police not quite standing in the middle of it, led to over 3,500 deaths across Northern Ireland, and many more were injured and maimed. Eventually, by the 1990s, all sides had come to the reluctant conclusion that they could not win. This realisation developed slowly over time but led eventually to what became known as the peace process, a negotiated settlement in 1998 and the painstaking process of building post-conflict institutions based on power-sharing and cooperation for mutual benefit. This has involved the painful task of confronting and coming to terms with the complexities of living in a post-conflict environment and facing uncomfortable questions about ourselves and the society that we want to live in. The magnetic pull towards binary identities remains strong in Belfast and across Northern Ireland more broadly, evident at the seemingly endless elections to the Northern Ireland Assembly over the last quarter of a century. However, the passage of time and the arrival of local political institutions has allowed more complexity and nuance to enter political debate and provided space for people to agree to disagree without resorting to force. Dr Paul Mullan, Director of the National Lottery Heritage Fund in Northern Ireland, reflected on the importance of pluralism and complexity when considering the past based on the concept of agonistic memory, which creates a space in which people can disagree with one another without feeling diminished or threatened by the experience. 'The problem in society that we find ourselves in is whenever we take against people because they don't think like us. That is where the binary approach comes in.'[13]

For Mullan, the key is to 'complicate the narrative'[14] and put the complexity back into conversations surrounding who we are and where we have come from. However, this remains at best a work in progress, as binary understandings of the past have remained stubbornly resilient in Belfast and across Northern Ireland more broadly. Antagonistic memory rather than agonistic memory has been easier to find and is often to the fore in media coverage of Belfast in part because it fits with the dominant narrative of what is anticipated and expected from the city. There are, however, concrete examples of where the post-Good Friday Agreement institutions have joined other civic groups and community-driven initiatives to develop more pluralist thinking around political and cultural identity. One such case is provided by the Urban Villages Initiative, supported by the Northern Ireland Executive as part of its 'Together: Building a United Community' strategy. This is focused on promoting positive community identities and enhanced community capacity and improving the physical environment of the five Urban Villages so far identified, four of which are in Belfast and the fifth in Derry. The areas selected have a history of economic deprivation and community tension, and the Urban Villages initiative is focused on supporting sustainable change by coordinating multi-agency activities around the core objectives linked to the promotion of positive community identities. The emphasis here is very much centred on the opening of shared spaces, the promotion of pluralism and the avoidance of binary narratives that exclude members of the community. At a wider level, the Urban Villages activities are directed at promoting a sense of pride in the city and a feeling of belonging within safe, culturally diverse and inclusive communities.

Peacebuilding work is painstaking, usually incremental in terms of visible outcomes, and it takes time to have an impact. As W.B. Yeats put it in 'The Lake Isle of Innisfree', 'peace comes dropping slow', and while this classic poem was first published in 1890 it remains just as relevant in 2023. It can be difficult for slowly percolating peacebuilding activities to cut through in media coverage or within the public consciousness, but that does not diminish the fact that they are taking place and having some level of cumulative impact on society.

While Belfast has found it difficult to shake off its reputation as a city defined by intolerance, instability and sectarian violence, the agreement reached in the 1990s has allowed it to develop a post-conflict economy. Since the nineties turned into the noughties, Belfast has emerged like the metaphorical phoenix from the flames into a vibrant cultural space with an economy transformed from the years of violent instability that plagued the city over previous generations. While politically Northern Ireland remains dysfunctional and unstable, Belfast's post-Troubles economy is gradually reshaping the city, in terms of both its physical space and its external identity. This revitalisation is particularly noticeable through the new tourism economy in Belfast and how that collides with the legacy of its past. Belfast provides a fascinating example of both the opportunities and the sensitivities that accompany a society that is in the process of coming out of violent political conflict. Constructing a narrative on the past can be controversial and divisive, especially when people have avoided confronting it. However, building a post-conflict identity for external tourists eager to learn more about what took place in Belfast during the Troubles has provided new economic opportunities for the city and many of those who live there. Belfast is not unique in that respect, and many regions that have emerged from conflict have had to confront similar dilemmas. Tourism can be a vital lifeline for cities emerging from war and long-term political violence, assisting their economic recovery while also allowing people to collectively and individually remember what their society has been through. However, this simultaneously frames the political and cultural narrative of that conflict and brings new economic resources that can divide previously warring factions as easily as it unites them.

The peace process has certainly allowed Belfast to blossom as a city, to build a new tourist product that was not available during the Troubles for obvious reasons. This treads a careful path in terms of how the conflict is remembered and represented and has replaced some of the more divisive and painful narratives of violence with more inclusive and positive messages that brand Belfast as a modern progressive society with a rich, if divided, heritage.

However, there are some people who fear that this is creating a political economy based on an exploitation of 'conflict hot-spots', rather than grassroots conflict transformation approaches that will benefit the post-conflict society that Belfast aspires to become. In this critique, the memory of the dead and injured during the Troubles has been cheapened and violated rather than cherished and commemorated. Critics of the new Belfast tourism believe that the profit motive has resulted in some of the most vulnerable people in Belfast, who are still living with the aftermath of the conflict, being transformed into a business commodity, in a dystopian zoo of enduring sectarian division.

Today Belfast continues to be at the centre of debates over the extent to which tourist initiatives that engage with the political history of the city, and the Troubles especially, are helping visitors develop a more rounded and complex understanding of the conflict and the city, rather than being instead consumed as a more voyeuristic form of entertainment. The fact that visitors can come to Belfast and be exposed to the city and its rich cultural heritage might be seen as progress in itself, certainly compared to the decades that went before.

However, if tourists had visited Belfast during the Troubles era, they would have witnessed a blossoming of cultural activity in the city, the violence and division driving people to express themselves artistically. Powerful cultural movements frequently emerge out of grievance, anger and suffering, which might have something to do with the sheer volume of artistic excellence that has come out of Belfast over the last fifty years. Certainly, if you grew up in Belfast during the 1970s or 1980s, you were probably either a poet yourself, or you knew one who lived on your street. If you weren't a poet then the odds were that you were in a band or were an aspiring artist or actor. In a city built across a sectarian fault line and fragmented by religion, political allegiance and cultural identity, it was inevitable that the arts would capture, absorb and refract that cultural inheritance.

Belfast possesses a unique cultural legacy, and poetry, in particular, continues to provide an artistic means of interpreting and understanding the city today. These poets have inevitably reflected the society they came out of, and their work has, in different ways, mirrored the political and cultural divisions of Belfast. A fellow poet once remarked that Seamus Heaney's breakthrough anthology, *Death of a Naturalist*, first published in 1966, with its 'bursting mortars' and similes between nature and violence, was not an account of what was happening in Northern Ireland at the time, but rather a predictive voice about *what was going to happen* in the future. And so it proved in the generation that was to follow, with Heaney himself becoming emblematic of the conflict that surrounded him.

Whether a safety pin on the political grenades being hurled around during the 1970s and 1980s, or a safety valve allowing people some outlet for their frustrations, anger and hope, poetry arguably helps to explain and understand Belfast and its people in unique ways. While pictures can speak a thousand words, so too can poems, and Belfast's past and its present can just as easily be understood through an examination of its culture as they can by studying its politics. Many of these poems have functioned as cultural archives of the city, message boards to display and refine identities, connecting people across generations with an understanding of who they were, where they had come from and where they were going. We can see the past, present and possible futures of Belfast through its cultural expressions such as poetry just as surely as we can from a detailed analysis of its political institutions. The poetry brings together, preserves and refracts different narratives of our historical past and our political present; it remembers and curates different readings of the past, and it frames our understanding of who we think we are or aspire to become.

Belfast is a city in transition from an illustrious but divided past into an uncertain but hopeful future. The city is the self-styled capital of Northern Ireland, which is just entering its second century as a political unit. Belfast is likely to be at the centre of future debates and decisions about the political direction of Northern Ireland over the next generation and whether it remains the capital of a region within the UK or reverts to its pre-1921 status as the largest city in the north of a politically and geographically united island.

Whatever lies in store for it politically in the years ahead, the city has been the crucible for the blossoming of the liberal enlightenment in the eighteenth century and an economic powerhouse in the nineteenth century, as well as a notorious focal point for sectarian violence and political instability during the twentieth century. The outlook and behaviour of its people has been framed by its geography and history as much as by the economic and political structures they have embraced, rejected or learned to tolerate.

While Belfast has been characterised in the past as being a one-dimensional city, where violent people have done awful things to one other in pursuit of intolerant beliefs and uncompromising political identities, the chapters that follow seek to add the other two dimensions to the story.

1

THE LAGAN AND THE LINEN

The Lagan is a tidal river, which means, among other things, that it smells – or at least it used to. When I was growing up in Belfast in the 1970s, the river was not the go-to destination for a good day out that it has become today. My childhood memories of it would definitely not be fit for a tourist brochure, as I recall it being dirty, smelly and at times a rather forbidding obstacle to be crossed in the car, and certainly not a place to stop or play. Its water was brown, and in shallower parts you could see bits of debris – old prams, shopping trolleys and other hazards – sticking up above its surface. The concept of industrial chic was not a thing when I was young, and we tended to regard it as a dangerous dumping ground that was best avoided.

In fact, in the 1970s people did not really live in the city centre at all, in part because that style of urban living in duplex apartment blocks had not really taken off in Ireland, and also because it would have been a very dangerous lifestyle during the 1970s, with bomb attacks a daily occurrence in the city. In any case, there was little open at night in the city centre, and socialising was done in the suburbs rather than in the centre of Belfast. So the appeal of living along the Lagan at that time was severely limited by the lack of facilities as well as by the political context of the time, and the prospect of being offered a chance to live there would have been seen as a punishment rather than an aspiration when I was growing up in the 1970s. This was not just a Troubles phenomenon, either, as throughout Belfast's history the Lagan was never really a sought-after place to live. As the town grew and the industrial revolution gathered pace, mills were built to service the cotton and linen industries and the population of Belfast exploded between the eighteenth and nineteenth centuries. None of this expansion made the Lagan any more desirable, as at low tide it was flanked by mud flats and sewage, with ground that was too soft to build on and with few materials to use in any case.

Obviously the political instability from the late 1960s and descent of the city into a daily onslaught of shooting and bomb attacks meant that Belfast was not seen as a place to live in unless you had to, or as a place to invest in either. It was not until the early 1990s that developers and other entrepreneurs began to realise the value of the Lagan and the opportunity it presented in the economic rejuvenation of the city. This was connected to the emerging peace process and prospects of greater stability, which saw capitalists of all political colours licking their lips at the investment potential of cheap land and public subsidies aimed at providing a 'peace dividend'.

THE LAGAN AS LIFEBLOOD

The story of the River Lagan is intrinsic to the story of Belfast itself. It is an indelible feature of the city and familiar to everyone who lives there. In this sense, the Lagan is more than a river or a geological feature of the physical landscape and forms part of people's cultural identity and sense of place. This can be seen through its representation in civic organisations across the cultural, economic and political spectrum. Its name derives from the Irish *Abhainn an Lagáin,* meaning river of the low lying district, and it has been used since by countless groups from book publishers (Lagan Press) to redevelopment enterprises (Laganside Corporation) and even electoral constituencies (Lagan Valley). It is part of the local vernacular and has even made it into prime-time television through characters like Superintendent Ted Hastings in the fictional police drama *Line of Duty*. Hastings, played by Northern Irish actor Adrian Dunbar, made the phrase 'I didn't float up the Lagan in a bubble' at least familiar to (if not exactly understood by) audiences in Great Britain.

It is not an exaggeration to say that Belfast would not exist were it not for the River Lagan, which has provided much of the lifeblood for the development of the city over the last 400 years, since it first became a major human settlement. Originating in Slieve Croob mountain north of the Mournes in County Down, the Lagan stretches for over 50 miles before bisecting the city and entering Belfast Lough. Belfast owes its economic fortunes and its political significance to the Lagan and its tributary rivers, without which there would in all likelihood have been no linen industry, no shipbuilding industry and no political revolutionaries. Without the Lagan, Belfast would have been undeniably smaller, and most likely the wider area would not have forged the separate industrial economy to the rest of the island, which was primarily based on agriculture, that it did.

The River Lagan is central, therefore, to the geography of Belfast and to its political, economic and cultural heritage. The river has become a key symbol of the city and is celebrated today through a regeneration and investment programme that began in the early 1990s and the commissioning of public artworks celebrating the river and its historical significance. One of the best known of these pieces is *Big Fish*, a 10-metre-long ceramic sculpture that sits in front of the old Custom House on Donegall Quay. *Big Fish* was created by artist John Kindness in 1999 and has become one of Belfast's most recognisable landmarks and a tourist attraction in its own right. It is composed of blue and white ceramic tiles decorated with text and images relating to the history of Belfast.

Many cities are built on the banks of rivers for obvious reasons, and Belfast is no different in that respect to Glasgow, which was built on the Clyde, Liverpool, built on the Mersey, Dublin, built on the Liffey, and London, built on the Thames. For the earliest settlers, rivers provided fresh water to drink, food to eat, fertile soil to grow crops and often wood to burn and to build houses. They also provided transport routes before roads were built for the movement of people and goods – and they all provided routes outwards to the sea. Belfast's evolution was no different in this respect to that of many other cities across these islands and more broadly around the world.

The Lagan is not the only natural feature of Belfast that defines the city, as Cave Hill looms over its metropolitan centre and provides a natural border with Belfast Lough on one side and it on the other. Cave Hill gets its name from a series of five caves cut out of its basalt escarpment, topped off by an Iron-Age structure known as McArt's Fort, believed to have been the base for the kings of the Ulaid, the ancient rulers of Ulster during the Middle Ages.[1] Cave Hill defines the city and provides a continuity between the first human settlements established under its shadow and the city as it is today. It has borne silent witness to the development of Belfast from village to town to city, from Neolithic farming settlement to artisan trading centre to full-blown industrial behemoth. It has also watched radicalism and revolutionaries blossom and wither from the eighteenth century to the present day. Its slopes have witnessed hope, horror and hate as generations fought for liberation or fled from persecution while the city below formed and reformed in multiple economic, political, social and cultural relationships. In her social history memoir of growing up in the White City area underneath Cave Hill just before the Troubles broke out in Belfast in the late 1950s and early 1960s, historian Marianne Elliott writes about its significance for many people brought up in Belfast: 'The Cave Hill dominates both the physical and the imaginative landscape of Belfast. It pervades the personality of north Belfast in particular and of all who have lived there.'[2] Like McArt's Fort, the Giant's Ring is another example of early human settlement close to the River Lagan seeing the establishment of a community with evidence of some coordinated and collective ritualistic behaviour. The Giant's Ring is an ancient stone henge monument dating back to the Neolithic period around 2700 BC and is located near the Lagan at Shaw's Bridge on the outskirts of Belfast.

All of these periods in Belfast's development relied heavily on the River Lagan, and the expansion of the cotton and linen industries in the eighteenth and nineteenth centuries and shipbuilding the century after that was inherently connected to the Lagan and shaped the political ecology[3] of the city as we know it today.

GENESIS: INTERVENTION AND INSECURITY

Today, if we visit a city it is unlikely that we will think too deeply about why it is where it is or what alternative settlements might have risen to prominence instead of it. But cities are normally established because they possess advantages and resources that other places do not, and Belfast provides a case in point of that evolutionary process. The emergence of Belfast in the sixteenth century and its transition from a small village to a town of significance was based in part on its strategic positioning and natural assets, such as a plentiful supply of fresh water from the Lagan and other major rivers, large forests in the area that provided shelter, food and an abundant supply of wood, and the surrounding hills that afforded protection from attack.

In addition to these natural advantages, the town was also given a helping hand in the shape of wider political and military objectives of the English government and its representatives who controlled Ireland at the time. Belfast is generally seen as having been formally established in 1613 when King James I issued a royal charter giving the town legal and political status and promoting its economic development and expansion. But this was driven not by a love of the location so much as by a desire to defend England from attacks coming through Ireland by foreign enemies, in particular Spain. In religious terms, Ireland was a predominantly Catholic country (as was Spain), while England had enthusiastically embraced the Protestant Reformation. This was a time when religion was much more than a private practice and was deeply embedded in people's understanding of personal wellbeing and whether they would achieve eternal salvation or damnation when they died. Religious heresy was akin to treason and was innately political, and it was treated accordingly by Christians on both sides, despite their worshipping the same God.

English military priorities were crucial to the early development of Belfast. The initial investment by the English Crown in what was then little more than a decent-sized village was driven by the desire to control Ulster and the rest of the island. Ireland was seen by Queen Elizabeth I in the sixteenth century and by her successor James I (James VI of Scotland) as representing both a political and a security threat to England to the point that conquest, occupation and control became key priorities throughout their respective reigns. It was considered, therefore, to be worth the blood and treasure required to subdue the local population and rebuild the country on more acceptable lines, as a place where the inhabitants spoke English rather than Irish and where forests were cut down to open up land for agriculture. The campaign to achieve subjugation was also aimed at ensuring that loyal Protestants (mainly English and Scottish) replaced disloyal Catholics (mainly Gaelic and Irish). So Belfast was invested in by Queen Elizabeth and by King James I in part as a base for carrying out their policy goals of Anglicisation and political control. Waves of religious intolerance and violent repression were an inextricable part of that effort, and the legacy of that tyranny is woven into the fabric of the city and its geography to the present day.

Converting people to Protestantism and rooting out Catholicism, as well as being seen as God's work, was also viewed as being a sensible security and defence policy, as 'Papists' could not serve two masters, the Pope on the one hand and their King or Queen on the other. Anglicisation was a political war against Ireland as much as it was a culture war, so replacing Catholicism with Protestantism, the Gaelic language with English, Brehon law with English law, as well as imposing English inheritance rights, land ownership and farming practices, was connected to political subjugation and a Hobbesian type of political transaction where loyalty would be given in return for protection.

A muscular deforestation policy was also pursued in an attempt to police the region more effectively, reducing the area where rebels could hide and launch surprise attacks on English forces. The Earl of Essex, Walter Devereux, landed in Carrickfergus in 1573 but decided that it was Belfast that should be developed as the centre of English fortification due to its strategic position as a harbour for ships, the plentiful supply of fresh water from the River Lagan and its tributaries and better-quality land and raw materials for building. Essex took to his mission with gusto, razing forests to the ground and decimating those who stood in his way. The rest of the century witnessed episodes of brutal violence on both sides, with Irish chieftain Shane McBrian O'Neill capturing the Belfast garrison in 1597, hanging all Englishmen that could be found and, according to contemporary accounts, sparing little brutality in the process: 'All the English men in the ward were hanged . . . and their throats cut, and their bowels cutt oute of their bellyes by Shane McBrian.'[4] Other atrocities followed on both sides as Belfast was hewn out of a bloody power struggle between the English Crown on one side and an array of Irish chieftains on the other. Essex was intent on building a more significant settlement in Belfast, but his tactics were so brutal this resulted in widespread instability that saw Elizabeth withdraw her support, and he was forced out.

By 1605 the role of Lord Deputy of Ireland had passed to Sir Arthur Chichester, widely regarded as the founding father of Belfast, and he would succeed where Essex had failed, using a relentless campaign of terror, destroying farmland and livestock to literally starve his enemies into submission. Grisly tales of famished Irish peasants eating grass – or even one another – are recorded in contemporary accounts of the period. On one occasion, when Chichester was returning from a raid, he came across the following harrowing scene in the Castlereagh Hills, as recorded by Fynes Moryson, Secretary to Lord Mountjoy, who had held the role of Lord Deputy of Ireland before Chichester's appointment:

> a most horrible Spectacle of three children (whereof the eldest was not above ten years old) all eating and gnawing with their Teeth the Entrails of their dead Mother, upon whose flesh they had fed 20 Days past, and having eaten all from the Feet upward to the bare Bones, roasting it continually by a slow Fire, were now coming to the eating of her said Entrails in like sort roasted, yet not divided from the Body, being as yet raw.[5]

This horrific episode was a direct consequence of Chichester's scorched earth approach to local resistance and to building the town as a bastion of English control in Ireland. So while Chichester was a founding father of Belfast, and gave his name to several of its main streets, like many other cities Belfast was built on the foundations of bloody conquest. It was a town developed and given investment in order to control and subjugate the surrounding population, and its founding father Sir Arthur Chichester, who won Belfast's charter of incorporation in 1613, was a man notorious for his ruthless enforcement of English control. Subjugation of the local population through repression and control of Belfast's natural assets (its rivers and access to Belfast Lough) were key to his success and the accolade that 'he was the true founder of the town of Belfast'.[6]

Sir Arthur was a fittingly colourful individual for a city that would later become synonymous with violence. Before Chichester became the embodiment of English rule in Ireland, and set about imposing England's version of law and order upon it in his role as Lord Deputy, he was on the run from law and order in England. Chichester was a member of the Devonshire nobility who had 'legged it' to Ireland and then fled to France after ambushing and robbing a 'Queen's Purveyor' (tax collector) during his youth. Like a scene out of the BBC sitcom *Blackadder*, Queen Elizabeth I apparently liked his risk-taking mentality and military prowess, and when he proved himself on the battlefield she later decided to pardon him. He arrived in Ireland in 1598 becoming Governor of Carrickfergus, before being appointed as Lord Deputy by Elizabeth's successor James I in 1605. The Lord Deputy was the monarch's leading representative in Ireland and effectively the chief executive in a role that combined both civil and military functions. They were the eyes and ears of the Crown and imposed its will, albeit with a considerable degree of latitude in terms of the day-to-day governing of the country. Typically, Chichester did not really want the job, as he claimed it was too much work and took him away from what he was really interested in doing, which was making himself rich.

One of the twentieth century's most renowned chroniclers of the city, Cathal O'Byrne, who published his celebrated collection *As I Roved Out* in 1946, was clearly not a fan of Belfast's founding father. This was perhaps due to his zealous persecution of Catholics, whom he murdered with evident enthusiasm. One of Chichester's letters to Queen Elizabeth detailing how he was carrying out his duties as Lord Deputy describes his journey around Lough Neagh, between Carrickfergus on the outskirts of what would become Belfast and County Tyrone: 'I burned all along the Louth within four miles of Dungannon and killed 100 people, sparing none of what quality, age or sex, soever, besides many burned to death, we kill man woman and child, horse, beast, and whatsoever we find.'[7] O'Byrne laments the fact that 'it is rather a pity the picturesque old street should be named after such a monster, for Chichester Street is to our thinking, one of the most picturesque streets in the Belfast of to-day'.[8] In retrospect, it seems rather fitting that Belfast, which has suffered a little unjustly from a tarnished reputation for violence and destruction, was founded by a man whose public reputation is not tarnished enough.

This is not an attempt to take Chichester out of his time in the seventeenth century and judge him against legal norms or moral values of the twenty-first. It is poor history to interpret actions of the past by today's standards, but with that caveat in mind, the fact remains that Chichester was by any estimation a tyrannical presence. Despite this, as the saying goes, we can choose our friends but cannot choose our relatives, and perhaps more than any other single individual, this former villain and fugitive turned military leader and civil servant was the founding father of Belfast. There is a campaign today to decolonise and ethically rebrand public spaces, cutting out the more egregious symbols of Britain's colonial past. This has seen statues being removed in towns and cities across the UK and beyond, but to date Chichester has escaped this fate just as he escaped English justice over 400 years ago.

Before being occupied by English planters, grasping landlords and merciless military enforcers like Chichester, Belfast was settled by less illustrious raiders in the Bronze Age at least 4,500 years before Chichester left such a formative imprint upon it. Aside from his 'own' Chichester Street, Donegall Street and Donegall Square (where Belfast City Hall stands today) were named after him, while he designed and designated several of the other main areas of the city centre including High Street, Ann Street and Waring Street. While buildings have come and gone since his initial foray into urban planning, most of the streets that Chichester designed for the town remain the backbone of its urban architecture to the present day.

Any celebration of Belfast and its achievements over the last 400 years has to take that bloody and shameful past into account at some level. Our appreciation of the city today has to guard against sanitising this past in a way that converts famine, disease, repression and campaigns of genocide against the native population into historical nostalgia or heritage linked to leisure and tourism. This does not mean we need to feel guilty or apologetic about our city and where we have come from, simply that we appreciate that the city we see today has been hewn from tragedy and failure as well as from fortitude and success.

As Belfast evolved during the seventeenth century, the struggle for power connected religion to economics and to politics in a transparent way, separating out the haves from the have nots, the loyal from the disloyal, the deserving from the undeserving. As a result of the Protestant Reformation in England, religion became *the* key divider between the dominant and the dominated sections of society, and the Protestant English Crown attempted to colonise and Anglicise Catholic Ireland for both political and economic advantage. Belfast, like Ulster generally, had resources such as land that the Crown could give to its soldiers in reward for service. As a result, resources were confiscated from the 'native' Catholic population and given to the newer Protestant community. This was done in a number of ways, through a combination of bribery and force, the carrot and the stick, and by changing the law to enable political goals to succeed. This might sound like a one-sided story – but that is because it was largely one-sided, with Irish Catholics progressively dispossessed, disenfranchised and delegitimised.

The most overt example of this policy was the plantation of Ulster in the early seventeenth century, when Scottish and English Protestants were encouraged to go to Ireland and were given land in return for their loyalty to the Crown. It is difficult to imagine the scale of this initiative in today's era, but in 1609, the plantation of Ulster was a staggeringly ambitious project. Over just a few years, 170,000 English and Scots settlers were given land in Ulster, 23 new towns were established and varying levels of protection were provided against the understandably unhappy Catholic natives who had been dispossessed. In the modern jargon of neo-liberal capitalism we might refer to the plantation as an early example of a public–private partnership, where the government provided some resources and the settlers put in their own capital as well, in order to farm the land and establish new communities.

While the impact of the plantation has been overstated in the subsequent political development of Ireland, it helped to provide a critical mass to the existing Scottish Protestant community that had built up in Ireland over previous generations. This connected the issue of religion to economic grievance and citizenship in a way that defined Catholics and Protestants in oppositional terms. While Antrim and Down (and thus Belfast) were less impacted by the plantation than other counties in Ulster (as it was already mostly Protestant by that point), this wider context still impacted upon the political, economic and social development of the town.

The arrival of such a large body of Scottish and English settlers changed the pattern of agriculture, as well as Irish educational and legal structures, making them more compatible with those in England. A series of 'Penal Laws' were also enacted at the end of the seventeenth century in reaction to the previous Catholic regime of James II, in an attempt to subjugate the Catholic population and deprive them of citizenship, religious freedom and economic means. As their names would indicate, these laws removed the right of Catholics to bear arms, hold public office, vote in elections or be members of parliament, as well as introducing other restrictions including rights over the education of their children. One of the overriding themes of the Penal Laws, in addition to the confiscation of Catholic property, was the obsessive fear of the Catholic Church and its clergy. While this might seem a little paranoid by today's standards, England was still recovering from the reign of Queen Mary (aka 'Bloody Mary'), who had attempted to reverse the Protestant Reformation in England and the religious revolution initiated by her father, Henry VIII.

For the remainder of the seventeenth century, the main story of the period was the enormous transfer of property ownership from Catholic into Protestant hands and the creation of what became known as a Protestant 'Ascendancy' and a Gaelic Catholic underclass.[9] It is important to note that this privileged Protestant position did not extend to the Presbyterian community which made up the majority of the Belfast population, especially among its merchant class. The Williamite Settlement that followed the victory of William of Orange over James II and his ascension to the English throne favoured the Anglicans in the Church of Ireland over the Presbyterian community. This would have political ramifications that will be examined in the next chapter, creating grievances within the Presbyterian community that gave them common cause with their Catholic neighbours in the city.

During all of this upheaval the river network that ran through the city was vital for the development of Belfast as a centre of English control, and together with the proximity of Belfast Lough it became pivotal to further growth during the seventeenth and eighteenth centuries.

RECLAIMING THE FARSET

While the River Lagan has shaped the modern landscape of Belfast and has been integral to its economic expansion and political significance for at least the last three centuries, it is not the only important river in the city. Today lying largely forgotten, the River Farset (*Abhainn na Feirste* in Irish) is a tributary of the Lagan originating on the County Antrim side and joining the Lagan just before the river enters Belfast Lough. The route of the Farset is largely invisible to the tourists who visit Belfast today, but they will almost certainly be standing over it at some stage, even though they may not realise it. The river begins at Squires Hill far above the city, its source having been traced to a small watercress bed at Horseshoe Bend close to the Ballyutoag Road. It then flows down through Ballysillan in the north of the city under Cave Hill, before cutting across the Crumlin and Shankill Roads, and it then parallels the 'peace line' between the mainly Protestant Shankill Road and Catholic Falls Road before dipping under the Westlink dual carriageway and into the city centre.

The main artery of the Farset still flows up High Street today, contained within large pipes under the road, some of which are so big you could literally drive a bus through them. These Victorian structures were made of brick and can be dated to around the 1840s, their continued survival being a testament to the construction standards of the mid-nineteenth century. After periods of heavy rain there can be upwards of 60,000 litres of water flowing under the road, and during high tides and periods of torrential rain, the water level can still flood parts of the city. If you visit High Street today, the only evidence of the Farset's existence is the curve of the road, which follows the shape of the original river. The Farset flows into the Lagan just past the famous Albert Clock on High Street, an underwater backwater outflow of the city's past. It is a little ironic that despite playing such a fundamental role in the development of the city, not least during the industrial revolution when it serviced the linen mills, the Farset is now largely ignored and forgotten by those who walk above it in the city.

In recent times there have been discussions about rediscovering the Farset and its important role in Belfast's past, opening parts of it back up in conjunction with redevelopment and leisure activities in the city. Cultural projects have also tried to regenerate the reputation of the Farset along with Belfast's other hidden waterways and acknowledge the formative role they played in the development of the city. The project *Resounding Rivers* by Sonic artist Matt Green in 2010 positioned six installations at key sites above the rivers in the city centre to project the sound of their water onto the streets of the city. When he was interviewed about the project, Green said:

Each of the installations is surrounded by a different body of noise – some loud and some quiet. All of the sound is supposed to mingle with what is around, never assert itself. I expect that some people will pass by the works and not notice them, for others they will hear the sound and be intrigued by it, perhaps becoming aware of it as an artwork or just experiencing it on their own terms for themselves.[10]

The sound installations followed the routes of the Farset and other hidden waterways and were intended to highlight the fact that the Lagan used to be a much wider river than it is today. Green's intention was to reconnect the everyday experience of people living in the city with its forgotten heritage in a subtle, creative and experiential way.

The names of our streets – Bank Street, Bridge Street, Skipper Street – allude to the importance of these waterways in the development of the city. But today, they are culverted and diverted, built over and hidden, and in only a few places are we aware of the presence of water in the cityscape. 'Resounding Rivers' aims to give them a renewed presence in the city centre.[11]

It seems entirely fitting that, culturally at least, the Farset is beginning to be rediscovered, if still not being a part of the city's everyday physical space. In 2016 the Arts Council of Northern Ireland (ACNI) in partnership with Belfast City Council (BCC) provided financial support for a project by Creative Belfast that sought to bring the river back into the public imagination for those who lived above it. Aisling Ni Labhrai from Belfast's Cultúrlann McAdam Ó Fiaich centre explained the purpose of the project and the way in which the river, despite being hidden from view, was a lasting legacy to other physical manifestations of the city's industrial heritage that had long since disappeared: 'It has such a story to tell. It is so much part of the beginnings of Belfast. Pre-Harland and Wolff, pre-shipbuilding we had Linenopolis.

The merchant houses that grew up [and] the mill houses that grew up, a lot of the physical heritage has gone.'[12]

The Farset Project was a cross-community initiative between the Cultúrlann McAdam Ó Fiaich on the Falls Road and the Spectrum Centre on the Shankill Road. The public artwork that resulted from this collaboration is a 6-metre-high sculpture known as *Origin*, comprising a stainless steel raindrop positioned at the Horseshoe Bend at Squires Hill, overlooking the city and commemorating the source of the Farset that flowed from that point into Belfast. Tracey McVerry, one of the artists from Solas Creative responsible for the creation of the sculpture, explained the connection between *Origin*'s appearance and its symbolic relationship with the river and city: 'The importance of the River Farset and the lifeforce which it gives to the people of Belfast is portrayed in the form of a granite ripple at the sculpture's base. ... Everything radiates out from the centre, just as a drop hits the water surface. The ripples represent the linen industry, foundries and the hard-working communities that built and shaped Belfast.'[13] The *Origin* sculpture did not win universal critical acclaim, its symbolism a little opaque for those without some knowledge of the wider historical context. The artwork had the dubious honour of receiving the 'What's That Thing' award from the *Spectator* magazine in March 2017.[14]

The Farset is not the only underground tributary in Belfast, as the Blackstaff River also wends its way underground before merging with the Lagan. Its source can be found in Black Mountain, which looms over the west of the city. From there it travels northwards, entering Belfast at the old Gas Works site under Botanic Avenue and continuing on towards the Lagan. Like the Farset, it runs relatively silently and largely unnoticed under several main roads in the city, including the always traffic-clogged Boucher Road at Tates Avenue, and Great Victoria Street under the main Europa Bus Station, before continuing onwards into the River Lagan.

It is highly likely that any tourist visiting Belfast today will stand unwittingly over the Blackstaff River, especially if they visit the Europa Bus Station on Great Victoria Street or walk around Queen's University, Botanic Gardens or the 'golden mile' around Botanic Avenue and Shaftesbury Square, with its large concentration of bars and restaurants. One of Belfast's most prestigious book publishers, many of whose titles are cited in this volume, is named after the Blackstaff River, and while it is no longer visible to most people, its cultural influence on the city remains. These underground rivers crisscross the city and are fundamental to how the town and subsequent city was planned out, built and expanded.

The River Farset is responsible for giving Belfast its name (*Beál Feirste* in Irish), and it seems a fitting allegory that today it is hidden in an underground tunnel under High Street in Belfast and largely forgotten.[15]

NAMING THE SANDBAR

The name Farset comes from the Irish word for sandbar, and *Beál Feirste* refers loosely to the 'mouth of the sandbar', though as Belfast's unofficial poet laureate Ciaran Carson notes in his personal memoir of the city, *The Star Factory*, there is some disagreement among historians and linguists about the precise etymology of the name.[16] Carson points out that Belfast is a city built on water from various rivers and springs that spout out of the hills of Antrim. Without the water, there would be no city, as its water was the lifeblood needed for the industries that built it, and without the Farset, Belfast would not have been given its name.

Carson also raises the interesting point about the pronunciation of Belfast, with most people over the last fifty years placing an emphasis on the first syllable *Bel* rather than the second, *fast*. A native Gaelic speaker himself, Carson notes that his father's generation would have emphasised the second syllable because in the Irish version, *Beál Feirste*, the weighting was on the second word. It provides an interesting example not only of how names are given, but of how their pronunciation alters when refracted through a different language. Carson also remarks on the serendipity of the Farset servicing in parallel the Catholic Falls and Protestant Shankill Roads, the mills along its length giving employment to both communities, enabling Protestants and Catholics to produce linen that neither community could afford to buy.[17] The cityscape itself is still shaped by the journey of the Farset, with mills having been positioned where the river was sufficiently deep to power the factories and more artisan activities and cottage industries such as linen-bleaching and weaving taking place where the Farset was shallow. In other words, the economy and urban architecture of Belfast were shaped by the course of the river rather than the river being moulded to shape the needs of the town. Before Belfast expanded into a city, its rivers were its boundaries, and in medieval times the Farset was the northern boundary and the Blackstaff was the southern boundary of the town.

The growth of the cotton industry in Belfast during the eighteenth century required mills to be built for the spinning process that were powered by water from rivers such as the Blackstaff, the Farset and the Lagan. Without the rivers there would have been no mills, and without the mills there would have been no cotton industry or linen industry. It would be reasonable to suggest that without its rivers, Belfast would be a much less significant place than it is, would not have experienced the population expansion of the eighteenth and nineteenth centuries and would not have ridden the wave of the industrial revolution as energetically as it did. The Farset and the Lagan were therefore the strategic arteries of Belfast's industrial expansion, allowing the city to grow and thrive in the centuries that followed.

The river brought employment in the mills, which brought people in search of jobs, which led to new roads and house-building programmes and to the urban and cultural landscape of the city that exists today. Streets were built by those with the money to build them and were named as they saw fit. This partly explains some of the more exotic street names in the city, which were a product of what was happening at the time the streets were developed. Former Sinn Féin President Gerry Adams remarks on this in his memoir of growing up on the Falls Road in Belfast during the 1960s:

> A number of the streets in the Lower Falls area have names connected with the Crimean War and the Balkans e.g. Raglan Street, Balaclava Street, Sevastopol Street, Inkerman Street, Odessa Street, Alma Street, Plevna Street, Sultan Street, Balkan Street, Cyprus Street, Varna Street, Servia Street, Bosnia Street, Belgrade Street, Roumania Street. These streets were built by the Ross family, owners of a local linen mill, who had prospered as a result of the Crimean War. They used their profits to expand their mill and to build houses for their workers and to rent.[18]

There is no doubting the strategic importance of the Farset to Belfast's physical and cultural development, but its usefulness was also its downfall, as constant activity led to chronic pollution. Eventually this became so unpleasant that it was gradually covered over until the whole river was banished to its ignominious subterranean existence. Ciaran Carson's prose about Belfast was rarely written through rose-tinted glasses, and he concludes his recollection of the Farset in a way that's befitting of a city where nostalgia always has a cutting edge: 'I did not know its name, then, but was mesmerised by its rubbish: a bottomless bucket, the undercarriage of a pram, and the rusty springs sticking out of the wreck of a sunken abandoned sofa.'[19]

This rather downbeat reminiscence seems apt given that by the end of the 1700s the Farset had become a dumping ground and little more than an open sewer full of animal carcasses, dye from the mills and human waste, which obviously worsened as the town's population expanded. Carson's imagery matches the prevailing damp climate of the city and the challenges presented by its immediate physical environment. Belfast sits in a bowl, with hills on one side and the sea on the other. It is a low-lying settlement which has in the past been susceptible to flooding, with much of the land composed of mudflats rather than firm bedrock, making building difficult.

The Lagan has come a long way since the 1970s and the generations before that when its low-lying situation used to result in an almost permanent shroud of smoke over the city. As Jonathan Bardon remarked, 'The choking atmosphere uniting with a penetrating dampness largely accounted for the alarmingly high rates of death from tuberculosis and bronchitis until very recent times.'[20] To this day, in fact, if you leave South Belfast in the afternoon via the Saintfield Road, which rises upwards to the suburb of Carryduff, you can often see the cloudy pall sitting over the city in your rear-view mirror as you drive into the sunshine.

While today the Lagan has become an economic and cultural asset to the city, a place where people want to live and socialise, it has been quite a journey and has taken over 400 years to get to that point. However, despite the ugliness, the smelliness, the mud and the squalor, Belfast has always had advantages that other towns in Ulster have not enjoyed, going back to the reasons why Sir Arthur Chichester was so keen to develop the town at the beginning of the seventeenth century.

What Belfast lacked in air quality and available bedrock for building purposes, it made up for in other areas – not least its location. Despite its low-lying geological challenges, its smelly rivers and its periodic flooding, Belfast was well located at the mouth of the Lagan and Belfast Lough, a strategic position from which to become Ulster's largest port, exporting agricultural produce to Britain, the river acting as a conduit to carry produce through Ulster's fertile farming land onto ships for export and profit. A series of locks were built around rapids and weirs in the river to allow boats to navigate the waterway and increase the capacity for goods to be moved for export and for the cotton and linen industries to develop in the eighteenth and nineteenth centuries. In fact, the Lagan was instrumental in the industrialisation of linen production in Belfast, to the point that the city earned the nickname 'Linenopolis'.

FROM THE LAGAN TO LINENOPOLIS

Linen is central to the story of Belfast, and its inheritance is woven into the fabric of the city as much as that of the Lagan itself. Belfast's street names, such as Linenhall Street, its buildings, including the Linen Hall Library, and what is informally known as the Linen Quarter today have all become part of the city's cultural infrastructure. What is now Belfast City Hall was initially the site of the White Linen Hall when the building opened for business in 1787. With its prominent position in the centre of the city, the White Linen Hall became an important centre for the linen trade before being demolished and replaced by Belfast City Hall in 1906.[21] Opinion differs as to the economic significance of the White Linen Hall, which was built to establish Belfast, rather than Dublin or closer linen-producing towns such as Lisburn, as the trading hub with England. Irrespective of its economic significance, the public money that was poured into the building of the White Linen Hall demonstrated the ambition of the Presbyterian entrepreneurs at the centre of Belfast's civic development during the eighteenth century.

Major infrastructure projects such as the Lagan Navigation, a canal that connected the River Lagan through to the port of Belfast Lough, were crucial for allowing the transportation of linen from across Ulster and positioning Belfast as the trading hub for this increasingly sought-after and lucrative product. Prior to this, heavy goods had to be transported by horse and cart on whatever roads or paths were available. However, having a waterway that allowed linen, coal, potash and other heavy materials to move around in large quantities was, in modern parlance, 'a game-changer' for the linen industry and those invested in it. While the arrival of railways helped enormously, these did not feature in Belfast until the late 1840s, and in any case the rail network was far from comprehensive beyond the central trading routes. The river was an obvious solution, and having a waterway that would allow transportation from the port in Belfast Lough, down the River Lagan and into the cotton and linen producing centres of County Down and further into mid-Ulster had clear attractions.

The Lagan Navigation connected Belfast to the neighbouring town of Lisburn, and the idea to develop the river in that direction had been around since the middle of the seventeenth century. Belfast is a much larger city today than it was in the eighteenth century, and as Lisburn was at the centre of the linen industry it made sense to connect them together via the Lagan to enable linen produced in Lisburn to get to the port of Belfast. The term 'navigation' refers to the widening and deepening of the existing river rather than the construction of a new waterway. The advantage was that it was much less expensive and faster to build than a wholly new infrastructure project. The Lagan Navigation followed the river as much as possible to keep the costs down, but short sections of canal were excavated at points where that was not possible, avoiding areas where weirs had been built or where the river dropped down rapids that would not be navigable for boats. In 1749, engineer Acheson Johnston developed a plan that would link Belfast right through to Lough Neagh by making the Lagan navigable as far as Moira and then cutting a canal through to the south-east corner of Lough Neagh, near Lurgan, giving Belfast access to much of central Ulster and thus making the import of coal and other raw materials, and the export of linen from Ulster farms, faster and cheaper for companies in Belfast than for their competitors in other parts of Ireland, notably in Newry. Getting the Lagan to Moira would mean that the river (and everything on it) would only be

10 kilometres from Lough Neagh, the largest lake in Britain or Ireland. If a canal could be built to take the Lagan to Lough Neagh then the majority of the rest of Ulster would be accessible, and that would benefit manufacturers, traders and other communities along the route. Acheson Johnston estimated that it would cost around £20,000 to get the Lagan to Lough Neagh, and finally, over a century after the idea was first mooted, work began on the project in 1756.[22] The Navigation section connecting the River Lagan between Belfast and Lisburn was completed in six years, with four new locks installed and a tow path built by 1763.

The section from Lisburn to Lough Neagh was the more ambitious and costly part of the project, and additional funding was required to complete it. Initially, in an early example of progressive taxation, a tax was placed on alcohol sales along the route of the canal. While this lasted for eleven years, it was not sufficient to fund the scheme. Like building projects the world over, there were snags, delays, unforeseen problems and engineering challenges that plagued the project. By 1765, and after £40,000 had been spent, new engineers determined that further development of the Lagan past Lisburn was a 'non-runner' due to its susceptibility to flooding and existing mill development along its route. A canal was the only other option but was delayed due to inevitable disagreements over the route and a lack of capital to finance the scheme. Eventually, in 1794, following the intervention of the Marquess of Donegall, an 18-kilometre-long canal composed of 10 new locks was opened that connected Moira with Lough Neagh at an estimated cost of £62,000.[23] While once reputed to be one of the richest men in Ireland, the Marquess was also beset by a spendthrift son, who ran up gambling and other debts that his father was forced to settle. George Augustus had the lavish title of Lord Belfast but not the wallet to match such grandeur. By his early twenties he had run up debts of over £200,000 on gambling and other pursuits that left him a guest in a debtors' prison for a short time.[24] The 'bank of mum and dad' had to come to the young rascal's rescue, and in the process the Marquess had to sell off most of his control of the Lagan Navigation to Belfast's merchant community before his death in 1799.[25]

The enterprise was certainly an engineering triumph but was less successful in practice due to periods of flooding and high rainfall that damaged the lower river section. Nevertheless, imperfect though the waterway was, the development of the Lagan helped Belfast to trade and transport linen that was manufactured beyond its town boundaries in Armagh and Tyrone.

Another key change that helped Belfast take advantage of its strategic positioning at the port was the creation of a new quay, built at Belfast's docks in 1769. At the beginning of the eighteenth century the water level at low tide was no more than a few feet in places at the quayside, with a very narrow channel running for over 2 miles to open water further out. This meant that most ships had to anchor up to 3 miles outside Belfast and have their cargoes and passengers unloaded and brought in on smaller boats, which was obviously a cumbersome, time-consuming and costly process.

The new quay, unsurprisingly named after Sir Arthur Chichester (like half of the town centre), allowed larger ships to berth on the edge of the city, making the transportation of linen faster, easier and cheaper. Other improvements to Belfast's maritime architecture were made in subsequent years, including the No. 1 Clarendon Graving Dock, completed in 1800, and No. 2 Clarendon Graving Dock, completed in 1826. This upgrading of Belfast's port allowed larger ships to berth much closer to land, which cut down on the time it took to load and unload cargo and thus reduced costs. This also had the effect of increasing demand for access to the port, which can be seen by the rapid increase in customs receipts and the volume of ships that passed through Belfast Lough over the next forty years.

These advances in the town's maritime infrastructure were matched by manufacturing innovations and the capacity to mechanise and scale up linen production in Belfast's mills. To make linen, you needed flax, fresh water and an array of chemical processes to treat the textile. Initially, the production of linen was a small-scale cottage industry, as the process for milling it had not been mechanised at the end of the eighteenth century. It was predominantly an artisan trade, in part because the flax had to be hand-spun and the brown linen that was produced then had to be bleached over a period of several weeks in the open air, in a place with easy access to fresh water and transportation. This is why the Farset, the Lagan, Belfast's access to the sea and export became so central to the development of the city. Early in the eighteenth century local farmers would turn their small amounts of flax into brown

41

linen, and this could be transported via the Lagan through the farms of mid-Ulster to Belfast, where merchants would buy the brown linen and use their bleaching plants around the town to turn it into the final product, and from where it would then be exported to England and further afield into North America and the Caribbean via ships in Belfast Lough.

It was a profitable trade but not on a scale that would set the world on fire, though ironically an actual fire did help to revolutionise the linen industry in Belfast early in the nineteenth century. On a Sunday morning in June 1828, Thomas Mulholland's York Street mill caught fire, the raw cotton keeping the inferno going for most of the day. However, like the metaphorical phoenix from the flames, out of the ashes of this disaster came opportunity for the enterprising manufacturer. He rebuilt the mill on a site close to the original factory, not as a cotton mill but for flax-spinning and linen production. Like many successful entrepreneurs, Mulholland had done his research and development, travelling to England to look for innovations that might improve efficiency, lower costs and increase profit. The problem with flax up to this point had been that it was not ideally suited for machine production, its greasy sticky texture clogging any machinery that attempted to spin it. Hand-spinning flax was the only option, which was labour-intensive work. As S.J. Connolly notes, in the early part of the nineteenth century flax was too brittle to be machine spun, and while attempts were made to do so, it led to an inferior and uncompetitive product.[26] However, while travelling around England, Mulholland and his partner John Hinds found that a competitor there had discovered that if flax was soaked in fresh water for six hours it could be spun into fine yarn through power-spinning machines.

Mulholland and Hinds took this idea back with them to Belfast and pioneered the technique of 'wet spinning' in their new rebuilt mill in 1830, which allowed flax to be spun into a fine enough yarn to enable it to be mass-produced and converted into linen. This new method was not only faster and more profitable – it was also of superior quality to the hand-spun yarn previously produced, allowing linen to replace cotton in the marketplace. Their mill was to become the largest linen mill in the world for the next 100 years, growing exponentially from 8,000 spindles in 1830, to 25,000 spindles in 1856. As historian Jonathan Bardon notes, 'only two mills spun flax by power in Belfast in 1830 but by 1846 there were 24 mills. Before 1830 all of Ireland exported not more than 4½ million pounds of yarn in a year; from Belfast alone 9 million pounds were exported in 1857 and 28 million pounds in the boom year of 1865.'[27] Linenopolis had been born, Belfast was its centre, and the rivers of the city provided its lifeblood.

A TRAGIC POLITICAL ECONOMY

It was not just the Lagan or industrialisation that built the cotton and linen industries in Belfast – it was also the wider context of the nineteenth century, an era dominated by poverty, famine and urbanisation. The 1838 Poor Law introduced workhouses (also referred to as poorhouses), Belfast opening its first in 1841, with destitution being the sole criterion for admission. The Poor House (later known as Clifton House) actually doubled up as a cotton mill, where its founder Robert Joy encouraged those within its protective walls to earn their keep. This was enlightened capitalism for its day, and by 1800 it was estimated that the cotton industry provided work for 13,500 people. The logic of connecting a poorhouse with a cotton mill was not driven by the profit motive so much as a form of economic liberalism that viewed self-help as a key life skill and charity as a dangerous descent into deskilling and demotivating people, sapping their drive and desire to pull themselves and their families out of destitution.

Robert Joy was an entrepreneur, printer, publisher and philanthropist from a wealthy liberal Presbyterian family. His father, Francis Joy, founded the *Belfast News Letter* in 1737, Belfast's first daily newspaper, which is still publishing today. Robert Joy took over the family printing business with his brother Henry and became an enthusiastic social reformer, playing a leading role in the Belfast Charitable Society and the funding and construction of what would become the Clifton Poor House.

Most importantly, Robert Joy was a forward thinker and a practitioner of what today we would term evidence-based research. Convinced of the need to provide some level of assistance to the most 'deserving' poor and destitute in the town, he went on a fact-finding tour of cities in Britain that had already established poorhouses. His research took him to Liverpool, Glasgow,

Birmingham and Manchester, where he visited the poorhouses and spoke to those who ran them. In advocating for a similar facility to be built in Belfast, Joy was convinced that productive work would have to be provided within any such facility to enable the children housed there to find a means of survival once they left. Robert and Henry Joy, together with their predominantly Presbyterian liberal reformer colleagues in the Belfast Charitable Society, spent several years fundraising to build a poorhouse through public lotteries and other philanthropic ventures. The foundation stone for the Clifton Poor House was laid in August 1771, and after many years of painstaking effort by the Belfast Charitable Society, the Clifton Poor House was eventually opened in December 1774.[28] Robert Joy was central to the entire project and even provided the plans that were used in the construction of the house, which remains one of Belfast's most recognisable public buildings to the present day.

During his fact-finding tour in Britain, Joy got first-hand experience of the cotton manufacturing process and realised that cotton-spinning could have great potential for the economic fortunes of Belfast. He had a cotton-spinning machine constructed and had children in the poorhouse trained to use it. By today's standards we might view this as exploitative child labour, but from Robert Joy's perspective this was a means of providing skills for the children that would allow them to survive when they eventually left the poorhouse. While the Belfast Charitable Society was initially reluctant, Joy persuaded them in 1779 to provide space for cotton-spinning machines to be installed. Children were paid to spin cotton yarn, and the business model, like many successful models, was scaled up by the society some years later. The cotton production in the poorhouse was effectively a start-up, and in 1784 Robert Joy, together with his business partners Thomas McCabe, a watchmaker, and John McCracken, a sea captain (and father of liberal reformer Mary Ann McCracken), opened a cotton mill in Francis Street in the Falls area of Belfast under the name of Joy, McCabe, & McCracken.[29] They employed over ninety people in the mill, many of whom had been children in the Clifton Poor House and were already trained in the new technique of 'spin-twisting', where the cotton was powered by a water wheel.[30]

By the end of the eighteenth century, the mainly Presbyterian merchant class in Belfast had invested heavily in the production of cotton, increasing its mechanisation by building mills along the main rivers and expanding trade routes between Belfast and England as well as internationally. Presbyterian entrepreneurs like Robert Joy recognised the economic opportunities that cotton provided and believed that such prosperity would also help deal with the social ills around poverty, destitution and public health that were growing as fast as the city. At the beginning of the nineteenth century, the population of Belfast expanded by nearly 50 per cent, between 1801, when it was estimated at around 19,000, and 1811, when it had risen to almost 28,000.[31] This put pressure on the town's infrastructure and resources – on housing, jobs and food – in a context where the price of cotton and the market for it fluctuated regularly. It was therefore an uncertain and uneven economy subject to boom and bust, expansion and contraction. This was fine in the good times when jobs and investment were high, but became more problematic during periods of economic slump when there was less to go around.

At the beginning of the nineteenth century the cotton industry was thriving in Belfast, which meant that the Presbyterian merchants in the city were thriving too. Entrepreneurs such as John McCracken (father of Henry Joy McCracken) and Thomas Mulholland built huge mills in Belfast around the Lagan, the Farset and the Blackstaff rivers. As Jonathan Bardon notes, 'In these years, cotton was king in Belfast; it was estimated that between 1800 and 1812, £350,000 was invested in cotton machinery there.'[32]

The problem with the boom-and-bust economic model was that cotton mills and those who owned them and worked in them could not adjust easily to cope with the fluctuating demand or the external political context. Tensions between Britain and America threw the cotton industry in Belfast into deep depression, while other British political and military problems during the period depressed the cotton trade. The Battle of Waterloo in 1815 was also a metaphorical Waterloo for Belfast's cotton industry at the time, depressing wages and leading to sectarian tensions within the town, which had expanded during the good times. Prices for cotton fell dramatically after Waterloo – by up to 40 per cent – which meant that wages also fell, people lost their jobs and those who still had them worried that they would be next.

While everyone suffered at points of contraction, it was typically the lowest-paid who felt the pain most acutely, and who were most susceptible to poverty, hunger, destitution and illness. When employers cut wages or jobs there were frequently attempts to mobilise against them, setting employers against employees, and violent incidents and attacks on employers' homes by disgruntled or desperate workers were not uncommon.

Even when there was plentiful employment in the linen mills it was often dirty work carried out by women and children. Around 70 per cent of linen workers were female, while the 1867 Factory Act made it legal for children as young as 8 years of age to work for 6 hours a day. The mills were noisy, full of fibrous dust from the flax and poorly ventilated. Female workers, in particular, were exposed to the worst of the conditions, working in dusty humid spinning rooms that regularly reached temperatures of 30 degrees centigrade.[33] Due to the heat, many women worked in bare feet, but due to the wet floors, nail infections and deformities were commonplace. The humid working conditions, together with poor ventilation, caused respiratory diseases and high rates of tuberculosis. While pay and conditions were poor for women working in the linen mills, there were strict hierarchies nonetheless, based on the type of job held and evident from the way mill workers were dressed: 'All round the hall were neater girls in smart hats and jackets, probably the girls from the wareroom of the city, but all down the center tables . . . were the mill-girls themselves. Ragged and tattered, with pinched wan faces, aged before their time, holding round them the shawls that barely hid the slovenly vest beneath.'[34]

However, it was the Irish Famine, *An Gorta Mór*, in the middle of the nineteenth century that provided the grisly shot in the arm for the linen industry. The famine from 1845 to 1849 resulted in a radical reshaping of the Irish population and the political economy of the country. It hit rural areas that were dependent on subsistence farming harder than Belfast, but it also accentuated the gap between the increasingly de-populated rural areas of Ireland and the urban metropolis of Belfast that saw a dramatic influx of people searching for work in the mills, factories and shops. It was a population explosion and a ready provider of labour for the burgeoning linen industry. As mills were converted to move from cotton to linen production in the 1830s and 1840s, and as new ones were built and subsidiary factories such as bleaching plants grew to replace the hand-bleaching process, job opportunities increased in Belfast, attracting in people from rural areas.

The rapid industrialisation of the linen trade in Belfast was not just facilitated by the abundance of labour from beleaguered rural communities and the advancement of spinning techniques in the mills, it also benefited from new market opportunities in the middle of the nineteenth century, as well as the introduction of machine weaving in the 1850s. Specifically, the American Civil War in the 1860s led to a global shortage of cotton, and Belfast was able to step in and offer linen as an alternative and more affordable textile. Journalist Frank Frankfort Moore, writing in the early 1920s and reflecting on the growth of Belfast in the nineteenth century, confirms the importance of external geopolitical events to the economic growth of Belfast and the growth of the linen industry in particular. He notes how the blockade of Confederate ports reduced the availability of cotton in the spinning districts of England that were dependent on America for its supply. As prices rose, it became much more viable for them to buy linen as an alternative to cotton.

As soon as the economic situation became apparent in Ulster . . . hundreds of acres were sown with flax, and there would have been hundreds more if seed could have been procured. . . . Fortunes were made in seed alone and the mills were working day and night turning out the finished material for the bleach greens. The merchants who supplied the bleach greens with their chemicals also made fortunes, as did the foundries who provided the machinery to the mills. At the R[oyal Belfast] A[cademical] Institution four boys out of every five were being apprenticed to the linen business. . . . Most of the privately owned mills were turned into limited companies, and clerks at £100 a year became managers at £1,000 – the foreign correspondents in the head offices sometimes drew over £1,000, I was told, and I stood breathless hearing it.[35]

The combination of a ready market due to conducive external trading conditions and the rapid mechanisation of machine-produced yarn as a result of the 'wet-spinning' innovation in new steam-powered mills saw the linen business booming by the 1860s. By this point, linen had almost totally replaced cotton, with only two of the thirty-two mills in Belfast producing the latter product.[36] For most of the next century Belfast was at the centre of production and trade for linen goods, and the industry left its mark on the fabric of the city long after the mills that were once so dominant had disappeared.

THE CHALLENGES OF GROWTH

Belfast's population rose exponentially between 1800 and the 50 years that followed, first stimulated by the cotton trade and then by the mechanisation of the linen industry. As the nineteenth century began, the population of Belfast was around 20,000, and in the next 30 years it grew to over 50,000. By 1851 the Belfast census put the population of Belfast at 87,000 people, while over the next decade its population climbed to 121,000.[37] This represents a staggering population expansion, a 505 per cent increase over the 60-year period, establishing Belfast as the second-biggest city in Ireland, only Dublin being larger. As with many rapid population expansions, while this lifted some out of destitution, it also created new pressures and competition for resources in the town, not least in employment, housing provision and public health.

Those who flocked into Belfast during this period were effectively refugees from the famine and disease that was, in every sense of the word, a blight on the subsistence lifestyle of rural communities. The new workforce that arrived in Belfast from rural parts of Ulster (and from other parts of Ireland) was weak and sick before it arrived in the city. Diseases such as typhus and cholera were the inevitable pock-ridden bedfellows of poverty and squalor, on the one hand, and Belfast's damp temperate climate, on the other. Epidemics are always felt more harshly by the poorest members of society, and as it has been with the Covid-19 pandemic in the twenty-first century, so it was with typhus and cholera in Belfast in the nineteenth century. It was the poorest and the weakest who suffered the most.

We have grown grimly accustomed over recent years to words and phrases such as 'lockdown' and 'social distancing' in response to the Covid pandemic, but back in the mid-nineteenth century, the Belfast Charitable Society and the Clifton Poor House were operating these policies (arguably more effectively) in response to cholera and typhus outbreaks in the 1830s and 1840s. On Christmas Eve 1831, the Belfast Charitable Society passed a resolution requiring that on the first appearance of cholera in the city all 'communication between the house and the town be immediately suspended to stop it [cholera] spreading [to the Poor House residents]'.[38] The response across the UK to the Covid pandemic in 2020–21 was characterised by incoherence and inconsistency, as policymakers failed to adequately understand the nature of the disease they were trying to manage and mitigate. However, Belfast was used to epidemics in the nineteenth century, having experienced regular waves of diseases such as cholera, and in 1831 civic leaders did what they could to moderate the impact on the weakest members of society.

The desperately weak who fled from rural areas in search of food and work after the Irish Famine hit in 1845 brought typhus with them, and the lice they carried infected others in the local population. In 1847 there was a full-blown typhus epidemic that ripped through the city – or at least through those without the economic means to distance themselves from it. Other diseases took hold, including smallpox, and people died in the streets faster than they could be buried in mass graves. Those lucky enough to survive the outbreak of typhus and smallpox had to cope with a wave of dysentery that ripped through Belfast at the same time. The hospitals and the graveyards filled up, while coffins became so scarce bodies were squeezed into them four or five at a time. Before long there were so many corpses they just gave up using coffins and reopened the old cholera pit to bury the dead.

The Belfast workhouse built in 1841 had a 1,000-bed infirmary, but, despite additional temporary accommodation being added, it was overwhelmed, with over 14,000 sick and dying inmates. Local newspapers reported that even more people 'for whom there remains no provision – are daily exposed in the delirium of this frightful malady, on the streets or left to die in their filthy and ill-ventilated hovels'.[39] A cholera outbreak, not unusual in the city during the first half of the nineteenth century, came on the heels of the typhus outbreak, killing over 1,000 people in 1849 – again wreaking most havoc in the poorest areas of the city. In 1849 the death rate from the cholera outbreak was twice as high as a previous epidemic in 1831, which was put down to poor housing conditions, overcrowding and a lack of adequate sewage facilities. It was clear that the excessive death rate was due to poor sanitary conditions in the poorest and most densely populated areas of the city. One finding that stands out from contemporary accounts by reforming medical practitioners such as Dr Andrew Malcolm, who sat on the Belfast Sanitary Committee, was the essence of a 'killer statistic'. It relates to another epidemic of the time, which was relatively unseen – infant mortality, as a result of which 'the average life expectancy in Belfast was no more than nine years'.[40]

So when we consider the growth of Belfast during the industrial revolution, the blossoming of entrepreneurship among the merchant class, the economic tiger of the linen industry that gave Belfast its nickname of Linenopolis, it should be remembered that this was a civic expansion that benefited some and not others. More specifically, like capitalism the world over, it was a success story for the rich but a traumatic and tragic experience for the poorer members of society.

It would be bad history to judge Belfast during this period by the standards that we would expect today in terms of public health, employment rights, educational provision or adequate social services, but it is still worth noting that its rapid expansion from a town into the second-largest city in Ireland came at a price. That price was borne by the poor, and Belfast's route to economic prowess was littered with the collateral damage of poverty, disease, overcrowding and sectarian violence between groups competing for jobs and food when resources were scarce.

Many of those who had been part of Belfast's economic success at the end of the eighteenth and start of the nineteenth century were well aware of the price that was being paid and decided to do something to address it. The Presbyterian merchants who had driven the cotton industry and become wealthy off the back of it were conscious of poor public health, of the squalor, disease and political discrimination that allowed some to prosper while keeping other sections of society from doing the same.

The enlightened capitalists who understood that healthy workers were more productive workers knew only too well that Belfast's economic success and expansion came at a price. Many of them joined progressive organisations committed to addressing the political, social and economic problems that became increasingly apparent as the town grew into a city. The Belfast Charitable Society had been established by key figures among the Presbyterian business community in 1752 to build what became the Clifton Poor House, and those involved in that project soon moved from addressing the economic ills of society to tackling its political shortcomings.

These were radical thinkers, and they had a radical political agenda for Belfast and for the rest of the country that reverberates to this day. They were largely Presbyterian, they were mostly liberal, and they left an indelible mark on Belfast that remains firmly rooted in its DNA today.

2

THE RADICALISM

Belfast has always had a radical edge, the city forged out of a combination of hardship and opportunity, with an economy as inconsistent as the weather. In a city that was sunny one minute and lashing rain the next, life was often unpredictable, and it paid to adapt quickly to the changing environment. It is a stereotype, of course, but there is a certain Belfast personality type that combines the warmth and humour of Southern Ireland with the blunt directness of the Scottish Glaswegian. What emerges is an amalgam of both dispositions, a fusion of optimistic hopes and pessimistic opinions. Our humour is often of the gallows persuasion, and our accent is more a guttural bark than the lilting brogue of our Southern cousins. As a child I was frequently admonished by my teachers and others for my 'broad Belfast' accent and told that I would get nowhere if people could not understand what I was saying. Elocution was the medicine prescribed, and lessons to straighten out our regional phonemes were a big thing when I was young – teaching us to pronounce our 'ings' and not to collapse words of multiple syllables down into one at all opportunities. It was a hopeless cause in my case, as I did not see any problem with the way that I spoke and felt that elocution lessons on Saturday mornings were eating into time that could have been more usefully spent playing football with my pals.

Perhaps we have a chip on our collective shoulders driven by decades of poverty and political conflict, an experience of endemic victimhood, failure and doomed fatalism that requires us to help ourselves and our communities because the state has proved unwilling or unable to do it for us in the past. Certainly, the desire to resist authority, to prove critics wrong and to fight the stubbornly persistent 'imposter syndrome' is a trait that I certainly recognise in myself and in many other people that I know from Belfast.

FROM RELIGIOUS FUNDAMENTALISM TO POLITICAL RADICALISM

The appetite to dissent from authority is certainly not restricted to one side of the divided community and has been woven into the cultural and political DNA of the city for centuries. The desire of people to resist rules imposed by those in authority highlights a literalism and a radical commitment to principle that is connected to the region's experience of religion and politics, within Belfast's Presbyterian community especially.

The Protestant Reformation in the sixteenth century spawned a 'dissenting' tradition that was integral to the Presbyterian focus on the individual interpretation of the Bible, rather than the writ of Rome that many Protestants believed forced Papists to do what they were told by their priests, bishops and popes. So Presbyterians emerged as an insurgent branch of Protestantism, outside the Anglican establishment, innately individualistic and suspicious of group-think and of the collective compromises necessary in large religious or political organisations. The Presbyterians were non-conformists, they were comfortable being thought of as 'Dissenters' and, in theological and political terms, they placed a great deal of faith in the relationship between the individual and their Creator – unfettered by human interference and the frailties that were assumed to go along with that.

While today we might consider someone's religious beliefs to be a private matter, this was certainly not the case in the seventeenth or eighteenth centuries. Religious belief was central to people's identity during a period when the concept of Hell was taken literally and avoiding going there after death motivated behaviour that would be regarded as unjustifiable zealotry by today's standards. Ireland has certainly secularised significantly over recent generations, but this goes beyond a general increase in non-attendance at church or even a growth of atheism within society. Even among believers there has been a shift away from the idea of 'God-fearing' among those who still do worship, regardless of whether they are Catholics or Protestants. The theologies of both of these forms of Christianity have liberalised enormously over the last two centuries and now downplay the idea of sin and the consequences of committing them.

When I was a child, sins were real and the distinction was clear between different categories of wrongdoing. Original sin was a given part of the human condition; we were all told that we had it and so were guilty on arrival. Mortal sins were for very serious crimes like murder and the various transgressions set out in the other commandments, although missing Mass on Sunday was said to be one too. Venial sins were reserved for less egregious matters, like stealing sweets from the newsagents when you were eight or nine years old, taking the Lord's name in vain or fighting in school. The sacrament of confession in the Catholic Church was about doing penance through prayer and being absolved of your sins so that you could avoid the fiery pit of Hell when you died.

So Hell was a real and present danger when I was young, and I was afraid of going there, just as my Scottish and Irish ancestors were afraid of it back in the eighteenth century. The generation before mine certainly believed in Heaven and Hell, and on one celebrated occasion my late Scottish father-in-law, a blunt former coal miner from Shotts near Glasgow, invoked it when speaking to my late mother-in-law. Margaret was from Bray in County Wicklow, and both her and Bill were the epitome of devout God-fearing Catholics. One evening when we were visiting them where they lived in Manchester, one of the street lights began flickering, but because of the red curtains it appeared like a rosy throbbing glow in the living room. When Margaret turned around on the sofa and asked us 'What in the name of God is that light outside?', quick as a flash Bill rasped back with a mischievous grin: 'It's the Fires O' Hell burnin fir Ye!' We all laughed our heads off, but she checked behind the curtain cautiously, just to be on the safe side.

Back in the early eighteenth century, Hell was real, the Devil was busy and sins of all types were thought to be in abundant supply. Religious faith could literally be a matter of life or death and was certainly a centre of political gravity and public policy. Wars were fought over it, and heretics and blasphemers were put to death for espousing what were perceived to be dangerous theological beliefs. Much of this was political and economic, of course, with religion used as the cover for more temporal motives.

In the Irish context, Protestant England had repressed Catholic Ireland, destroyed as many Catholic monasteries and churches as they could lay a torch on, outlawed Catholic priests and taken land off Catholics and given it to Protestant settlers. But again, this had more to do with politics and economics than theologically driven bigotry. However, it appears that even religious intolerance had its limits, as the attempt by Episcopalian Protestants in Ireland to enact a penal law in 1719 to castrate unregistered Catholic priests was resisted by the powers that be in London, who considered it to be 'unnecessarily inflammatory'. It was eventually decided that such undesirables should be dealt with after 1 May 1720 by being branded with a 'large P' on their cheek with a red hot iron, an act of leniency that may have come as a dubious relief for those unfortunates at the receiving end of the practice.[1]

Beyond the spiritual realm, your religion was inextricably linked to a range of other more temporal factors, including class, political and cultural belief systems and economic interests. So to understand the Presbyterian community in Belfast in the eighteenth century and why they thought and acted the way they did, we have to understand where they came from in the first place.

The first point of reference here is that, while today Protestants are often seen as being a homogeneous religious grouping in Northern Ireland (the Yin to the Catholic Yang, in binary understandings of political division in the region), this was certainly not the case in the eighteenth century. The Presbyterians were predominantly of Scottish heritage, a settler community, either as a result of the natural process of economic migration over the centuries, or as a result of the organised plantation of Ulster by the English government at the start of the seventeenth century. The Presbyterians were therefore a settler community of traders and merchants who were quite distinct from other Protestant denominations in Ireland. These Dissenters, as they became known, flirted briefly with radical liberalism and revolutionary political reform at the end of the eighteenth century.

The Presbyterian community in Belfast were not the same as the Protestants in the Church of Ireland, who were in effect the landed gentry, the landlord, farming and land-owning class, socially and theologically connected to English Anglicans. This group, often referred to as the Episcopalians, had a monopoly of political control in Ireland by the beginning of the eighteenth century, in large part due to a body of legislation known as the Penal Laws imposed after 1695 to subjugate the Catholic population.

When Protestant William of Orange defeated Catholic King James II in 1690 at the Battle of the Boyne, confirming the Protestant hold on the English throne, he quickly demonstrated that he was no friend of the Presbyterian population in Ireland. While his Dutch Calvinist background was relatively close to Presbyterianism in theological terms, he was constrained politically by the Anglican-dominated parliaments in Dublin and London. The 'Williamite Settlement' that followed his victory strengthened English control over Ireland by connecting legal entitlements and political represen-tation more closely to land ownership. But it was mainly the Episcopalians in the Church of Ireland who owned the land – not the Presbyterians. These laws were directed at dispossessing the majority-Catholic population of land ownership, disenfranchising them politically and ensuring that they were not allowed into key areas of employment such as the law, medicine or the civil service. Additional legislation, such as the Test Act in 1704, imposed further legal restrictions on Catholics, but these laws also damaged the standing of the Presbyterian community, who were seen by the Episcopalians as posing a potential economic and political threat to their interests.

So while Protestant King William of Orange might have defeated Catholic King James II at the Battle of the Boyne, the Williamite Settlement that followed ensured that Presbyterians, like Catholics, were subjected to legal discrimination. This provides another good example of the fact that religious differences were not just about a theological disagreement between Christians but were also linked to different political and economic interests. In blunt terms, the Episcopalians, who are also often referred to as the Protestant Ascendancy, while periodically afraid of Catholicism and the real potential of uprisings, did not see them as posing a threat to their political and economic position, but the large group of Presbyterians were viewed in precisely those terms during the eighteenth century. So the Williamite Settlement scooped the Presbyterians up in its net of legal and political discrimination, even though it was aimed more at the Catholic population.

Presbyterians, who formed the overwhelming majority of Belfast's popula-tion in the eighteenth century, found themselves therefore in an invidious position, as while some of them emerged as an affluent merchant and artisan class, they found themselves excluded from power by the Episcopalians in the Church of Ireland. As the eighteenth century progressed, tensions between the Presbyterian Dissenters and Episcopalians intensified, with the main focus being over religious emancipation and parliamentary reform in Ireland. The Presbyterian Dissenters were mostly artisan merchants, traders, weavers and factory owners, and they had little representation among the land-owning class or the gentry. By the beginning of the eighteenth century, legislation brought in by the Episcopalians such as the Test Act of 1704 – more accurately the 'Act to Prevent the Further Growth of Popery' – included a specific clause that was aimed at the Presbyterians. Under this legislation, no person could vote in elections or hold public office without taking the Oaths of Allegiance and Abjuration and receiving communion in an Episcopal church. This demand, known as the Sacramental Test, was obviously anathema to the Presbyterians, as it required them to deny a core aspect of their theological belief. The Test Act resulted in mass resignations of Presbyterians from public office, as they effectively would have had to renounce their faith as the price of remaining in their jobs. So despite the fact that Presbyterians represented the overwhelming majority of the population in Belfast, they were indirectly discriminated against by the Episcopalian minority, who were desperate to hold on to their dominant position.

The Presbyterian Church was given no legal recognition in a further attempt to 'incentivise' the Dissenters to convert to the Episcopalian wing of Protestantism, and if they refused to do so, they had to accept their political exclusion. Writing in the 1930s, early-twentieth-century historian Edmund Curtis pointed out the parlous state of the Presbyterian community as a result of the religious discrimination directed against them: 'The State regarded the Popish Priest indeed as an enemy, but did not deny that he *was* a priest and that his functions of marriage etc., were valid. The Presbyterian or Dissenting minister was not an ordained clergyman according to law, unless he had been ordained by a bishop, and the marriages he performed were not marriages by law.'[2]

The Test Act had a huge psychological and political impact on the Presbyterian community, and it was not rescinded until 1780. Given that marriages carried out by Presbyterian ministers were seen as invalid by the state, the children produced by such marriages were deemed to be illegitimate, which had obvious knock-on effects for inheritance entitlements. The temptation to leave Ireland or to metaphorically bend the knee in the Episcopalian Church and thus overcome the discrimination aimed at the Presbyterian community must have been overwhelming.

This puts the legacy of the Battle of the Boyne into a different perspective and shows that, throughout most of the eighteenth century, religious tensions were not so much between Catholics and Protestants as they were between the Church of Ireland and its Presbyterian cousins. A mere fourteen years after William of Orange had 'saved' them from the clutches of Catholic King James, therefore, Presbyterians found themselves being deprived of some of the most basic rights of citizenship. This poetic irony was not lost on the Presbyterian community, with contemporary writer Daniel Defoe pointing out the injustice of their situation:

> It seems somewhat hard, and savours of the most scandalous ingratitude that the very people who drank deepest of the Popish fury, and were the most vigorous to show their zeal and their courage in opposing tyranny and Popery, and on the foot of whose forwardness and valour the Church of Ireland recovered herself from her low condition, should now be requited with so injurious a treatment as to be linked with these very Papists they fought against. This will certainly be no encouragement to those Dissenters to join with their brethren the next time the Papists shall please to take arms and attempt their throats.[3]

The Presbyterian indignation is understandable, especially when the Church of Ireland even suggested that landlords should not give leases to Presbyterian tenants or, if they did, should charge them higher rents than their Church of Ireland neighbours. However, such intolerance and petty vindictiveness was driven not so much by internal theological disagreements between Protestant denominations than by different political and economic interests. The Presbyterian mercantile class was increasingly regarded as being a political and economic threat by the Episcopalian land owners in the Church of

Ireland. This intensified as the cotton trade and the embryonic linen industry made the Presbyterians more wealthy and more influential than their Church of Ireland cousins, and nowhere were they more wealthy and more influential than in the city of Belfast. As a result, Belfast became the crucible for a Protestant power-struggle between the numerically strong, economically powerful but politically excluded Presbyterians, and the numerically smaller but politically dominant Episcopalians.

The disadvantage experienced by Presbyterians during this period is one of the reasons why so many of them emigrated to America and established such a strong bond with those fighting for independence from the British Crown. By the time of the American War of Independence, it is estimated that around 200,000 Presbyterians had arrived in America seeking relief from the Penal Laws and joining the democratic fight against British Crown forces. Their enthusiasm for the American cause led President Theodore Roosevelt to remark a century later that 'the fiercest and most ardent Americans of all were the Presbyterian Irish settlers and their descendants'.[4] Indignation tinged with criticism was expressed in the House of Commons by Lord Newhaven at the irony of a situation in which George Washington was able to make common cause with Irish Presbyterians to 'oppose our armies with our own Irish subjects, whom our own narrow policy had driven from their country'.[5]

During the second half of the eighteenth century the grievances of the Presbyterians in Belfast and the insecurity of the Episcopalians were beginning to heat up, and leading Dissenters in Belfast sought to turn the temperature up to boiling point in an effort to achieve political reform. The Presbyterians who left Ireland to fight in the American War of Independence were changed by the experience, and many related that through letters to family and friends back home. As the eighteenth century entered its final three decades, many Presbyterians in Belfast were becoming liberal in their politics, well-organised and wealthy enough to take action. They had supported the American struggle for independence and welcomed the Revolution in France. They aspired to a new and liberated Ireland where there would be no oppression or discrimination on the grounds of religion. They had been, in the modern vernacular, radicalised.[6]

BELFAST RADICALS

In the second half of the eighteenth century the position of the Presbyterians in Belfast was increasingly anomalous. Numerically dominant in the city and affluent – extremely wealthy, in some cases, due to the growth of trade and commerce – they were, at the same time, politically powerless. Presbyterians were not able to vote for either of the two MPs sent from Belfast to the Irish Parliament in Dublin, who were effectively the appointees of the Marquess of Donegall. The undemocratic nature of political representation in Belfast became increasingly ridiculed among the city's Presbyterian middle class in the latter half of the eighteenth century, as they mocked the charade of Donegall sending his minions to do his bidding in parliament.

This clear injustice festered among the Presbyterians in the city and led to increasing calls for reform of the parliament. The Dissenters, living up to their name, looked at George Washington's campaign against British rule and were encouraged by the American War of Independence. They were further enthused by the French Revolution and the vocabulary of liberty, equality and fraternity that went along with it. The Presbyterians were a highly educated and literate community, and they were attracted by the radical liberal philosophy of Thomas Paine, John Locke and other writers and intellectuals who preached the gospel of rational humanism. The revolutionaries in France were looked up to intellectually and admired culturally by many Presbyterian reformers in Belfast in the late eighteenth century, such as Samuel Neilson. This even extended to the fashion of the day as a self-conscious revolutionary style was adopted by some, such as Lord Edward FitzGerald (a Dublin Anglican rather than Ulster Presbyterian), who cropped his hair in the French revolutionary style and began wearing a green cravat, a radical departure from the Irish aristocratic fashion at the time of wearing wigs. FitzGerald provided an element of charismatic bohemian chic to the radical cause, as an aristocrat, a romantic and a soldier who spurned his prospects in the Irish Parliament and took his inspiration from France. FitzGerald was the essence of the bon viveur. He loved to love and to be loved in return and, aided by his charm and conviviality, he provided stylistic flair and panache to the radical movement.

By the 1780s a group of radical thinkers, including Samuel Neilson, Thomas Russell (an Anglican from County Cork), Mary Ann McCracken and her brother Henry Joy McCracken, Samuel McTier and his wife Martha McTier, Dr William Drennan and several other notable activists, began to think aloud and advocate not just political reform of the Irish Parliament but the complete political separation of Ireland from Britain. The fact that they were able to do this, openly, provides an interesting window into the political culture of Belfast at the time. It was undemocratic, certainly, even by the standards of the day – but it was not a repressive society. It was a city alive with discussion and civic activism, with a vibrant array of groups and societies meeting, arguing and campaigning for change around a range of political, economic and cultural issues.

A LYING OLD SCOUNDREL

Belfast embraced the Enlightenment, and the Presbyterian community of the city, especially, wallowed in its literature, political ideas and idealism – at least until those ideals became bloodstained and riddled with moral ambivalence and the stony flavours of failure. Martha McTier often used to exchange letters with her brother Dr William Drennan, in which they discussed their readings of the works of Voltaire, Montesquieu, William Godwin and Mary Wollstonecraft. Thomas Paine's *The Rights of Man* was a particular favourite and was to become the secular catechism of the Belfast radical movement in the early 1790s.

These were highly educated and literate people attracted to Enlightenment thinking, and they watched developments in revolutionary France with a mixture of envy and admiration. The ideas of Ulster-born philosopher Francis Hutcheson (tutor of Adam Smith), Professor of Moral Philosophy at Glasgow University, were also a formative influence in building up the belief that the individual could not be free if those around them were not also at liberty and that the health of society in general was connected to the individual citizens being treated with equity in terms of freedom from discrimination and oppression. This led the Presbyterians to make an obvious connection between the abolition of the slave trade and the abolition of autocratic English rule in Ireland.

It would be inaccurate to portray these Presbyterian merchants as completely altruistic, as many of them had grown wealthy on the back of the political and economic exploitation that they were now objecting to. While it might seem odd that these Presbyterians were arguing for Catholic emancipation, that they were able to do so at the end of the eighteenth century was because, firstly, they were much larger in number than Catholics in Belfast at the time, so did not feel threatened by them economically in the way that might have been the case had the Presbyterian and Catholic populations been more equal in size. Secondly, this was not an alliance of equals but much more of a patron–client relationship, where the middle-class Presbyterian community were able to develop friendships with the Catholic working class in the same way that a progressive and enlightened employer builds a sense of loyalty among their employees.

It would not be condescending or inaccurate to say that the Presbyterians of Belfast acted with patrician charity towards the Catholics of the city, rather than seeing them as their kith and kin. The relationship was generally a good one, illustrated by the fact that the first Catholic church in Belfast, St Mary's in Chapel Lane in the centre of the city, was paid for largely out of subscriptions from the Presbyterians in Belfast. St Mary's Chapel was opened in 1784, and a donation for over half of the building costs raised by Presbyterians was handed over to the parish priest at the opening ceremony. This was an extremely generous act of both religious tolerance and social friendship, but it is hopefully not too cynical to suggest that the population imbalance between the two allowed such generosity to emerge in Belfast in a way that was much more difficult in other parts of Ulster, such as Armagh, where the Protestant/Catholic population balance was much narrower. It was in Armagh, where the Protestant and Catholic populations were relatively similar in size, that sectarian secret societies flourished, especially at times of economic hardship and depressed wages. It was in County Armagh that the Battle of the Diamond in 1785 between the Catholic Defenders and the Protestant Peep-O-Day Boys led to the formation of the Orange Order following a series of sectarian attacks between the two groups.

The patron–client relationship works as long as both sides know their place and act accordingly. However, it can become a little more complicated when the client wants to run the business for themselves or take their own decisions. This brings us back to the point that the emergence of liberal radicalism in Belfast was a story about complicated and often conflicted people, not a black-and-white tale of progressive versus regressive forces. There were class and religious structural barriers that created something of an invisible force-field between the Presbyterian radicals and the Catholic community in the city and beyond that were the target of their intended liberation. So while Belfast's Presbyterians had the space and security to act with generosity towards Catholics, many outside the town had less capacity to do so. Also, the theological difference was always going to be a structural barrier in their relationship that would limit the extent to which the two groups could align with one another. In the end, Presbyterians, with their commitment to individualism, found it difficult to empathise with the theological beliefs or cultural traditions within the Catholic Church. There was always a sense that, while hard done by, Catholics were different to Protestants – superstitious, even.[7]

In addition, many of these Presbyterian reformers were on a political journey themselves, none more so than Waddell Cunningham, one of the most successful businessmen in Belfast in the second half of the eighteenth century. Cunningham's political journey was longer than most, and he began it in dubious circumstances as a trader and a smuggler in the most egregious business of all – slavery. Cunningham exported wood from Honduras, but his ships also transported slaves between a number of islands in the Caribbean. As a young man he sailed to New York to make his fortune – and certainly succeeded in that endeavour. He built one of the largest shipping companies in the US and used it to trade weapons illegally with the French in the West Indies. Once described by Theobald Wolfe Tone, the grandfather of eighteenth-century revolutionary liberalism, as 'a lying old scoundrel', he was not the typical Presbyterian liberal. Cunningham was the essence of an aggressive business mogul, and he showed little signs of nurturing an ethical conscience or a desire for liberal reform as he diversified from shipping to factory building to imports and exports and capital accumulation. He had a finger in every business pie going, including shipping, sugar refining, flour milling, animal exporting and even tobacco smuggling.[8]

In 1786 Cunningham, along with his brother-in-law and business partner Thomas Gregg, called a meeting of business and civic leaders at the Exchange and Assembly Rooms in Waring Street in the centre of Belfast. The central objective of this was to discuss a plan to establish a slave-ship company out of Belfast that could capitalise on the slave trade in the way that other cities such as Liverpool and Bristol were doing in Britain. As noted by Cathal O'Byrne writing about the episode in 1946, while the agenda for the meeting used the euphemism of promoting the 'West India Trade' for the benefit of everyone in Belfast, it was really about slavery, and everyone knew it:

> It was not in tea, brandy, rum, molasses, cotton or hardwood only that those gentlemen were interested – the West India Traders of Belfast were Slave Dealers also. Liverpool had at least sixty slave-ships on the high seas at that time, and if the Belfast 'traders' lagged behind the Liverpool 'merchants', it certainly was not the fault of Waddell Cunningham and his wealthy friends.[9]

The business model was based on shipping goods to the Gold Coast in Africa, purchasing African slaves and transporting them to the sugar plantations in the West Indies, then returning to Belfast with cargoes of sugar and brandy. By this time, Cunningham and Gregg had built up their fleet of ships and had already become involved in the slave trade through their business interests in New York. So the 1786 meeting was effectively about scaling up their business model and bringing it back to their home city.

However, at the public meeting where Cunningham and Gregg unveiled their 'new opportunity' to the citizens of Belfast of a company for slave-ship trading between the port of Belfast and the West Indies, a local jeweller and watchmaker called Thomas McCabe denounced the plan with the following memorable intervention: 'May God wither the hand and consign the name to eternal infamy of the man who will sign that document.'[10] This threat of a celestial curse struck a chord with the gathering, and even Cunningham himself was shaken by the prospect. No signatures went on the paper that day, no hands risked the wrath of the Almighty and no slaving company was formed in Belfast.

In any case, the law was also a potential concern, as the British Navigation Acts had banned Irish ports from participating in the slave trade until 1780. The idea itself withered and a slave-trading business was never established in Belfast, even though individual businessmen like Waddell Cunningham continued to trade in the slaving industry. He even owned his own 150-acre plantation with Gregg in Dominica in the West Indies (which they renamed Belfast),[11] and by the time he died, Cunningham was reputedly the richest man in the city.

Thomas McCabe, the goldsmith and watchmaker from North Street in Belfast and issuer of frightening curses to would-be slave traders, was regarded as something of an agitator following his intervention, and because of his friendship with leading radicals such as Samuel Neilson, he became a target. His shop was looted by a mob of drunk soldiers in March 1793, who smashed his windows and ransacked his merchandise. He refused to repair his shattered windows afterwards, preferring them to remain as a monument to the aggression of the military. He famously had a new sign put up above his shop after the attack which demonstrated a flair for marketing as well as a pugnacious commitment to his liberal principles: 'Thomas McCabe, an Irish Slave, Licensed to sell Gold and Silver.'[12]

Despite his heinous business practices and egregious moral stance on slavery, Waddell Cunningham was still an advocate of some level of political reform, and he had enough common cause with other Belfast reformers to attend a dinner hosted by leading Presbyterian radicals Samuel and Martha McTier in October 1791. Theobald Wolfe Tone was another guest at the dinner, as he was in Belfast to inaugurate the newly minted Society of United Irishmen, and he later noted in his journal that his conversation with Cunningham ended up in 'a furious battle, which lasted two hours, on the Catholic question'.[13] While Cunningham wanted reform, his conservative instincts and opposition to core objectives, such as Catholic emancipation and the abolition of the slave trade, meant that he never actually joined the United Irishmen.

A RADICAL SOCIAL NETWORK

As Cunningham's story suggests, ideas were in flux in the second half of the eighteenth century, and radicalism could be a double-edged sword. There was space for people to evolve, for their ideas to change and for enlighten-ment to flourish, and that is what many within the Presbyterian community did. Waddell Cunningham represented the more conservative gradualist reformer, driven by self-interest rather than liberal idealism. Others, like Samuel McTier, Martha McTier, Samuel Neilson, Mary Ann McCracken and her brother Henry Joy McCracken, were ideologically committed to the goals of liberty and equality regardless of their own political and economic interests and were advocates of immediate reform.

What connected these people to one another was in part a liberal idealism but also, more directly, their religion – the vast majority of the Belfast radi-cals were Presbyterians, not Catholics. They were also drawn towards one another by their political and business interests and through their experience of exclusion from legislative institutions by the land-owning class. Finally, at a very basic level, they were connected through their social networks, as they either worked with one another, prayed with one another or were related to one another – or all of the above. It is often said that Belfast is a small place and that everyone knows everyone else, a truism that could certainly be used to describe the narrow Presbyterian merchant class in the city at the end of the eighteenth century. Mary Ann McCracken was the sister of Henry Joy McCracken, and Martha McTier was the wife of Samuel McTier and also the sister of Dr William Drennan. They were bound together by family and social ties as much as by their ideas – but that did not prevent tensions from emerging between radical and conservative elements as the political and economic context changed.

Mary Ann McCracken was at the centre of this Presbyterian family and social and business network, and to some extent she represents a counter-point to Waddell Cunningham's more guarded and conservative approach to reform and his enthusiasm for the slave trade. Mary Ann McCracken was ideologically committed to the cause of the United Irishmen and to their revolutionary goals and methods. She was also a committed feminist (before that term had been invented) and wrote passionately about female education and female equality as prerequisites for a happy and stable society. McCracken was an active social reformer within the Belfast Charitable Society and a champion of the oppressed, and she outlived her brother by over sixty years.

Aside from the cause of Irish independence, one of Mary Ann's central concerns was the abolition of the slave trade. She was a founding member of the Belfast Women's Anti-Slavery League, along with Martha McTier, and even in her late eighties was regularly seen handing out anti-slavery leaflets at Belfast docks.[14] She refused to consume sugar, molasses or rum because of the connection of those items with the slave trade and joined other Presbyterian radicals in arguing that anyone who did not also boycott those products was complicit in the slave trade indirectly. While Mary Ann McCracken despaired that she might never see the end of slavery, it was finally outlawed in America in 1865, a year before her death. She died in 1866 and is buried in Clifton Street cemetery overlooking the Poor House that dominated her life. As an indication of Mary Ann McCracken's enduring legacy and importance, Clifton House[15] in Belfast marked International Women's Day on 8 March 2021 with an event celebrating her life and work in association with the newly formed Mary Ann McCracken Foundation, started in her memory by the Belfast Charitable Society.[16]

McCracken was particularly close to Thomas Russell, the first Secretary, in 1788, of the Belfast Society for Promoting Knowledge, which would later become known as the Linen Hall Library and remains a thriving part of the city's cultural life to the present day.[17] Russell, like McCracken, was an unlikely revolutionary, beginning his career as an army officer like his father and brothers and seeing military action in India, where he received a commendation for bravery for carrying a wounded colleague off the battlefield. When he returned to Ireland he became a magistrate, before he resigned in disgust at the anti-Catholic bias of his colleagues. He was quickly drawn into Presbyterian social circles in Belfast and became a vital link between them and radicals in Dublin, notably Wolfe Tone. By late 1791 he had been (in the modern security vernacular) radicalised to the point that he established the Dublin branch of the Society of United Irishmen and helped to develop the intellectual case for Irish independence. His role running the Belfast Society for Promoting Knowledge provided a good opportunity for Russell to quietly organise this secret society and to publish articles in the *Northern Star* that made the case for radical political reform – and eventually for insurrection.

A historian writing in the mid-twentieth century referred to the political culture of the time as an 'oligarchy tempered by discussion',[18] but the more the radicals talked and the longer they spent doing so, the more difficult it became to take action. They were split internally, riddled with informers who succeeded in further destabilising them and undermined by limited reforms that reduced discrimination against Presbyterians without emancipating Catholics. For Waddell Cunningham and those like him, the case for change became less and less convincing as time went on, while the risk of repression became more and more immediate. While the coalition of conservative and liberal Presbyterian reformers could hold together while they were both subject to political and economic discrimination by the Episcopalian-dominated landed gentry, it was only a matter of time before they split apart. Political reforms and economic inducements aimed at addressing Presbyterian grievances (but not Catholic discrimination) divided the Presbyterian community in Belfast, inducing the liberal radicals to crystallise into a new organisation demanding immediate Irish independence while the conservatives like Cunningham backed away and made their peace with the establishment.

As the more conservative reformers peeled off – or were bought off – Belfast radicals got more radical and came to the conclusion that political change would only come through a new society of united Irishmen committed to revolution and insurrection. Dr William Drennan was a key catalyst in the formation and radicalisation of the United Irishmen and has perhaps a stronger claim than Wolfe Tone to be regarded as the father of the movement.[19] Educated in Glasgow and Edinburgh, where he qualified as an obstetrician, Drennan became the physician in the Clifton Poor House and saw first-hand how British government policies were impacting on the most vulnerable people in Belfast. He was also an inveterate letter writer and wrote regularly about the need for action, often criticising the respectability and moderation of his liberal colleagues. Drennan was an advocate of a secret organisation committed to a 'benevolent conspiracy', namely the complete independence of Ireland from Britain. He wrote to his brother-in-law Samuel McTier advocating this course of action, who in turn put it to his friends in Belfast on 1 April 1791 in a tavern in Crown Entry off High Street in the centre of the city:

I should much desire that a society were instituted in this city having much of the secresy and somewhat of the ceremonial of Free-Masonry. . . . A benevolent conspiracy—A Plot for the People—No Whig Club— no party Title—The Brotherhood its name—the right of Man and the greatest happiness of the greatest numbers its End. Its general end Real Independence of Ireland, and republicanism its particular purpose.[20]

The spark had been ignited that would lead to the formation of the Society of United Irishmen in Peggy Barclays Tavern in Belfast in October 1791, and the organising committee included Samuel Neilson, Thomas McCabe and Henry Joy McCracken, as well as McTier himself.

FROM UNITED TO DISUNITED IRISHMEN

Russell, Neilson, Simms, McCracken and one or two more of us, on the summit of McArt's fort took a solemn obligation, which I think I may say I have on my part endeavoured to fulfil – never to desist in our efforts until we had subverted the authority of England over our country and asserted her independence.

Wolfe Tone[21]

Over the months that followed, the radicals widened their social network of Presbyterian drapers and merchants in Belfast and invited a young charis-matic lawyer to speak about a pamphlet he had recently published entitled 'An Argument on Behalf of the Catholics of Ireland'. His name was Theobald Wolfe Tone, and his visit to Belfast in October 1791 would change the city and Irish politics forever.[22] The radicals devised the key tenets of what would later become Irish Republicanism in line with the liberal thought of the French Revolution and formed the Society of United Irishmen in Belfast in October 1791.

Tone, along with his key Belfast allies, including Samuel Neilson, Henry Joy McCracken and Thomas Russell, drafted three key resolutions to guide the activities of the United Irishmen. As recorded by Richard Madden in his history of the society published in 1846, these resolutions were read out to the first meeting of the Society of United Irishmen in Belfast on 12 October 1791 along with the following exhortation from Tone setting out, in vivid terms, their central grievance against the English political control of Ireland: 'We have no national government. We are ruled by Englishmen and the servants of Englishmen, whose object is the interest of another country, whose instrument is corruption and whose strength is the weakness of Ireland.'[23]

While it would later become more militant, separatist and republican, the initial aims of the Society of United Irishmen in October 1791 were fraternal and progressive. The constitution of the society was proposed by Samuel Neilson, an elder of the Presbyterian Church in Belfast and the son of a Presbyterian minister (Rev. Alexander Neilson), with the first Secretary, Robert Simms, also a Presbyterian elder. A year later Neilson founded the *Northern Star* newspaper, which became the public mouthpiece of the United Irish Society. This was a remarkable publication, which ridiculed British policy in Ireland and promoted the ideas surrounding equality and liberty that fuelled the French Revolution. Neilson poured a lot of his personal fortune into the *Northern Star* and developed a healthy readership within and beyond Belfast. Wolfe Tone was apparently fond of referring to Neilson as 'the Jacobin', a reference to the most radical political group to emerge at the beginning of the French Revolution.[24]

On 3 May 1792, the anniversary of the revolution in Poland was celebrated by the United Irish Society in the Donegall Arms pub in Belfast, and the toasts that were made and drunk to by those celebrating provide an illustration of the international liberalism at the heart of their movement at the time. The following were just some of the toasts raised that evening:

The Revolution in France.

'The Rights of Man' and Mr. Paine.

The sovereignty of the people.

The constituting and legislative assemblies of France.

The American Congress and the illustrious Washington.

The Society for the Abolition of the Slave Trade.

The memory of all good citizens who have fallen in the cause of liberty.

The liberty of the press.

An equal representation of the people of Ireland in parliament.

May the people of Ireland be united and all enjoy equal liberty.[25]

Who was in the chair presiding over these progressive liberal sentiments? None other than Waddell Cunningham, would-be slave trader, owner of a plantation in Dominica and the richest man in Belfast. However, while he was there physically, by this time his ardour for reform had cooled significantly and he was doing what he could to slow down the pace of change. For the more committed that night in the Donegall Arms, a number of practical political reforms sat alongside their lofty aspirations and ideals, chiefly the removal of all legal discrimination against the Catholic population and the restoration of full rights of citizenship within the political system. They also demanded a reform of parliamentary representation to reduce the stranglehold of the Episcopalians and land-owning class on political power.

It did not take long, however, for the Society of United Irishmen to become disunited, in part due to the excesses of the French Revolution and the souring of the liberal dream, aided and abetted by political reforms designed to cool the revolutionary ardour of the Belfast radicals. In September 1792 Martha McTier declared 'I am turned, quite turned against the French' in response to the violence and sectarian warfare that had followed the revolution.[26] Yet some of the leaders within the United Irish movement, along with the *Northern Star*, were slow to call out the excesses in France, according to historians such as Roy Foster: 'It could always be relied upon to explain and rationalise the reverses and convulsions of events in Paris through the early [seventeen] nineties – supporting the execution of the King, as did Tone and Drennan.'[27]

As early as 1792 the cracks in Presbyterian unity started to appear, with disagreements emerging not about the goals of the movement, but rather about the speed at which they should be pursued. The reasons for this difference of emphasis were linked to a realisation that if Catholics were given immediate political emancipation it could create a significant Catholic-voting bloc in Belfast, which could pose a threat to their own economic and political position. While this disagreement over timing of reform started as a difference in emphasis, it grew into a much wider schism over political objectives, leading to two distinct strands in Presbyterian political activism. The first of these can be traced through the Society of United Irishmen, to the 1798 Rebellion in Ireland, political failure and a more sporadic form of liberalism in the nineteenth century. The other strand led to a gradual co-option of the Presbyterian community by the government, to the point that it became an enthusiastic supporter of the Union with Britain and conservative ethno-religious groups such as the Orange Order.

As the Society of United Irishmen became more and more frustrated at the pace of change from 1792 to 1798, those who wanted to arrest the momentum for change retreated more and more from the original manifesto of the society. From this point, uniting Protestant, Catholic and Dissenter and establishing an independent and secular Irish Republic became the mission of the United Irishmen, alienating the more reformist sections of the movement.

By 1794 the United Irishmen had become more directly connected to the goal of republican separatism and were more closely aligned with radical Catholic groups such as the Defenders, a secret society dedicated to breaking the constitutional connection to England. The Defenders were dominated by the Catholic peasantry and engaged in frequent and violent sectarian attacks against Protestant rural vigilante groups such as the Peep-O-Day Boys. This fused Presbyterian radicalism with militant separatism and pushed the other strand of Presbyterian activism more firmly in the direction of loyalty to the Crown and an alliance with their religious cousins in the Church of Ireland.

THE DECLINE OF RADICALISM

Eventually, at the end of the 1790s, these social ties fractured as the prospect of liberal reform diminished, British government repression of political dissent increased and some radicals were pushed towards support of violent insurrection. While a hard core pushed on to armed rebellion against British rule in Ireland, many others drew back from the brink, either because of concern about the implications of militant action or because they were placated by limited British government reforms that they felt they could live with. The end result was the 1798 Rebellion, a mass uprising against British rule in Ireland organised by the United Irishmen and led in Ulster by Henry Joy McCracken. However, many of McCracken's fellow radicals had long since deserted the cause of insurrection, and in any case the United Irishmen were actually quite divided by 1798, poorly equipped and hopelessly outnumbered by the British.

The defeat of the United Irishmen is often associated with their rout in the 1798 Rebellion, but that was the culmination of a decline that had begun several years earlier. While the excesses of the French Revolution had cooled the ardour of many radicals, especially the Belfast Presbyterians, the response of the British government was just as big a factor in their decline. The outbreak of war between Britain and France in 1793 changed the context significantly, as the Presbyterian radicals suddenly found themselves backing the ideals of a country at war with Britain. Their agitation was then framed as being a security risk by some and as treasonous by others. When the Society of United Irishmen was proscribed the following year, many of the more conservative Presbyterians in Belfast took fright at the idea of being on the wrong side of the law and quickly melted away. The rest went underground, plotting rebellion in secret and hoping for external assistance from France.

At Westminster, Prime Minister William Pitt was genuinely worried about the radical spirit of the Presbyterian community and the commitment of the United Irishmen to political independence. As a result, his government made concessions to the Catholics with Relief Acts in 1792 and 1793 which addressed many of their grievances. This helped to raise the tension among the Presbyterian reformers who remained split between those ideologically committed to Irish independence and those who became less convinced of the urgency for change. In 1792 Catholics were permitted to join the legal profession, and the government began discussing the possibility of Catholic emancipation – if not actually granting it. Such talk, together with financial inducements linked to the payment of the royal grant given to the Presbyterian clergy, the *regium donum*, was enough for conservative Presbyterians to further question the need for radical action.

By 1795 it had become clear that concessions from the British government were of a limited nature and would not include anything approaching full Catholic emancipation, never mind democratic self-government or political independence. The hope of peaceful parliamentary reform had been extinguished, and revolution became the only alternative to the political status quo.

Increasingly isolated and hopelessly riddled with spies and informers, the rump of the United Irishmen ploughed on with their attempts to foment and execute an armed insurrection. By this stage, Belfast and its radical Presbyterian community had ceased to be the driving force behind the movement, and it became more aligned with the Defenders and with United Irish activity in other parts of Ireland, including Dublin.

One of the largest blows to the United Irishmen came in 1796 in the shape of an aborted invasion from France masterminded by Wolfe Tone, who sailed to Ireland with an armada of French war ships. It was an audacious move, the stuff of Hollywood movies, as Tone sailed on board the *Indomptable*, bringing the very thing that the British had feared for generations and that many of the Irish had prayed for – an invasion of Ireland from France that could seriously challenge England's grip on the country.

When Wolfe Tone's attempt to land in Bantry Bay in 1796 failed, two things happened. First, the ranks of the United Irishmen swelled with Catholics hopeful that their ship had come in, or at least would come in from France the next time around. In Ulster alone, membership of the United Irishmen doubled in the first four months of 1797 as beleaguered Catholics who had been so cruelly let down by the parliamentary process of reform felt that the French invaders would soon return to liberate them. The second thing that happened was that the British government also thought, like the United Irishmen, that the French would be back as soon as they had patched up their ships and the weather improved. It was time to act and root out the insurgents, and as a result the response of the government was both harsh and swift. An Insurrection Act effectively imposed martial law in Ireland as the British abandoned its policy of conciliation and, frightened not just by Tone's audacious attempt to land French soldiers in Ireland but also by the encouragement this provided to would-be rebels across the rest of Ireland, moved to suppress the insurgents.

General Gerard Lake was sent to Belfast to quell the growing rebellion in Ireland, and his observation on arrival that 'nothing but terror will keep them in order'[28] was an early warning of the harsh tactics he was prepared to employ. Known United Irishmen and those who sympathised with them were arrested and imprisoned without trial, offices were raided and property was destroyed. Suspects were flogged in the street or shot without anything approaching due process. Lake's military tactics were crude and one-dimensional, but they were also terrifying. He was merciless in his quest to root out the rebels, and his war of attrition certainly weakened the United Irishmen in Belfast and County Antrim. However, there is also a view that Lake's campaign of terror helped to precipitate the very thing he was trying to avoid – their armed insurrection against British rule.[29] It was Lake who annihilated the United Irishmen at Vinegar Hill in Wexford, one of the defining battles of the 1798 Rebellion, killing so many rebels that even he seemingly regretted it.[30]

A year before the final denouement, in May 1797 the office of the *Northern Star* newspaper was attacked by an armed militia who destroyed its printing presses and the building itself, finally putting the paper out of business. Those who escaped the net went on the run or underground, with only the most committed continuing with their plans for an armed uprising. By this point most of the ideological, intellectual and organisational energy had leaked away, and coordinated repression from government forces, including torture, took its toll on the rebels. Instead of a coordinated insurrection, the following summer in 1798 saw a series of localised uncoordinated attacks doomed to failure before they had begun. The 1798 Rebellion was poorly executed by insurrectionists who were inadequately armed, organisationally divided, without French support and infiltrated by informers. It is instructive and perhaps a little ironic that in the summer of 1798, when the rebellion took place, there was little if any action in Belfast, the intellectual birthplace of the United Irish movement. A contemporary observer recorded 'the death-like silence which pervaded the streets [of Belfast] while the counties of Down and Antrim resounded with the noise and tumult of battle.'[31]

Henry Joy McCracken persevered and led the Rebellion in Antrim and Down, but after inevitable defeats in a number of battles in County Down he went on the run, before his equally inevitable arrest, after which he was tried for treason, convicted and sentenced to death. His sister Mary Ann remained committed to her brother (and to the cause he fought for) until the end. She brought him food when he was in hiding in the Belfast hills and accompanied him to the gallows when he was hanged, even attempting to organise his revival afterwards. She had negotiated that her brother should not be decapitated, the usual fate meted out to insurrectionists, and had arranged for his close friend Dr James MacDonnell – who happened to be Ireland's leading specialist in resuscitation – to be close by the gallows. However, MacDonnell did not show and sent his brother instead, who could not prevent McCracken from dying. In truth, MacDonnell was falling out of sympathy with the radicals, afraid of the militancy that had taken over their idealism – and he would fall out with the radical spirit a great deal more in the years that followed. McCracken's account of her brother's public execution in the centre of Belfast provides a glimpse of the trauma she had to go through in his last moments: 'I took his arm, and we walked together to the place of execution . . . Harry begged I should go. Clasping my hands around him (I did not weep till then), I said I could bear anything but leaving him . . . fearing any further refusal would disturb the last moments of my dearest brother, I suffered myself to be led away.'[32]

Despite this personal tragedy, the disintegration of the United Irish movement and the annihilation of their attempted armed insurrection against British rule in 1798, Mary Ann McCracken's commitment to the original liberal goals of the Presbyterian radicals never wavered, and she lived out her life dedicated to the pursuit of liberty, equality and fraternity for the most vulnerable in society. When she discovered after his execution that Henry had an illegitimate child named Maria, Mary Ann sought her out and effectively adopted her for the rest of her life. Trite though it might sound, Mary Ann McCracken walked the talk of radical liberalism with a consistency that makes her one of the most revered radical daughters of the city to the present day.[33]

While Henry Joy McCracken led his followers to certain defeat in Antrim, insult was added to injury for those Presbyterian radicals who remained in Belfast when reports emerged of sectarian massacres of Protestants in the south of Ireland. One of the most infamous was the Scullabogue Barn massacre at New Ross in County Wexford on 5 June 1798, when up to 100 non-combatant men, women and children were murdered by the rebels in reprisal for the actions of English soldiers who had just killed up to 3,000 rebel fighters in the Battle of New Ross. Fleeing from this battle, some of the rebels came back to the barn outside which their prisoners were being held, executing up to forty men in groups of three on the lawn before the rest of the prisoners ran into the barn. When the desperate survivors slammed the doors closed on their attackers, they were shot at and stabbed with pikes, and then the barn was set on fire to literally smoke them out. If they did not burn to death, they were put to death while fleeing the inferno, in a blood bath of hatred, anger and rage on the part of the United Irish rebels responsible for it.[34] Most (though not all) of those murdered in this attack were Protestants, and their attackers were Catholics, giving the massacre a sectarian dimension that both scared and appalled the remaining Presbyterian radicals in Belfast. In June 1801, Dr William Drennan recollected that 'the savagery of the lower Catholics was even greater than the rule of retaliation could account for'.[35] This was the judgement of an intelligent liberal, aware of his own inherent suspicion of Catholics and striving to be impartial. The reaction of less sophisticated Presbyterians in Belfast and across Ulster was much sharper, as they saw their worst fears of Catholic payback for centuries of oppression seemingly coming to pass.

The spirit of radical Presbyterian separatist activism had already diminished dramatically in Belfast by 1798, and the Scullabogue Barn massacre and reports of other sectarian atrocities by the insurrectionists during the Rebellion removed much of the enthusiasm for revolution that remained. As government reforms reduced political, economic and social discrimination against them, Presbyterians in Belfast were drawn towards their Protestant co-religionists and away from the Catholics. The realities of a politically liberated Catholic population left Belfast's Presbyterians with little appetite for the cause of emancipation that they had championed so enthusiastically at the beginning of the decade. Former activists such as Belfast's most prominent physician of the era, James MacDonnell, had turned against the radical cause of the United Irishmen due to the rising militancy before the 1798

Rebellion. Previously, MacDonnell had been an ally of Thomas Russell's, an urbane member of the Belfast intelligentsia, a believer in the Enlightenment ideas shared by other Belfast radicals and a founder of the Belfast Academical Institution in 1810 and the Belfast Reading Society (which later became the Linen Hall Library) in 1788.[36] MacDonnell was a key cultural and philanthropic figure in Belfast in the early 1790s, was spoken of warmly by Wolfe Tone in his diaries and even had Thomas Russell as a lodger for two years, helping him get the job as the Linen Hall's librarian. Yet, by 1803, MacDonnell had signed a public petition for Russell's arrest and even contributed £50 of his own money towards the bounty for Russell's capture, causing some of his erstwhile colleagues to condemn him as a 'contemptible cold blooded Judas'.[37] Martha MacTier was no less scathing in her conclusion, denouncing MacDonnell as 'the Brutus of Belfast'.

As the eighteenth century came to a close, Belfast's liberal radicalism had dimmed and attention went elsewhere, notably into commerce, the linen industry and manufacturing. As the Act of Union was passed in 1800, Presbyterians in Belfast made their peace with the Protestantism of the English Crown and the politics of the government in London. Their radicalism morphed into loyalty, their liberal sentiments moved away from nationalistic goals towards civic initiatives, and their attention turned increasingly from politics to business. Guy Beiner has written convincingly about the post-1798 transition in Presbyterian politics and maps the way in which the radical spirit found new forms. While the memory of 1798 was de-commemorated through a process of 'social forgetting', the radicalism remained and re-emerged in future generations.[38] This provides a nuanced explanation of the way in which collective memory changed and was reshaped by the political, economic and social context that surrounded it. In this sense, the past is never wholly behind us and how we remember it is always in flux. It comes and goes, and how we remember our past morphs over time.

Nevertheless, as the eighteenth century ended and the nineteenth began, there was money to be made, there were linen mills to be built and a whiff was in the air of an industrial revolution around the corner.

3

THE SHIPS

I was brought up in East Belfast under the shadow of the Harland and Wolff shipyard, which was the engine room of the city during the industrial revolution in the nineteenth century and which remains central to the city's economic and cultural heritage. The shipyard dominates East Belfast, its two huge banana-yellow cranes Samson and Goliath bestriding the Musgrave Channel on Queen's Island, close to the point where Belfast Lough meets dry land, like two enormous square tusks. I have a painting of the cranes in the living room of my house in England's Peak District that I bought from the Yard Gallery in Holywood, a stone's throw from where I went to primary school. The painting is a prized possession, not just because it was a rare piece of art that my partner and I could agree on, but because it reminds me of 'home' and growing up under the shadow of the cranes during my childhood. They are more than cranes to me, therefore; they are part of my identity and my sense of place and belonging.

Some years ago a friend of the family who stayed with us for a few days proceeded to tell me all about the cranes as soon as they arrived and saw the painting. 'Hey, nice painting!' they exclaimed, breezing into the living room. 'That's David and Goliath in Belfast, you know.' 'No, it's actually Samson and Goliath,' I responded – politely but firmly. 'No, I'm sure it's David and Goliath,' they ploughed on. 'You should check it out.' I walked out of the room, my face burning with indignation, muttering through clenched teeth not entirely *sotto voce*: 'Well I lived under them for nearly two decades so I think I should know what they're called!' My partner, her laugh stifled by the fear of a meltdown at the beginning of a social visit, rapidly changed the subject to a less divisive one as I harrumphed upstairs. 'So let's talk about Brexit then . . .' she said.

Today the cranes have become part of the skyscape of Belfast, co-opted for better or worse into the city's corporate identity and incorporated into all sorts of merchandise, from tea towels to Christmas tree baubles. (I do, of course, have the Christmas tree baubles and the tea towel – as well as the artwork.) The cranes are thus an authentic part of the city, while also providing a visual stereotype for every ubiquitous media story from Belfast or fictional cop show using the city as its backdrop. The cranes were built in Harland and Wolff shipyard between the late 1960s and early 1970s and are located on Queen's Island where the shipyard meets Belfast Lough.[1] Far from being museum pieces, they are still very much a part of Belfast's current industrial capacity, even though the shipyard itself is long past its prime and now employs a fraction of the 35,000 people that worked there during its heyday.

While the history of the shipyard and those who worked in it is predominantly a unionist one, the cranes do have a cultural resonance inclusive of the nationalist community. In 2020 the newly formed East Belfast GAA club used the cranes as a central part of its logo. The club was founded with the intention of opening up Gaelic games beyond an Irish nationalist audience to all communities within the city. The designer of the club crest, Rory Millar, explained that the brief was to design something that not only was aesthetically attractive but also delivered an inclusive message: 'What was required was an authentic tribute to the area's unique character that also clearly communicates the progressive ethos of the club itself.'[2] So the cranes are iconic symbols that connect the past with the present and economic prowess with culture in a manner that allows unionists and nationalists (as well as the growing number of people who sit beyond this binary group) to identify with them on some level.

That was not always the case, as the history of the shipyard is a metaphor for political and economic exclusion by the unionist community of their Catholic neighbours. This reflected the wider malaise in Belfast before and after Ireland was partitioned in 1921, as the unionist majority attempted to maintain its authority and power over a smaller but growing nationalist minority that was too small to compete with unionists in elections but too large to ignore.

The significance of the shipyard concerns not just the ships that were built there but also the wider resonances the yard had on the city, on the people who built the ships and on those who were not allowed in to build them or were driven out while doing so. Like many other themes in the book, the shipyard was therefore a microcosm of the city and of those who lived there, their economic fortunes and misfortunes, their political tastes and distastes. In this sense, the shipyard is woven into the cultural fabric of the city, binding its past to its present and connecting us to it, as a result of experiences of either inclusion or exclusion. To understand the role of the shipyard, we need to turn to poets and playwrights as much as historians, anthropologists or political scientists.

Luckily we have access to all of the above, not least the unofficial Poet Laureate of the shipyard, Thomas Carnduff. Born in 1886, Carnduff remains one of Belfast's most authentic voices, and, like the city he was born into, he was undervalued, enigmatic and a jumble of contradictions. Like many other people who feature in this book, Carnduff was a radical. Shipyard worker, gang member, Orangeman, working-class labourer, UVF member, proud unionist and proud Irishman, Carnduff was also a writer and poet who gave a voice to the workers during times of economic hardship. Made redundant from the shipyard during the recession in the 1930s, Carnduff turned to writing, typing poems and plays centred on the working-class people he knew in the shipyard on his portable Corona.[3] With an authenticity gained from having been there himself, Carnduff painted pictures with his verse, bringing the shipyard and the people who worked there to life.

Towards the end of his life, Carnduff cemented his move from labourer to writer by becoming the caretaker of the Linen Hall Library from 1951 until 1954, two years before his death. He earned the soubriquet 'the Shipyard Poet', though he worked at the 'Wee Yard' rather than in Harland and Wolff itself.[4] A verse from his poem 'Men of Belfast' is inscribed on the Atrium floor of the Titanic Belfast museum, so while Carnduff remains one of Belfast's hidden gems, his work is etched into one of the city's foremost tourist attractions and thus the consciousness of all who visit it.

THE EARLY DAYS OF THE SHIPYARD

Belfast was always a maritime town. As explained in the Introduction, it was developed as a settlement because of its geographical advantages – its relatively easy access to the sea and into surrounding villages through its river networks, including the Lagan and the Farset. Shipbuilding therefore existed long before the shipyard, and before Belfast's transformation from a small town into an industrial city.

There are paintings and engravings depicting small boatyards on the banks of the River Lagan dating back to the sixteenth century, but the first significantly sized ship to have been built in Belfast is thought to be the *Eagle Wing*, a 150-tonne vessel that set sail from Belfast to North America in 1636 carrying a group of dissenting clergy and other emigrants away from a religious dispute in the town. Dubbed 'the Irish *Mayflower*', the *Eagle Wing* carried passengers who took their inspiration from the pilgrims who left England's shores in 1620 and subsequent years for Cape Cod near Boston, Massachusetts, to escape their religious persecution at home. The predominantly Presbyterian group on board hoped to escape from oppression and discrimination by the Episcopalian Anglicans in the Church of Ireland. Sadly, the voyage was cut short as, after two months at sea and despite being closer to America than to Ireland, they incredulously sailed home again without making shore in America. The ship had been badly damaged by rough seas and awful weather, but the God-fearing passengers and crew took the storms as a sign of celestial disapproval. In what would make a great film screenplay, the mast broke and the rudder of the ship failed, but they were saved by one buccaneering passenger who went over the side of the boat with a rope around his waist and somehow managed to fix the rudder while suspended in mid-air. But the decision to turn back was not taken on the grounds of the sea-worthiness of the vessel so much as a fear that God 'himself' was against the trip. One of the organisers, Rev. John Livingstone, wrote that 'if ever the Lord spoke his winds and dispensation, it was made evident to us that it was not His will that we should go to New England'.[5] Miraculously, there were only two deaths during the journey, but in spite of its ill-fated voyage, the *Eagle Wing* was to become the forerunner for a shipbuilding industry in Belfast that would help to turn the town into a thriving city.

In 1791, William Richie, a Scot from Ayrshire, arrived in Belfast with a team of ten men and an array of basic materials to start a shipyard. The following year he launched the 300-tonne *Hibernian*, a ship which helped to kickstart Belfast's reputation for shipbuilding in the nineteenth and twentieth centuries. However, shipbuilding as a significant manufacturing concern began unpromisingly during the nineteenth century, starting as an ironworks in the centre of Belfast. This enterprise in the Cromac area of the city faltered to the point that the owners, two Liverpool businessmen, Robert Pace and Thomas Gladstone, struck a deal with the Belfast Harbour Commission to transfer their ironworks to Queen's Island at Belfast docks and use their equipment to manufacture iron ships. Queen's Island was an unlikely hero in the story of Belfast's rise to fame as a shipbuilding mecca. Once again we see how the political ecology of the city played a major part in how those who lived there adapted to the opportunities available to them. Just as the River Lagan and the River Farset had facilitated the rise of the cotton and linen industries in the eighteenth and nineteenth centuries, Queen's Island was to play a similar role in the growth of shipbuilding in the nineteenth and twentieth centuries. In the early nineteenth century, as maritime trade increased, Belfast business interests and civic leaders saw the potential of the port but also its limitations. Belfast Lough was just too shallow to allow large ships to dock close to the city, and investment was needed to develop the docks if it was to expand as a significant maritime port. At low tide there was barely 1 metre depth of water at the quay in the centre of the town. From the quay to the first significant depth of water in the Lough, known as Garmoyle Pool, the depth was no greater than 6 metres at low tide, so large ships had to dock further out in Belfast Lough and transfer people and goods into smaller boats to get them ashore, all of which took longer and cost more money. Some ships were marooned 3 miles out of port, and the transfer into small open boats made trading less competitive and made passengers uncomfortable, especially in the winter months.

This problem was addressed with the passing of the Belfast Harbour Act in 1847, and with a newly constituted Belfast Harbour Commission plans were made to upgrade the port. Ireland's most renowned railway engineer, William Dargan, was contracted to make a cut to allow access for large ships into the docks from Garmoyle Pool right to the quayside. This was opened to much fanfare on 10 July 1849 and together with other upgrades to the docks saw a significant improvement in business and profits, demonstrated by the rise in both tonnage and ships passing through the port from 288,133 tonnes and 2,724 ships in 1837 to 1,372,326 tonnes and 7,817 ships in 1867.[6] By 1852 Belfast had become the leading port in Ireland.

In a very Belfast type of way, the dirt, mud and silt from the cut that Dargan had made between the docks and Garmoyle Pool in Belfast Lough formed an island that was to become the epicentre for shipbuilding in Belfast over the next 150 years. Initially named after Dargan but subsequently rebadged as 'Queen's Island' following a visit from Queen Victoria in 1849, the island became the focal point of what would become Harland and Wolff shipyard. Today it accommodates the Titanic Belfast museum and the studios where blockbuster film and television series are recorded, including *Game of Thrones*. Back in the 1840s it is unlikely that William Dargan would have realised that the cut he had made or the mud he had piled up would contribute to over 3.5 million tourists visiting the city a century and a half later. Whether or not Dargan anticipated the full impact of his new island, this change in the political ecology of the city created economic opportunities in the generations that followed.

Before these improvements to Belfast docks and the creation of Queen's Island had taken place, English entrepreneurs Pace and Gladstone had leased their by now debt-ridden company to another Liverpool entrepreneur by the name of Robert Hickson, who, recognising his lack of experience in shipbuilding, employed Edward Harland as his manager. While he would not have known it at the time, Hickson's decision to hire Harland would have a significant impact not just on his business but on the future of the city itself. Historians such as Kevin Johnson have gone as far as saying that when Hickson offered Harland the job of shipyard manager, 'he had no reason to suppose that he was bringing to Belfast the man who would define, more than any other individual, the industrial future of Belfast'.[7]

Harland was undoubtedly a great engineer, but his importance owes just as much to those around him and to the political, social and economic structures that allowed his entrepreneurship, engineering skill and managerial ability to flourish. Harland was young, ambitious and ruthless, arriving in Belfast to take up his post at the relatively young age of twenty-three, and he was determined that he would succeed and make his fortune. He certainly took a career risk, as when he arrived in Belfast there was only one ship-building contract on the order book and it was far from certain that others would follow.

Harland was born in Scarborough in Yorkshire and had an interest in engineering from a young age, gaining an apprenticeship at the esteemed Robert Stephenson company in Newcastle on Tyneside. Here he learned the fundamentals of his trade as an engineer and developed a keen interest in shipbuilding design. He combined a flair for engineering with a hard-nosed and merciless business style, cutting workers' wages, banning smoking and bringing in 'scab labour' from the Clyde to break strike action in the Belfast shipyard. On a more positive note, Harland, for want of a better phrase, turned the ship around, paid off the debts of the yard, kept impatient credi-tors at bay, personally guaranteed the wages of his staff and slowly started to turn a profit.

Harland was assisted by the shipping magnate Gustave Schwabe, who met him when he was apprenticed at Stephenson's and, recognising ability when he saw it, looked for an opportunity to invest in him. Schwabe's nephew Gustav Wolff became Harland's personal assistant in 1857, and so began one of the greatest business partnerships in the history of Belfast. By this point, Harland was frustrated working for Hickson and was keen to open his own yard. Serendipity came calling in 1858, when Hickson offered Harland his interest in the Queen's Island yard for the princely sum of £5,000, the deal being sweetened considerably when Schwabe's company Bibby's promised three new shipping contracts to Harland's yard. It has also been claimed that Schwabe bankrolled Harland to enable him to buy out Hickson's share in the yard, and that the appointment of Wolff as his personal assistant was part of the deal. The three men formed a formidable team. Harland was the engineering brains of the operation, Wolff was the partner who filled the order book, while uncle Schwabe was able to commission ships from the Belfast yard that were designed to his company's exact speci-fication and were delivered on time and to a high degree of engineering quality. It was the essence of a win–win scenario for all involved, and the money flowed in as the ships sailed out. Eighteen of the first twenty-five ocean-going ships built by Harland and Wolff were commissioned by Schwabe, which provides some sense of the importance of the connection between the supply and demand side of the business, not to mention the family ties inherent in the relationship. Reflecting on his career later in life at a social event, Wolff chose to downplay his own role in the growth of the shipyard: 'Mr Chairman: Sir Edward Harland builds the ships for our firm; Mr Pirrie [Chairman of Harland and Wolff after Harland died] makes the speeches, and as for me I smoke cigars for the firm.'[8] This was a severe attack of false modesty on Wolff's part, however, as his business acumen and contacts in the shipping industry were crucial to the yard's success.

By 1860 business was booming, with over 1,000 employees working at Queen's Island. Bibby's placed orders for more ships, and in 1861 Gustav Wolff became a partner in the business, not because Gustave Schwabe wanted it but because Edward Harland wanted it. Over the 30 years that followed, Harland and Wolff expanded from under 2 acres to an 80-acre site, with a workforce that exploded from 100 to 10,000.

The partners pioneered steam ships with innovative designs such as square, flat hulls that were nicknamed 'Belfast bottoms'. These became much sought-after by the Confederate Army during the American Civil War due to their speed and manoeuvrability.[9] Predictably, war was a boon for the shipbuilding industry, and Harland and Wolff prospered as the civil war raged in America. Harland and Wolff understood that pioneering new designs and innovations that would appeal to their customers gave them a market advantage over their competitors, and they used their creativity and engineering skill to great advantage, focusing on designing ships that could travel further without refuelling, that could carry heavier cargoes and that were more manoeuvrable in smaller ports.[10]

As the business grew, so the Belfast Harbour Commission improved and invested in the Queen's Island site, building the Hamilton Graving Dock and a floating dock known as the Abercorn Basin in 1867, speeding up the completion of three more significant cargo ships, the *Istrian*, *Iberian* and *Illyrian*.[11]

SECTARIANISM AND SHIPBUILDING

Politics was never far away from economics in Belfast, and as the shipyard grew it became the site of sectarian rivalry between Catholics and Protestants. When Catholic labourers were brought in to excavate the site of the Abercorn Basin, tensions grew with the predominantly Protestant workforce. This spilled over into violence and rioting, with Protestant workers physically attacking the Catholic navvies and forcing them out of the site in August 1864. Harland reacted in typically pugnacious style, putting up posters announcing that the shipyard would be closed until every Catholic evicted had been reinstated.

Harland himself was a unionist and went on to become a fierce opponent of Gladstone's Home Rule Bill in 1886 and a Unionist MP. The overwhelming majority of people employed in Harland and Wolff were Protestants, and it would be naïve to ignore the fact that the shipyard became the economic embodiment of Protestant and unionist political and cultural domination over the Catholic nationalist population. Shipbuilding in Belfast was a Protestant unionist occupation, and the small number of Catholics who worked in the shipyards were vulnerable to the wider political and economic tensions endemic within the city during the mid-nineteenth century.

There was a strict hierarchy in terms of jobs at Harland and Wolff, but in practice they were all controlled by Protestants. In terms of day-to-day operations, the foremen were the top of the pile, effectively the line managers of the workforce with the power to hire and fire casual labour. In times of recession it was these foremen who decided who worked and who did not and thus who would eat and who would starve. These labourers would gather every morning in the section of the shipyard known as the Village Square, hoping to catch the foreman's eye and get a day's work. By today's standards this might be thought of as an unacceptable employment practice (like a particularly bad form of zero-hours contract), but back in the nineteenth and early twentieth centuries it was an entirely normal and generally accepted part of the economic ecosystem.

Under the foremen were the skilled trades, welders, riveters, joiners and other craftsmen, who were employed following periods of apprenticeship, which were controlled within families and handed down like heirlooms from fathers to sons. These were not free, as families still had to pay large sums of money to help support their children through the five-year training periods. Apprenticeships were much sought-after, especially when Harland and Wolff began expanding and work looked reliable and relatively well paid. But families would have to pay up to £100 for their children (sometimes as young as fourteen) to be taken on, and the apprentices would have to provide their own tools, bring their own food and be effectively mentored and championed by an existing member of the workforce who would also be expected to contribute financially themselves.[12] This ensured that apprenticeships were kept within families or close social networks, which indirectly, of course, kept apprenticeships in Protestant hands and excluded Catholics.

At the bottom of the shipyard pecking order were the unskilled labourers and casual workers, poorly paid and badly treated.[13] Most of this group were Protestant, but some Catholics were also employed during periods of economic expansion when a larger workforce was required. Catholics were tolerated rather than welcomed, but during periods of economic contraction or wider political tension outside the shipyard walls, they became a focal point for intimidation and attack by their Protestant co-workers.

Working conditions for everyone were tough. Shifts were long, normally starting at 6 am and finishing at 5.30 pm, freezing in the winter, boiling hot in the summer (at least on the rare occasions when it was boiling hot in Belfast), and little if any attention was given to health and safety conditions on the site. Injury and accidents, sometimes fatal ones, were relatively commonplace, and the environment was universally noisy and chaotic.

The expulsion of Catholic workers from the Harland and Wolff shipyard in 1864 reflected wider waves of rioting between Protestants and Catholics during the 1860s. Outside the shipyard, riots took place that targeted churches and schools and were coordinated and organised. The street disturbances lasted for eighteen days and left twelve people dead and many more injured. In one instance, a Protestant mob destroyed the Catholic Malvern Street National School in reprisal for an attack the previous day on a Protestant school. The school principal claimed that it was all done calmly and deliberately rather than in anger. 'The mob worked intently, like furniture removers. And the inhabitants of Malvern Street stood at their doorways watching all.'[14]

On 16 August 1864 a citizen of the city wrote a letter to his friend with an account of the violence, which provides a flavour of the scale and severity of the sectarianism and the inability of the police to contain it. The police were themselves part of the problem, as they were overwhelmingly drawn from the Protestant community and were at times complicit in the violence and partial in attempts to apprehend those responsible for it.

> Reports are brought in of men shot in the streets like dogs, of bloody affrays between the rival parties, of school houses wrecked, of churches attacked, of shops plundered, of inoffensive persons beaten, of the law set openly at defiance till we are at length until we are inclined to think that we are living among savages. The press give harrowing pictures of the scenes in the hospitals, dead dying and wounded [and] of the surgeons up to their elbows in gore, of the coolness and fury of the mobs.[15]

So while Harland and Wolff was busy expanding and building ships, there was regular violence taking place outside its gates between Catholics and Protestants, and the 1864 riots filled the city's hospitals with the wounded, with nearly one hundred being treated for gunshot wounds and at least eleven fatalities recorded.

The background to the riots in 1864 was economic decline, together with the fact that Belfast was geographically segregated along religious lines (roughly two-thirds Protestant and one-third Catholic) and had a job market that was similarly divided. During periods of economic recession, Catholics and Protestants competed for the scarce resources and jobs that were available, Protestants dominating the higher-paid skilled jobs while Catholics were more likely to be employed in the unskilled sector of the economy as labourers or navvies. Another trigger point was provided by the calendar, with the summer months being a high point of tension when the Orange bands would march in the city to commemorate military victories of the past, especially the Battle of the Boyne. Public displays of community loyalty and commemorations of historic battles from the seventeenth century were really demonstrations of territorial control and helped to foster a basic sense of communal loyalty within the Protestant unionist community. During economic recessions, when unemployment rose in working-class areas, the Orange identity was an important means of reinforcing the notion that Protestant workers had long-term cultural and religious connections with the factory owners despite their short-term interests in common with Catholics who were also unemployed.

While the 1864 riots were an infamous case, similar sectarian breakdowns in Belfast had occurred in previous years during the Orange 'Marching Season', July 1857 being a notable precursor to the 1864 riots in the city. On 12 July 1857, Rev. Thomas Drew, a well-known evangelical preacher in Belfast and Orange pamphleteer, gave a special sermon for Orangemen that drew a capacity crowd of around 2,000 to his church. He whipped the congregation into a near hysteric fervour in a style of preaching that was similar to the Southern Baptist revivalists in America. The following excerpt from Drew's sermon provides a flavour of the way in which the Orange celebrations in July heightened tensions in Belfast and why it was difficult to prevent these going beyond church walls and exploding out into the workplace and onto the streets:

> The Sermon on the Mount is an everlasting rebuke to all intolerance. . . . Of old time lords of higher degree, with their own hands, strained on the rack the limbs of the delicate Protestant women, [Catholic] prelates dabbled in the gore of their helpless victims. The cells of the Pope's prisons were paved with the calcined bones of men and cemented with human gore and human hair. . . . The Word of God makes all plain: puts to eternal shame the practices of persecutors, and stigmatises with enduring reprobation the arrogant pretences of Popes and the outrageous dogmata of their blood-stained religion.[16]

This was interpreted by some working-class Protestants in Belfast as a call to arms, and while the sermon fired the starting pistol for rioting, the cause was that the Protestant and Catholic communities in Belfast had by this point determined that their political and economic interests were mutually exclusive to one another. While Drew was the trigger in 1857, both sides were perpetually ready for a fight, stockpiling their ammunition, organising their streets and in 1857 indulging in rioting that lasted for over a week. One of the commissioners appointed to look into the causes of the riots afterwards underlined the point that Drew was a symptom of a much more structural schism between Catholics and Protestants in Belfast, and he compared the interface areas where the violence had been concentrated as being akin to a war zone: 'The aspect of those localities was that of the camp of two armies, waiting only for a convenient time of actual battle.'[17]

As the 1857 riots demonstrated, in July and August the city was a tinderbox of sectarian tension and it did not take much for the sparks to light the bonfire. The particular trigger that led to the 1864 riots in Belfast was linked to a large group of Catholics who journeyed by train from Belfast to Dublin for an event honouring Irish nationalist leader Daniel O'Connell. The Liberator, as he was known, had died in 1847, and Dublin City Council had commissioned a monument to be erected as a memorial to his work in securing Catholic emancipation. A ceremony to lay the statue's foundation stone was held in Dublin on 8 August 1864 that drew people from all over Ireland into the city. The Belfast contingent travelled down to Dublin with Irish nationalist emblems, including green-and-white flags and rosettes, much to the annoyance of Protestants in Belfast. The following day, Protestants in the Sandy Row area of the city staged a mock funeral for O'Connell, marching their cortege, complete with a huge uncomplimentary effigy, towards the Catholic Pound area. The effigy was set alight in time for the nationalists returning from Dublin on the evening train to get a full view of their hero being burned and mocked by a Protestant mob that by this time was over 5,000 strong. Catholic residents of the Pound who had expected trouble and stockpiled paving stones and other missiles confronted the Protestant crowd, and the rioting began, barely stopping for ten days once it had begun.

That is the context for the friction inside Harland and Wolff shipyard in 1864, and this would be an endemic feature during the second half of the nineteenth and the first half of the twentieth centuries. When the rioting outside the gates of the shipyard led to the death of one of the Protestant ringleaders, John McConnell from Sandy Row, a group of 150 shipwrights walked out of the yard and marched into the centre of the city vowing revenge. A group of them walked into McNeill's gunshop in High Street and demanded every weapon in the shop, saying that they would otherwise burn the premises to the ground. Within minutes they calmly emptied every gun from the building, distributed them and sorted out all of the ammunition for the respective weapons. They marched through the city gathering people and more weapons and on to the Pound area to join a three-way riot with the Catholic residents and the military. The point here is that the workers of the shipyard were not immune from the sectarian bitterness outside its gates, and many became willing protagonists in violence that erupted in the city, such as riots in 1857 and 1864 and later episodes in 1886 and 1920.

PREACHING TO THE DISCONCERTED

While the shipyard expanded, so too did the population of Belfast, and the more it grew, the greater the pressure on housing and other civic amenities became. It was a heady mix of population density, segregated housing and employment along religious lines in an era of economic and political instability. Membership of the Orange institutions such as the Grand Orange Lodge of Ireland rose during the second half of the nineteenth and beginning of the twentieth centuries because of the emergence of the Home Rule debate, and due to the growth of the Catholic population in Belfast. Many working-class Protestants looked for people to blame for the political and economic threats that they felt surrounded by, and populist leaders provided them with clear targets to aim at.

The Harland and Wolff shipyard developed in the midst of this sectarian soup, which was stirred enthusiastically by religious leaders within a Presbyterian community that had long since abandoned any sense of political solidarity with their Catholic neighbours. Two of these leaders who gained particular notoriety at the time were Rev. Henry Cooke and Rev. 'Roaring' Hugh Hanna. Both men were radicals who sought to promote a conservative form of Presbyterianism in both a theological and a political sense. They became activist preachers, going out of their churches onto the streets to recruit believers. The religious dimension of the message was welded onto a conservative loyalist political identity, a cultural identification with Orangeism and loyalty to the Crown as defender of the Protestant faith. They both sought support within working-class Protestantism, and the Belfast shipyard was the crucible within which tensions were played out during these periods of political instability.

During the 1850s and 1860s these conservative clerics preached a gospel of religious fundamentalism and intolerance in outdoor sermons that enraged the Catholic community and incited Protestant mobs. They were aided and abetted by the Catholic clergy, who gave Cooke and Hanna plenty of ammunition to allege to their flocks that Catholics were hopelessly infected with the virus of 'popery'. This pejorative term was often used by Protestant evangelicals such as Hugh Hanna as what we would now refer to as a form of 'dog whistle' politics. Popery was a deliberately delegitimising and accusatory title designed to feed a dominant narrative concerning the Catholic community. Its substantive meaning was that papists were superstitious idolaters, fanatic blasphemers in theological terms, but also that they were suspect politically. Papists ultimately owed their political allegiance to Rome rather than to temporal authority such as the English Crown. Those who adhered to popery were therefore, by definition, disloyal citizens with ulterior motives.

Cooke was a gifted orator committed to a brand of Calvinist conservatism known as the 'Old Light' movement, which fought a battle within the Presbyterian Church with the 'New Light' advocates, who were more theologically and politically liberal. Cooke was a firebrand, preaching the gospels of evangelical Protestantism and political conservatism. He connected this to the industrial development of Belfast and to the driving role of the Protestant community that had delivered such progress.

For Cooke, Hanna and their legion of followers, Roman Catholicism was anathema to the concept of individual liberty, and so being anti-Catholic or anti-papist was 'baked in' to being an evangelical Protestant. From their perspective, as historian Fergus O'Ferrell notes, 'Rome would not permit liberty of conscience. It retained the authority to direct the spiritual, and, ipso facto the civil and religious life of its adherents.'[18] The belief that Roman Catholicism was as much a political project as it was a religious one was thus hard-wired into evangelical Protestantism, fanning the flames of hatred among those who were afraid and providing certainty for those who were insecure. It was a heady populist cocktail that intoxicated many of those Protestants in the shipyard and other areas of Belfast who were afraid that Catholics were increasing in numbers, becoming a clearer economic, political and existential threat to the Protestant unionist position in the city.

Hanna was also a rabble-rousing preacher, whose charismatic sermons caused what we would now refer to as 'interface tensions' in Belfast. He joined the Orange Order, serving briefly as Deputy Grand Chaplain for Belfast in 1871, and predictably he became an ardent opponent of Home Rule in the 1880s.[19] Hanna founded his own church, St Enoch's at Carlisle Circus in North Belfast, which became one of the largest in the city, his particular brand of evangelical Protestantism mixed with populist loyalism and anti-Catholicism filling the pews, many of the congregation being workers from the shipyard. A statue erected to commemorate Hanna at Carlisle Circus was blown up by the Provisional IRA in 1970, but the statue of Henry Cooke can still be found outside the Belfast Royal Academical Institution in Belfast city centre.

In the disturbances of August 1857, Hanna played a leading role in stirring up anti-Catholic feeling, refusing to observe a request from the Belfast Presbytery, the governing body of his own church, to cancel open-air religious meetings and rallies in order to calm sectarian tensions that were running high at the time. Hanna refused, claiming that the rights of Protestants were forged out of conflict and would only be maintained through such conflict.[20] Hanna was an agitator who developed a reputation as a radical firebrand due to his conservative theological and political views and the regularity with which he aired them. He intervened in public controversies, inciting violence that led directly to public disorder on several occasions, such as the street riots involving Protestant shipyard workers in September 1857.[21] His message was that Protestantism was under attack, the Church of Rome was behind much of it, and so any action taken by Protestants to counter that threat was both defensive and legitimate. But while Hanna provided the spark that lit the bonfire, he was typically never to be found when the fighting started, protected by a sympathetic police force and handpicked bodyguards from the shipyard who would step in as his personal protection unit at the first sight of trouble.

The rise of evangelicalism and political conservatism in Belfast's Presbyterian community in the second half of the nineteenth century was reflected not just in the activities of clerics such as Henry Cooke and Hugh Hanna, but also in the emergence of other civic associations. A proliferation of devout societies and what might be termed 'good living' projects that targeted public and personal morality emerged alongside the religious conservatism of these clerics. The Auxiliary Bible Society, the Ladies Bible Association and the Ulster Temperance Society provided a social outlet for those Presbyterians who were sympathetic to the evangelical focus on sin, guilt and control.

As the political climate became more febrile towards the end of the nine-teenth century with the emergence of the campaign for Home Rule within Irish nationalism, religious tensions in Belfast increased. The shipyard was clearly not immune from this sectarian feeling, and the expulsion of Catholic workers from Harland and Wolff by the numerically superior Protestant workforce was not uncommon. During the 1864 riots Catholics had to dive into the River Lagan to escape Protestant mobs, while the partition of Ireland in 1920 witnessed an equally notorious expulsion of Catholic workers from the yard.

Despite the pervasive sectarianism within the shipyard, there was work to be done and there were ships to be built, and, like the city itself, sitting along-side the dark side of intolerance and prejudice were tales of inspirational achievement and romantic adventure. None of these was more emblematic than one particular supership built by Harland and Wolff at the start of the twentieth century and thought to be unsinkable. This ocean liner was the biggest and the best, a vessel that would become both infamous and iconic, forever welded to the shipyard and the city that built it.

ONWARDS TO DISASTER

For months and months in that monstrous iron enclosure there was nothing that had the faintest likeness to a ship; only something that might have been the iron scaffolding for the naves of half-a-dozen cathedrals laid end to end . . . at last the skeleton within the scaffolding began to take shape, at the sight of which men held their breaths. It was the shape of a ship, a ship as monstrous and unthinkable that it towered there over the buildings and dwarfed the very mountains by the water.[22]

In July 1908, the shipping company White Star Line gave Harland and Wolff another huge contract to construct three equally massive ships. The second of the three vessels, No. 401, would become the most famous ship since Noah's Ark. It was, of course, the *Titanic*, and just a matter of months after its launch, on its maiden voyage to America, it would become synonymous with the most infamous maritime failure in modern history. It seems fitting that Belfast cherishes this failure to the point that it has become a central part of the city's cultural landscape. We have constructed our present-day brand and our tourist offering around the *Titanic* and its epic failure. This is perhaps a harsh judgement on Belfast and the shipyard, in that it was in perfect working order when it left the shelter of Belfast Lough. We are pleased that we built the biggest and most opulent passenger ship that the world had ever seen and that has become such a reference point in our shared social and cultural history. Books have been written about it, films made about it and documentary television series broadcast about what happened then and what should happen to the ship now. Poems have been written about it and, over a century later, primary school children around the world learn about the *Titanic* disaster.

It all began on 22 March 1909 in No. 3 Slip under the Arroll Gantry, when the keel of ship No. 401 was laid. However, before the contract for the *Titanic* had been awarded in 1908, Harland and Wolff had been struggling, and the boom-and-bust nature of the shipbuilding industry had resulted in periods of contraction and difficult labour relations, as wages were cut and workers were laid off. In truth, the success story of Harland and Wolff shipyard has had its share of hiccups, with periodic economic downturns being an additional headache to the endemic sectarian violence within and beyond its gates. By the late 1860s the order book had all but dried up and the shipyard was in the doldrums. However, the day was saved yet again by Gustave Schwabe, who persuaded the White Star Line to commission Harland and

Wolff to build five Atlantic passenger liners in 1869. The second half of the nineteenth century was an era of long-haul travel, by the wealthy for leisure, by the middle class for business and by the poor out of desperation. For various reasons, people were increasingly moving around, especially to America and further afield, and they needed ships to get them there – and hopefully back again.

The relationship with the White Star Line was a significant boost for Harland and Wolff and led it to expand its portfolio into the building and design of large-scale passenger ships focused on long-haul transatlantic travel. The first of these ships, which came down the slipway in Belfast docks in August 1870, was the *Oceanic*, which at the time appeared to be the last word in luxury travel. It catered for all budgets, from the first-class travellers with their rooms in the middle of the ship away from the noise of the engines, to those in third class, popularly known as 'steerage', housed at the rear and bottom of the boat where it was noisier, less comfortable and darker due to smaller windows. Even in steerage the *Oceanic* was an upgrade on previous vessels, and due to its speed, the other selling point was that you had to spend less time in it, as it set new record-breaking speeds, putting its competitors to shame.

The *Oceanic* was a big success for Harland and Wolff and was joined by its three sister ships, the *Atlantic*, the *Baltic* and the *Republic*, all of which were launched down the Queen's Island slipway within two years of the *Oceanic*. These massive-scale ocean liners became the template for a new phase in the history of Harland and Wolff that cemented the company's reputation as a world-leading shipyard. The success of the first wave of liners encouraged the White Star Line to commission two larger ships, the *Britannic* and the *Germanic*, which were launched in 1874. These were even faster and more luxurious than their predecessors, cutting the sailing time across the Atlantic, with the *Germanic* reaching America in seven and a half days, which set a new record at the time.

The alliance between Harland and Wolff and the White Star Line was immensely profitable for both parties and led to a rapid rise in the Belfast workforce. As it expanded, so did the size of the yard to accommodate the increasing scale of the operation. The workforce rose from 500 in 1861 to around 10,000 at the end of the century, and Harland and Wolff acquired more land from the Harbour Commission, amounting to a 80-acre site in the latter decades of the nineteenth century.[23]

This expansion coincided with changes at the top of the shipyard's management structure as both Harland and Wolff stepped back from day-to-day involvement in the company and devoted their energies to politics and civic life. Harland became Lord Mayor of Belfast in 1885 and Unionist MP for North Belfast until his death in 1895. Wolff also went into politics, becoming the Unionist MP for East Belfast in 1892, a role he retained until 1910.

By this time, the shipyard was being run by William Pirrie, a local Belfast draughtsman who joined Harland and Wolff as an apprentice in 1862 and worked his way up until he was appointed partner in 1874 – a meteoric rise, though entirely based on his merit and ability. Pirrie was the brains behind a new fleet of superliners including the *Olympic* and, infamously, the *Titanic* – larger, faster and more luxurious ships, maximising comfort and speed while minimising the time it took to cross the Atlantic. Pirrie's managerial skills were so highly regarded he was put in charge of all shipbuilding activities in the UK during the First World War. Like his mentor Edward Harland, Pirrie was a hard-nosed businessman who could be ruthless when he felt he needed to be, cutting the workforce from over 5,000 to 3,500 in the mid-1880s during a slump in orders, locking 900 riveters out of the yard for a month until they accepted lower wages and laying off those who took strike action. Jimmy Raymond, a former shipyard worker, recollects how Pirrie was loved and feared on the shop-floor: 'Lord Pirrie always had the name of being a hard man. They used to tell a story that when he was on his death bed he called out, "Hand me my sword!" "Your sword, Lord Pirrie? What do you want your sword for at this time?" "I want to take another cut at the wages before I go!"'[24]

Harland and Wolff was also in competition with the other shipyard in Belfast, Workman Clark's 'Wee Yard', which by the 1880s was more than holding its own, with clients on its order books that included the main competitors of the White Star Line, namely Cunard, as well as P&O, Royal Mail and Ellerman Lines. The Wee Yard was not so wee, either, as its site extended to over 50 acres at the end of the 1880s, and it was recognised in its own right as a major Belfast shipbuilder, rather than simply as Harland and Wolff's smaller competitor. By 1914 the two shipyards alone were responsible for an eighth of the global shipbuilding trade, employing over 20,000 people.

However, at the end of the nineteenth century and in the first two decades of the twentieth century, Harland and Wolff surged past the Wee Yard in terms of the volume, prestige and design innovation of the ships it built for the White Star Line, culminating in the *Olympic* in 1910 and its sister ship the *Titanic* in 1911. Cunard had stolen the maritime bragging rights a few years before with the launch of the *Lusitania* and the *Mauretania*, which earned the reputation of being the largest and fastest passenger ships in the world. Pirrie was tasked by the White Star Line to come up with something better, and so the *Olympic* was devised and designed, with work on it commencing in Belfast in December 1908.

It was Pirrie and his team who masterminded the design and production of these superliners, which became the largest and most luxurious ever to set sail, bringing a prestige to the vessels, to Harland and Wolff shipyard and to Belfast itself. The *Olympic* and *Titanic* were iconic ships that grabbed head-lines even before they were launched owing to the audacity of their scale and the opulence of their design. They were kitted out with electric lifts, squash courts and gyms for the first-class passengers, and in all respects they were regarded as better than anything that had gone before.[25] The launch of the *Olympic* was a major social occasion, with Lord Aberdeen, the British Viceroy, in attendance, as were other members of the gentry, along with Prime Minister Herbert Asquith's daughter and the leading executives from the White Star Line and Harland and Wolff, including, of course, Pirrie himself.[26]

The *Titanic* was launched on 31 May 1911 with less fanfare than the *Olympic*, but was heralded nonetheless as 'the unsinkable ship', a label that was to become tragically ironic less than a year after it entered the waters of Belfast Lough.

The sheer scale of the *Titanic* is still jaw-dropping to consider today, more than a century after its construction. Weighing in at a hefty 46,000 tonnes, it was nearly 270 metres (880 feet) in length and 53 metres (175 feet) in height from its keel to the top of its funnels. It cost £1.5 million to build, which in today's money would be upwards of £150 million, and was considered state of the art in terms of both its build quality and its internal finish. Everything about the ship was titanic. Even its two anchors were enormous, and each one, weighing 15.5 tonnes, had to be hauled on board by teams of 20 horses.[27] Over 3 million rivets were used to keep the ship watertight by the five-member rivet squads, who worked swiftly and in synch with each other, not least because the squad would be paid collectively based on how many rivets they had worked through in the week. They would then split the wage between them (often in the pub), with the two riveters getting more money than the three other members of the squad, based on their higher skill level and seniority. Herbie Atkinson, who joined Harland and Wolff in 1934, indicates the level of admiration that the riveters attracted:

> Well, I thought that the riveters were the greatest buggers I had ever seen in my life. Real craftsman ... A left-hander and a right-hander, a holder-up and a heater boy, bang, bang, all day. They never stopped. Unbelievable, great workers, craftsmen, no doubt. Nicest craftsmen I ever seen in a shipyard, and the hardest workers. They had to work, because they didn't get a penny piece until they pushed their first rivet in.[28]

It was tough work undertaken by tough men in poor working conditions, and injuries were commonplace, up to and including fatalities from falls or from heavy machinery. A report from 10 April 1912 detailing the accidents during the construction of the *Titanic* documented 8 fatalities, 28 severe injuries and over 200 minor accidents.[29]

All of this toil and capacity was to accommodate nearly 900 crew members and over 2,400 passengers. The latter figure is perhaps the most poignant, in that the *Titanic* was fitted with 20 lifeboats, sufficient for only 1,178 people. Elementary arithmetic is sufficient to work out that a lifeboat capacity of 1,178 and a human capacity of just over 3,500 was a considerable mismatch and would result in thousands of deaths if the ship were to sink, which is of course what came to pass in the freezing waters off Newfoundland in the North Atlantic a mere four days into its maiden voyage in the early hours of 15 April 1912. While this might seem like a horrific health-and-safety omission in a ship today, at the time, the lifeboat provision on the *Titanic* was in line with maritime regulations. The inquiries into the disaster that followed led to significant improvements in lifeboat provision and functionality, as well as other protocols to ensure that lessons were learned from the tragedy. There was clearly not enough lifeboat provision, those that were used did not launch properly when the *Titanic* was sinking, and several of them were only half full when they were launched. To heap tragedy upon tragedy, approximately 500 of the 1,500 or so who died in the freezing water that night could have been accommodated by the lifeboat capacity that was actually available.

Hindsight is of course a wonderful thing, but at the time the belief was that the ship had cutting-edge safety features, such as watertight compartments, and was built to withstand an impact accident and the flooding of its hull. This was part of the reason why the *Titanic* was described as 'the unsinkable ship', as it was designed to withstand up to four of its sixteen watertight compartments flooding. At 11.40 pm on 14 April 1912, the *Titanic* struck an iceberg that buckled its starboard side and flooded five compartments – it was one too many. The largest and most prestigious ocean liner to ever set sail was doomed from that moment to become an iconic disaster, the unsinkable ship doing just that on its maiden voyage. Of the estimated 2,224 passengers and crew on board the vessel, only 710 people survived the journey, and it remains the largest recorded single maritime death toll of a peacetime passenger ship.

Today the *Titanic* plays a key role in the cultural identity of Belfast and in its economy. The award-winning Titanic Belfast museum built on Queen's Island is the most-visited tourist attraction in the city and brings to life the story of the ship, the people who sailed on it and the men who built it. The angular building, designed in homage to the front hull of the ship, juts out at Belfast docks as an unmistakable statement. There is a brashness to it, a presence that is in no way apologetic, and the experience is as much a pilgrimage as it is one of tourist entertainment. This connects to the point that the *Titanic* might have been a historic tragedy and may be lying broken in two pieces 12,000 feet below sea, but it is very much alive as part of

Belfast's contemporary identity. When I visited Titanic Belfast, I was fully prepared to quibble and nit-pick about commercialisation, simplification or bastardisation of such a painful episode in the city's history. Actually, I was blown away by the detail, accuracy, empathy and sensitivity with which the story has been told. I was also impressed by how many school groups I saw there learning not just about the *Titanic* but about the people who built the ship, the conditions they worked in and the sheer scale of the engineering task they accomplished. I left via the gift shop with everyone else and enthusiastically loaded up with all the 'merch' I could get my hands on.

The other interesting aspect of my visit was, perhaps surprisingly, in the underground car park. I was amazed to see that every other car I could see in my section of the car park had a car registration plate from the Irish Republic. Obviously this has something to do with those visitors perhaps coming from further away and being less able to use public transport to get there – but it does say something about how Titanic Belfast and other high-profile attractions in the city are helping to connect the two political regimes on the island. Also, when I was growing up in the city in the 1970s and 1980s, cars from the Irish Republic were as rare as hen's teeth, so it was a nice surprise to see so many of them there thirty years later.

The urban architecture of Belfast reflects the importance of the *Titanic* to the contemporary life of the city, and the Titanic Quarter now formally defines the area where the museum and other entertainment, hotel and leisure facilities are based. Not everyone is convinced by the commercial imperatives that have revived the *Titanic* as a jewel in the crown of Belfast's post-conflict economy. Writing in *Causeway* magazine in 1996, Michael McCaughan reflected an uneasiness about the *Titanic* being raised metaphorically from the ocean floor and repurposed as an asset in Belfast's twenty-first-century post-conflict economy: 'Within this commercial frame, irony and parody are unconsciously present and the proposed transfiguration of Titanic from substance to pastiche is a retro-visionary proclamation that millennial postmodernity is alive and well in the city of Belfast.'[30]

From this perspective, where should the line be drawn in terms of how the *Titanic* is commemorated, monetised and consumed as a cultural product, and who gets to decide that? Thankfully, Belfast itself has not yet succumbed to tawdry representations of what was in reality a searing tragedy for those on board and a shocking failure for White Star and the wider ocean-liner industry. However, as we will discover in chapter 6, the dividing line between pilgrimage and pillage in a post-conflict economy is a fine one. Decisions about how to remember and represent tragic events and why they are being remembered are fraught with political and ethical considerations. In the end, the story of the *Titanic* is a human tragedy that for some should be mourned rather than celebrated. While Belfast has recognised the commercial opportunities presented by the fact that its iconic shipyard built the world's most iconic ship, there is also unease at the extent to which the tragedy is today being exploited and consumed as a leisure activity. As McCaughan reflected, 'Today, the gravesite of hundreds of people has become a tourist destination for cruising sightseers and a mega souvenir hunting ground for predatory promoters. . . . For many, the Titanic disaster is not quite history, it's still too close to the present.'[31]

There is certainly an irony in the extent to which the *Titanic* has become emblematic of the city as a thriving tourist brand, its tragic end successfully reinvented for the twenty-first century. It is also a little ironic that the *Titanic* is marketed today as an 'experience' that is accessible to everyone, as the rigid class boundaries of the early twentieth century were welded into the fabric and architecture of the ship. The *Titanic* had three classes of passenger, and while third-class accommodation on board was adequate, it had none of the opulence of first-class travel. Passengers experienced the tragic denouement very differently, with most deaths coming from the third-class compartments of the vessel. While the policy of prioritising women's and children's access to the lifeboats was the working principle on the vessel, in practice those women and children in first class were clearly a greater priority than their fellow travellers in steerage. This is evidenced by the list of fatalities, as only 3 per cent of female passengers in first class died, compared with 54 per cent of women in third class. Similarly, fifty-two out of a total of seventy-nine children in third class perished, while the vast majority of children travelling first class survived.

THE SHIPYARD'S 'ROTTEN PRODS'

While Harland and Wolff attracted some notoriety after the sinking of the *Titanic*, the disaster did not damage their order book, the more immediate impact for them being the death of their lead designer Thomas Andrews, who was on board when it sank. However, shipbuilding was always a boom-and-bust type of industry, and when the yard contracted and jobs became more precarious, relationships between Protestants and Catholics in the workforce became more frayed.

The shipyard was also hampered by events beyond its gates and, just as Hugh Hanna and Henry Cooke had done in the nineteenth century, other leaders such as Sir Edward Carson raised the political temperature in the shipyard in the early decades of the twentieth century. By this point, religious differences within the workforce had been welded onto political affiliations, and loyalty to Crown and Empire had been reinforced by the harrowing experience of the First World War. Tensions within the shipyard over loyalty to Britain were exacerbated by wider events taking place in Ireland, and specifically the rise of militant Irish nationalism. The Easter Rising in 1916 and guerrilla warfare between the IRA and the British state, along with the political ascendency of Sinn Féin, raised the collective temperature of Protestants in Belfast. The landslide victory of Sinn Féin in the 1918 general election, where they won 73 seats out of a total of 105, posed an existential threat to the Protestant unionist majority in Belfast, many of whom were employed in the shipyard. The co-existence of Protestant and Catholic workers in the shipyard became increasingly problematic during these tumultuous years, and sectarian tensions grew, fuelled by political leaders who promoted a binary narrative of loyal unionists and disloyal Sinn Féin separatists.

It would be too simplistic to characterise sectarianism in the shipyard as one-way traffic between Protestant perpetrators and Catholic victims, as violence at times went in both directions. Protestants were not a unified or homogeneous grouping with the same political outlook. As demonstrated later, in chapter 6, there were many Protestant workers in the shipyard who sympathised with their Catholic co-workers and defended them from attack.

This has been overlooked at times by a narrative that paints sectarianism in binary colours but ignores the fact that liberal Protestants and those from a Labour or unionised background actively opposed attacks against Catholics in the shipyard and expulsions such as those in 1864 and 1920. These workers, offensively termed 'Rotten Prods' by their co-religionists, showed solidarity and courage by standing shoulder-to-shoulder with Catholic workers threatened with expulsion, intimidation and violence and have often been overlooked in accounts of sectarian conflict in the shipyard in 1920 and on other occasions. This provides another example of the radical individualism within Belfast and the capacity of some to go against the grain, despite the pressure to conform. Dissenting is in the DNA of the city, and the 'Rotten Prods' in the shipyard were the latest example of an inclination that went back to the Presbyterian radicals two centuries earlier.

The passage of time has a way of simplifying the complexities of history, perhaps due to the way it gets repurposed for contemporary political arguments, its inconvenient wrinkles being ironed out in multiple retellings to the point that it becomes smoothed into binary narratives of us versus them and good versus bad. In the case of Belfast, the dominant narrative was that the numerically superior Protestant unionist workers in the shipyards and in other key manufacturing industries in Belfast, egged on by extremist political leaders and the Orange Order, intimidated and forced their Catholic co-workers from their jobs. While this certainly did happen, most infamously in July 1920, there were plenty of 'Rotten Prods' who dissented and tried to protect their Catholic colleagues and suffered the consequences of doing so, with one in four of those expelled from the shipyard in 1920 being Protestant.[32]

No one deserved the term 'Rotten Prod' as much as the man in charge at the shipyard, Protestant Home Rule supporter William Pirrie. While it is perhaps understandable that Harland and Wolff get most of the attention, Pirrie did as much as anyone to put the shipyard on the world stage as a global design and manufacturing hub for cutting-edge ships – most notoriously the *Titanic*. Pirrie was originally anti-Home Rule but switched his allegiance at the turn of the century, much to the alarm of unionist leaders at the time. Pirrie presented a conundrum for his unionist opponents, as by

1902 he was running Harland and Wolff very successfully, filling the order book, increasing profits for the company and providing secure employment for the largely Protestant and unionist workforce. Pirrie was a liberal unionist, not a conservative, and his success at the helm of the shipyard seems to have insulated him to some degree from criticism from Protestant workers who disagreed with his position on Home Rule at the same time as supporting his leadership of the yard.[33]

The 'Rotten Prod' label really gained traction after the end of the First World War when there was an economic downturn and a rise of unionised labour in the shipyard. This presented a threat to political unionism that had been desperately trying to maintain a cross-class alliance. To counter the threat of the newly formed Belfast Labour Party and the Independent Labour Party, the Ulster Unionist Council formed the Ulster Unionist Labour Association and attempted to steal the clothes of Labour by connecting a labour wing within the unionist movement and developing the idea that the interests of labour and the working class in Belfast were the same as the interests of the Union. Political unionism was keen to differentiate between pro-unionist labour and loyalty on the one hand, and the remainder of the labour movement which they painted as Bolshevist and disloyal on the other. The 'Rotten Prod' label emerged out of this attempt to delegitimise the labour movement and those unionists from labour and liberal perspectives who identified with their Catholic workmates or defended them from sectarian attack.

This group was of course the exception rather than the rule, as the prevailing mood among the Protestant working class in the Belfast shipyards was sympathetic to the unionist analysis and antagonistic towards Irish nationalism. This was especially true of the unskilled Protestant workers who were the more vulnerable in the shipyard during times of economic contraction and who eyed Catholic workers as a buffer between themselves and unemployment. It was the Protestant unskilled workers, for the most part, who welded their economic precarity to a muscular and religiously intolerant unionism.

By the end of the First World War, politics and economics had fused along sectarian lines, and the wider backdrop beyond Belfast was one of political uncertainty, with Home Rule legislation delayed, a landslide victory for Sinn Féin's militant separatist agenda in the 1918 UK general election and the Irish War of Independence raging between the IRA and the British state. After their election in 1918, the seventy-three Sinn Féin MPs boycotted the House of Commons in London and set up their own parliament, *Dáil Eireann* in Dublin, proclaiming Ireland a republic on 21 January 1919.

This febrile atmosphere fed into the Belfast shipyard expulsions in July 1920, the fear of Sinn Féin and Irish independence encouraging unionist leaders to heighten fears within the Protestant working class and stimulating those who were intolerant of their Catholic co-workers to take action. On 21 July 2020, notices went up in Belfast's two shipyards, Harland and Wolff and the Workman Clark 'Wee Yard', calling Protestant and unionist workers to a lunchtime meeting. At least 3,000 and possibly as many as 5,000 Protestant workers attended this in their lunch break, where they were encouraged to drive out the 'disloyal' workers from the yards. Everyone knew that this meant Catholics, socialists and the liberal 'Rotten Prods'. Following the meeting, hundreds of Protestant shipyard men, in the main apprentices and unskilled workers such as 'heater boys' (riveter assistants), marched into the yards and forced the Catholics and others they deemed disloyal out. It was brute-force thuggery, as the Protestant workers literally kicked and stoned their former Catholic colleagues out of their jobs, pelting them with rivets as they fled. The phrase 'Belfast Confetti' was coined as a sardonic metaphor for the expulsions and popularised later by local poet Ciaran Carson's poem of the same name. The expulsions quickly spread across the city from the shipyards to other manufacturing plants, including Mackies and the Sirocco Works, in copycat acts of violence. It was later established that over the tumultuous summer of 1920 around 10,000 Catholic men and 1,000 Catholic women were expelled from their jobs. While there were calls for them to be reinstated, including by Pirrie himself, the vast majority were not. Other historians estimate the overall figure to be closer to 7,500 men and 2,000 women expelled or intimidated out of their jobs from the shipyards and the surrounding manufacturing and textile factories in Belfast.[34]

While Pirrie threatened to close Harland and Wolff and lay off the entire workforce if those expelled were not allowed to return to work, he tacitly accepted the sectarian nature of his workforce and made excuses for not backing up his words with deeds. His business head, in any case, saw the advantages to be gained from a more religiously homogeneous workforce, which would likely result in greater harmony and productivity at a time of political turmoil outside the yard.

Since the infamous events of 1920, the shipyard expulsions have been seen by the nationalist community in Belfast as part of an anti-Catholic pogrom and a fascist-style zeal to eradicate them from the city. This has stirred some debate between Irish historians, with some pointing to the expulsion of the 'Rotten Prods' and socialists as evidence that it was not exclusively directed against Catholics. Others refer to the fact that, while the unionist political leadership may not have directly orchestrated the expulsions, the comments of one of the unionist leaders, Sir James Craig, in October 1920 (who went on to become the first Prime Minister of the newly minted Northern Ireland the following year) demonstrated that the expulsions were endorsed by the unionist leadership. Speaking at a ceremony to unveil a huge Union flag inside the Harland and Wolff plant, Craig posed and answered his own rhetorical question: 'Do I approve of the action you boys have taken in the past? I say "Yes".'[35]

Sporadic rioting and violent attacks spread across the city, with vigilante groups carrying out reprisals and premeditated violence. People deemed to be shipyard workers sympathetic to or involved in the expulsions were pulled off public transport and beaten up by angry Catholic mobs, while businesses and public houses were vandalised across the city. The buildings themselves were sucked into the political turmoil in 1920, some of them identified as either important symbols of unionism or venues for Catholic social or cultural recreation. Catholic churches, Orange halls and public buildings identified with either the unionist or the nationalist communities became targets in the incendiary atmosphere of sectarian conflict that followed the summer of 1920. This culminated in December 1920 with the passing of the Government of Ireland Act and the effective creation of Northern Ireland. The British 'solution' to the 'Irish Question', as the debate about Home Rule had become known, was to partition the island. As it was pithily observed at the time, 'when British diplomacy is confronted with one insoluble problem, it divides it into two insoluble problems'. Partition permitted a de facto independence for twenty-six of Ireland's thirty-two counties (within the British Empire) and allowed six counties in Ulster to opt back into the UK under the political and legal identity of Northern Ireland.[36]

The establishment of a majority-rule unionist-dominated political system led to widespread violence and mayhem on the streets of Belfast and across the six counties of Ulster that were now to be known as Northern Ireland. It is easy in retrospect to view history as a series of static events where A led to B and then to C, D and so on. However, when you are in the maelstrom of rapid political change and nascent civil war, nothing is fixed or certain and rumour is your guide. Both Protestant/unionist and Catholic/nationalist communities in Belfast and the island as a whole were convulsed by the partition of the country, fearful not just about what had taken place with the implementation of the Government of Ireland Act but also by what might happen in the months and years ahead.

Between the shipyard expulsions in July 1920 and the end of 1922, more than 400 people lost their lives in Belfast, with many more injured and displaced from their homes. There was large-scale destruction of property during this period, too, especially if buildings were particularly identified with either the unionist or nationalist communities. There were over 180 fires in August 1920 alone, which caused an estimated £1 million of damage, with buildings torched and families displaced from their homes.

The buildings were more than just bricks and mortar; they were manifestations of identity and representations of history, religion or cultural commemoration. They also became sites of confrontation between those who accepted and those who rejected the new political arrangements that had been made for them. So the buildings themselves got sucked into the political tumult, their reputations tarnished for those on the losing side of the increasingly bitter and visceral arguments taking place in and around them. Several buildings became the venues for dispute, not least the Ulster Hall in the city centre during the first election to the new Northern Ireland parliament in May 1921. When three Labour candidates booked the Ulster Hall for an election rally on 17 May, loyalist shipyard workers barricaded the doors to prevent the event from taking place, and unionist leader James

Craig, who was lined up to become the first Prime Minister of the new provincial government, sent a message of approval at how the Ulster Hall had been occupied by his supporters: 'I am with them in spirit. Know they will do their part. I will do mine. Well done big and wee yards.'[37]

As the new provincial government emerged after 1921, several of these public buildings become home to the unionist political class, symbols of political and economic dominance, control and an industrial heritage located firmly within the British Empire. In part, their unionist tinge was a result of nationalist boycotting of what they regarded as a fundamentally undemocratic political regime. But nonetheless, Belfast's civic buildings became aligned with a unionist and a British image when the first Northern Ireland parliament met in Belfast City Hall, as nationalists boycotted it in protest.

Several of these buildings are worth exploring in greater detail, as they act as time capsules for the historical, political and social development of Belfast. Thankfully, some of them still exist today and have become iconic features of the city's architectural and cultural heritage.

Buildings have stories, and the next chapter explores some of them.

4

THE BUILDINGS

One of the best things about Belfast when I was growing up was the fact that our evidently broken political system meant I could play football with my friends on the perfectly coiffured flat lawns up at the Stormont estate in East Belfast. The gardeners of Parliament Buildings thankfully kept cutting the grass during the years that the devolved government in Northern Ireland had collapsed, and what it lacked in the quality of democratic governance it more than made up for in being a great football pitch.

It was about 2 miles from where we lived on the Holywood Road, and during the summer months we would often cycle up to Stormont on our bikes for a kick-about. It was the stereotypical 'jumpers for goalposts' scenario, and we scarcely paid any attention to the massive, forbidding white(ish) building that loomed over us. We were much more alert to the poor security guards who would lumber over to chase us off when they could be bothered. But like urban pigeons flocking back onto discarded food wrappers after being shooed away, we would jump on our bikes and race off, reconvening the game once they had left.

These trips outside the protective shell of my street rarely brought me into any physical danger – the bike route from the Holywood Road to Stormont went through one of the most affluent parts of East Belfast, via the Circular Road, where C.S. Lewis grew up, and past Campbell College, where the posh Protestant boys (including Lewis) went to school. The fact that Stormont was dormant also meant that there were few politicians to protect, which decreased the security presence near our self-proclaimed football pitch.

We were relatively immune to the fact that we were playing under Carson's nose, or in front of a parliament building that for several generations had been a hated symbol of discrimination for the Catholic nationalist community. In retrospect, it is curious how invisible the police and army had become in our lives; they were armed and patrolling, and you could be stopped and questioned about where you were going and why, but through a child's eyes it was just part of the everyday scenery, like the traffic or the drizzle.

What is officially known as Parliament Buildings is referred to simply as Stormont by just about everybody who lives in Belfast. If you live in East Belfast, it is part of the skyline of everyday life and, like the big yellow cranes in the shipyard, is something you see every day. The Stormont parliament is one of several iconic buildings in Belfast whose stories are emblematic of the political, economic and cultural history of the city. These buildings combine functionality with aesthetics, connecting the political and economic history of Belfast with its urban geography. Beyond the bricks and mortar and their original role when they were constructed and occupied, these buildings are repositories of the city's political, economic and cultural heritage. The story of Belfast lies in the fabric of these buildings, and several of them have amazing tales to tell.[1]

THE LINEN HALL LIBRARY

I am proud to say that I am a member of the Linen Hall Library, the oldest membership library in Ireland and, for my money, one of the most significant civic institutions that has ever existed in Belfast. Founded in 1788, it is located in a former linen warehouse and perfectly situated opposite Belfast City Hall in Donegall Square North.

However, the Linen Hall is much more than the building and its curated materials, as the institution itself embodies the liberal enlightenment tradition in the city going back to one of its first librarians, Thomas Russell. Famously known as 'the man from God knows where', Russell was one of the key members of the Society of United Irishmen in 1798. He served with Henry Joy McCracken on the committee of the library in 1795, and both men were radical idealists who became militant Irish revolutionaries, and the library became a central part of that activism.

A History of the Linen Hall Library 1788–1988, written by former chief librarian John Killen, charts the importance of the library as well as its formative role in the social history of Belfast. The library was founded on 13 May 1788 out of the Belfast Reading Society and was originally named The Belfast Library and Society for Promoting Knowledge.[2] This quest for independent knowledge and education remains its guiding principle, and the library is recognised as being an independent and politically non-aligned institution which commands respect across Northern Ireland's divided community and internationally. It began as an intellectual project before it became a bricks-and-mortar institution with materials to preserve. While the language and bearing of the times might suggest a formality and seriousness, those involved were young, confident and wealthy and took their socialising seriously. The first committee meetings of the society took place in pubs such as the Donegall Arms in Castle Place, and those involved were not shy about getting stuck into the drink while they worked through the agenda of their meetings. Clearly the society had to move out of the pubs to make serious progress, and it has found several homes over the years, originally in the residence of its first librarian, Robert Cary, then finding a larger rented space in Ann Street in 1794, from where it relocated to the White Linen Hall (today the site of Belfast City Hall) in 1802, before finding its permanent home at the corner of Donegall Square North and Fountain Street, opposite what is now Belfast City Hall, in January 1892.

Its founders were part of the Belfast radical movement of the late eighteenth century who sympathised with the wider European liberal and enlightenment philosophy and with the American and French revolutions. They were the Presbyterian mercantile elite and they were on a mission to push the city forwards. To do that, they realised that an informed, literate, culturally aware citizenry was needed.

Those who founded the library were committed to promoting wider educational goals within the city, including the improvement of literacy across the community and providing books and other reading materials for those unable to buy them. In this sense, the emergence of the library was part of a wider flourishing of liberal initiatives in education, the arts, architecture and political activism with the rise of the United Irish movement. The people most active on the committee of the library were also active contributors to the *Northern Star*, the newspaper of the United Irishmen, including its editor Samuel Neilson. There was support among the founders of the library for the liberal goals of the Belfast radicals, and one of its first public interventions was to argue in favour of Catholic emancipation. This was in effect a statement of intent by the society that it was interested in more than just the curation of books, and it was from its earliest days a civic organisation committed to progressive political and social reform.

These were optimistic times for the merchant class in Belfast, who were an enterprising, educated, philanthropic community with time to devote to social enterprises such as developing libraries, schools, newspapers and activist societies. The Linen Hall was the outcome of that intellectual melting pot and its inherent energy and vitality. Killen's history suggests that the library was modelled on Benjamin Franklin's Library Company of Philadelphia, which he founded in 1731 to educate and mobilise the wider citizenry of Philadelphia.[3]

The Linen Hall has survived revolution in the 1790s and the arrest and execution of several of its key members, such as Thomas Russell and Henry Joy McCracken, for high treason, economic decline during the nineteenth century and even the Belfast Blitz during the twentieth century. In 1941 German bombing raids ravaged Belfast, but the Linen Hall managed to remain unscathed despite the destruction wrought upon the rest of the city. The Troubles in the 1960s brought new problems, not least the fact that getting in and out of Belfast was a hazardous business. Daily bomb attacks, and shooting incidents that were just as frequent, combined with the physical militarisation of the city centre, made it difficult to travel around. However, as had been the case during the Blitz in 1941, the building largely escaped unscathed during the Troubles, though there was some occasional blast damage to its windows and doorframes during the 1970s.

This period also brought new opportunities, as the conflict that surrounded the library spawned an abundance of literature and pamphlets from all sides that grew into the Northern Ireland Political Collection. This contains an unrivalled range of materials relating to the political conflict in Northern Ireland gathered over several decades. It has been supported financially by a number of organisations, including the National Lottery Heritage Fund, the Department for Communities and Belfast City Council. The collection was the brainchild of former librarian Jimmy Vitty, who came up with the idea in 1968 when he was handed a leaflet about a civil rights march in a city centre bar. Vitty realised that this was part of a living history that needed to be curated without regard to the political stance of those involved and in line with the non-partisan ethos of the library. Over the decades, this has grown into an invaluable resource for academics, students and the media, and it is used by researchers around the world who want to investigate the violent conflict and subsequent peace process over the last fifty years. As well as every book, journal, magazine and election manifesto produced during the period known as the Troubles (and many items that predated the 1960s), the Northern Ireland Political Collection has other treasures, such as posters, out-of-print and unpublished or embargoed papers and an amazing ephemera collection, with an assortment of items such as rubber and plastic bullets, badges and audio recordings of speeches, including some ripsnorting sermons from Rev. Ian Paisley's Martyrs' Memorial Church on the Ravenhill Road.

While the Troubles presented obvious challenges to the library, given that it was bang in the centre of town and surrounded by a daily barrage of bomb attacks and security alerts, it prevailed. In fact, much more harm was done to the fabric of the library by general economic decline, which brought regular financial crises, perhaps the most severe being in 1980, when a proposal was put forward to the governors to effectively sell off the building and the collections to the Belfast Education and Library Board and Queen's University. This was the result of years of financial decline, as year after year the library made annual losses, and its reliance on support from the Department of Education rose from 25 per cent at the beginning of the 1970s to 40 per cent towards the end of the decade. Something clearly had to be done to arrest its decline, and a feasibility study in 1978 produced a rather stark plan that boiled down in the end to two options: continued independence or merger with a larger and more sustainable partner. Of these two, it was clear that the first was a non-starter, as it was the status quo option that had got them into their financial hole in the first place. The remaining option, amalgamation, stared back at the governors of the day as the only remaining possibility but would in effect emasculate the library as a private charitable organisation. Over the next two years, protracted talks were held over the terms of amalgamation, until the Department of Education gave the library an ultimatum at a meeting in November 1980: agree to the scheme for amalgamation or the annual grant to the library would be terminated within two years. The governors felt they had no option but to agree to these terms, as it was out of alternatives, out of time and almost out of money. The terms of the deal were to be formally ratified at the last meeting of the board of governors on 18 December 1980, normally a festive event in the library calendar but feeling more like a wake than a Christmas party on this occasion.

Rather incredibly, and in line with the library's indomitable dissenting spirit, all was not lost, as one of the governors – Dr Brian Trainor, Director of the Public Record Office of Northern Ireland (PRONI), who had not been present at the previous meeting – objected strongly to the plan and spoke convincingly against it. In the space of five minutes, his colleagues had reversed their previous decision to support the amalgamation plan that had taken two years to develop and Trainor was tasked to come up with a viable alternative by the New Year.[4] The new plan included the selling off of some assets, including artwork, the recruitment of experienced and entrepreneurial governors and a public campaign launched in 1981 to 'Save the Linen Hall Library' that was supported by a wide array of political and cultural figures across civil society as well as through donations from the general public. Slowly but surely, the finances of the library improved, as membership rose, corporate donations increased and public money continued to come in, as its governance structure solidified.

Despite all of the political and financial crises over the last 200 years, the Linen Hall Library has endured, and it has arguably never been in better health, now financially supported by a number of private and statutory sources and professionally led. There are few institutions that manage to attract loyalty and public support from across the political spectrum, but the Linen Hall Library is one of them. The building that houses the Linen Hall is one of the most important in Belfast, but the library is an idea as much as a physical institution, and for as long as it exists it will indelibly connect the city of Belfast to its radical enlightenment spirit.

THE ASSEMBLY ROOMS

No building in Belfast has experienced the arc of ascent and decline as vividly as the Assembly Rooms, once a proud central hub for eighteenth-century merchants doing business and holding town meetings, today a largely forgotten derelict eyesore in the centre of the city. According to historian S.J. Connolly, the building was Belfast's most important social venue for over half a century.[5] It also provides a good example of the way in which buildings are much more than bricks and mortar, or whatever other materials hold them together, as the Assembly Rooms became one of the focal points for the emergence of radical revolutionary ideas at the end of the eighteenth century. These ideas, which included political independence from Britain, fell out of favour in the generation that followed, as did the building itself. A building that sits at the centre of the city's history is now occupied by pigeons rather than people and deemed 'at risk' by the Ulster Architectural Heritage Society. It was left vacant in 2000 when the Northern Bank relocated and was added to the Heritage at Risk register in 2003. Twenty years later, it still lies dilapidated as investment goes on around it in other parts of the city.

How could it be that a building with such a rich heritage and historical importance has been left to rot unloved, unwanted and unacknowledged by those who use the city every day and walk past its boarded-up exterior? The answer is that the building reflects a period of history that Belfast's civic leaders have had difficulty celebrating until very recently. The Assembly Rooms was built in 1769, originally a single-story structure known as the Exchange, and it became the hub for civic and business activities in the city. An upper storey was added in 1776, and there were several other additions and alterations made to its structure and function in the years that followed, including a major renovation by eminent architect Sir Charles Lanyon in 1845, when the elaborate stucco façade was added and the building was repurposed by the Belfast Banking Company, which later became the Northern Bank.

The Assembly Rooms stood at the intersection between Waring Street, Bridge Street and North Street at the centre of the area known as the Four Corners, the geographical and commercial hub of the town. Today, this part of the city is in a chronic state of disrepair and underinvestment, but back in the mid-eighteenth century it was the thriving epicentre of trade and civic life in the city. It was dominated in the second half of the eighteenth century by the Presbyterian merchants of Belfast, many of whom were radical liberals, some of the most prominent forming the Society of United Irishmen in the early 1790s, inspired by the events in Philadelphia and in Paris during the French Revolution. These Presbyterians were wealthy political activists, and the Assembly Rooms became a key venue to meet up, do business and engage in progressive ideas. The Assembly Rooms was the place where Thomas McCabe single-handedly prevented Waddell Cunningham, the richest man in Belfast, from becoming even richer by setting up a slave-shipping business out of the city.

The Assembly Rooms was the venue for the revival of Irish traditional music in 1792, with the hosting of the Belfast Harp Festival. This was much more than simply a musical event; its political focus was the preservation of Irish culture and a celebration of liberal sentiment timed as it was to coincide with the 1792 Bastille celebrations in France.[6]

Perhaps most notoriously, it was inside the Assembly Rooms that prominent United Irishman Henry Joy McCracken was tried in 1798 and sentenced to death before being marched around the corner to the junction between High Street and Corn Market and publicly hanged. Henry Joy McCracken remains one of the most important figures in Belfast's illustrious history, yet there is little evidence of his significance at the Assembly Rooms and nothing at all to mark the place where he was put to death. It is ironic that McCracken's memory has been eviscerated from the place he was executed while Sir Arthur Chichester's memory still lingers on the streets, even though Chichester is by far the more obvious villain of the piece. Sean Napier, guide on the 1798 Walking Tour of Belfast, has stated that he wants the street on which McCracken was hanged to be renamed after the revolutionary figure as a tribute to his role in the history of the city.[7]

The unloved Assembly Rooms sits as a testament to the political imbalance in the city over several centuries, which has only recently been rebalanced as unionists have lost political control. After partition created a permanent unionist government in Northern Ireland from 1921, there was little enthusiasm for celebrating that part of the city's heritage. The narrative of Protestant liberal radicalism born in Belfast, which pioneered democratic ideas and supported the political separation of Ireland from England, was not the story that unionist civic leaders wanted to celebrate. Their project was first and foremost to remain British in the face of antagonism from nationalists marooned within the new 'state' and chaos in the rest of the island, where a civil war took place in the early 1920s over the terms of the Anglo-Irish Treaty in 1921. The final boundaries of Northern Ireland were not ratified until the Boundary Commission rubber-stamped them in 1925, so during the 1920s and the decades that followed, an insecure political unionism sought to reinforce its claim to a British identity and shore up the political and cultural dimensions of the Union.

Belfast was clearly branded as being British, not Irish, and laws were brought in to reinforce that effort, including the Special Powers Act in 1922[8] and subsequently the Flags and Emblems Act in 1954.[9] This canopy of legislation helped unionist governments exert political and cultural control and equate Irish nationalist activism and cultural symbols with disorder and disloyalty. Irish nationalist parades and festivals could be banned, and while the Irish tricolour flag was not banned specifically, the legislation allowed it to be removed if it was deemed likely to cause public disorder – and so of course it regularly was considered to be provocative by the police and removed. The Union flag, by contrast, was protected, and it became a criminal offence to interfere with its display. As Belfast was spray-painted in red, white and blue by political unionism from 1921 until nationalists exerted some political control in the 1990s, its history of radical Protestant Irish separatism was airbrushed out of the public consciousness of the city.

That is the context for why the Assembly Rooms is lying derelict and rotting today, a largely forgotten part of the civic history of the city that tourists are likely to learn more about than local residents thanks to groups such as the 1798 Walking Tour and other organisations keen to revive that part of the city's forgotten history. The Presbyterian radicals in the 1780s turned Belfast from a town into a city, made it a global centre for the linen industry and set it up to take advantage of the industrial revolution. They were also the founding fathers of liberal democracy in Belfast and on the

119

island of Ireland itself, yet they have been all but forgotten in the twenty-first century. It is hard to imagine Philadelphia selling off Independence Hall and burying the memory of those who developed its own Declaration of Independence or American Constitution from a very similar era.

Not all of this can be laid at the door of unionists, however, as the Assembly Rooms has only been derelict since 2000, when nationalist politicians shared power with unionists, and Belfast City Council has been led by nationalist politicians as well as unionist ones. Putting public money into a building that was so integral to Presbyterian radicalism and the emergence of liberal enlightenment in Belfast has not been a priority for those in control of the city irrespective of whether they were unionists or nationalists.

Today the future of the Assembly Rooms is uncertain. It is a listed building, which means it cannot be flattened for site redevelopment, and its current owners, Castlebrooke Investments, the company behind the Tribeca Belfast[10] development on the edge of the Cathedral Quarter in the city, have plans to convert the building into a hotel. Whatever the future holds for the building, the fact remains that it is currently in a state of disrepair and decline. The Ulster Architectural Heritage Society does not mince its words when pointing out the urgency required to save the Assembly Rooms as a part of the city's unique heritage and its importance as one of the oldest and most historically significant buildings in the city:

The restoration of the Assembly Rooms would be an exemplar of heritage regeneration for Belfast and an indication that the City is revaluing its pride of place and character. However in the short-term, remedial works to the façade, removal of vegetation and safeguarding of the building is urgently required. Action that may be encouraged by way of enforcement. If not, the loss of more of the remaining historic fabric of this important heritage asset will be assured.[11]

However, a campaign is underway to have the Assembly Rooms brought back into public ownership and converted into a visitor and heritage facility centred on the United Irish movement. In December 2021 a new civic group came together under the banner of the United Irish Historical Society to discuss ideas including saving and repurposing the Assembly Rooms.[12] A less politically driven option would be for the Assembly Rooms to convert into a hotel that pays homage to the history of the building but with little acknowledgement of the radical edge of the times, a politically neutered and commodified space of five-star accommodation and themed artefacts. However, the worst of all worlds would be if the Assembly Rooms continued to decline, decaying slowly and disappearing from public memory and the physical fabric of the city.

THE ULSTER HALL

The Ulster Hall was built in 1862 and is located on Bedford Street in the centre of the city, a stone's throw from Belfast City Hall. From its opening in the nineteenth century until recent times, the Ulster Hall was the most prestigious theatre in the city and was used for all sorts of concerts and events, including political rallies by both unionists and nationalists. Charles Dickens read excerpts from his recently published *A Christmas Carol* at the Ulster Hall in 1867, while at the other end of the cultural spectrum, legendary rock band Led Zeppelin debuted their classic 'Stairway to Heaven' there in 1971.

The Ulster Hall is perhaps most famous for being the site of unionist political resistance, in the late nineteenth century to the possibility of Home Rule and in the late twentieth century after the signing of the Anglo-Irish Agreement. In February 1886, Tory grandee Lord Randolph Churchill travelled to Belfast to campaign against the First Home Rule Bill, the main focus of his visit being a speech to a huge crowd of unionist supporters packed into the Ulster Hall on the evening of 22 February 1886. Churchill left his listeners in no doubt about the urgency of the task that faced them or the calamity that the Home Rule Bill represented for the Protestant people of Ireland. He cautioned unionists against sleepwalking into Home Rule, which could come upon Ulster 'as a thief in the night',[13] and his message was to prepare, organise and resist by all means at their disposal.

In reality, Randolph Churchill actually had little regard for the people of Ireland, including unionists, but he viewed them as a necessary evil in terms of pursuing his own wider political agenda. Unionists did not trust Churchill, either, with Colonel Edward Saunderson telling him to his face that he was more distrusted than any of his other colleagues.[14] While their distaste for each other was mutual, it did not show that evening in the Ulster Hall when Churchill addressed his adoring audience for an hour and a half. His message was that unionists needed to prepare for a fight, and he dropped heavy hints that armed resistance against Home Rule would be supported by him and many of his senior colleagues in London: '[I]n that dark hour there will not be wanting to you those of position and influence in England who are willing to cast in their lot with you, whatever it may be, and who will share your fortune and your fate.'[15] This statement of solidarity was met with rapturous applause by his Ulster Hall audience but was seen by Irish nationalists and his political opponents in London as irresponsible incitement to violence.

Just over a quarter of a century later, the Ulster Hall was once again at the centre of the Home Rule debate. While Randolph Churchill had helped to see off the First Home Rule Bill, which was defeated in the House of Commons in April 1886, he had failed to kill it altogether. A second Home Rule Bill was introduced in 1893, and while it passed in the House of Commons it was defeated in the Lords, where there was a strong Tory majority. The issue receded but came back with a vengeance following the January 1910 general election, when Irish nationalists once again held the balance of power in the House of Commons. Another election in December 1910 left Asquith in power with the support of the Nationalist Party and Labour, allowing him to pass the Parliament Bill, which removed the veto power of the House of Lords. The last obstacle to the introduction of Home Rule for Ireland seemed to have been overcome, and unionists in Belfast prepared for the worst.

Ironically, it was Randolph Churchill's son Winston, who had joined the Liberal Party, who was at the forefront of the argument that promoted Home Rule for Ireland. Demonstrating a spectacular lack of understanding of the mood of unionists in Belfast, he accepted an invitation from the Ulster Liberal Association to give a speech in the unionist citadel, the Ulster Hall, where his father had previously spoken so memorably against the policy a quarter of a century before him. In response to threats of violence that accompanied the news that the Ulster Hall was to be defiled by a pro-Home Rule event, Churchill diplomatically withdrew and made it clear he was happy to appear at a different venue. However, in a further snub to Churchill's pride, the man who was at the time First Lord of the Admiralty and effectively the minister in charge of the British Navy was informed that there was no other hall or hotel available in the whole of Belfast to host the event. It was later claimed by the owner of the Grand Opera House in Belfast that he had been offered a knighthood as well as a significant financial inducement to allow the event to be held in his theatre but had declined. Instead, Churchill was diverted to a tent in the nationalist-dominated Celtic Park football ground, where, in the pelting rain, he made the case for Irish Home Rule to a smaller-than-expected crowd of 5,000. Before Churchill got there, his car was mobbed by angry unionists at his hotel in Belfast, the rear wheels lifted off the ground before police batoned the protestors back. Unlike his father, Churchill left Belfast a chastened figure, deciding not to go back to his hotel, where a unionist mob awaited him, after his speech. Instead, he slipped out of the city (as unionists put it, 'like a thief in the night') and took the back roads to Larne before sailing back to the safety of England. The Ulster Hall had remained unsullied by the Home Rule faction, and unionists had learned that organised resistance and a whiff of violence could achieve results.

The Ulster Unionist Council (UUC) became the main hub for the plan to resist the Third Home Rule Bill, up to and including through armed insurrection against the state to which they pledged allegiance. A provisional government for Ulster was planned in preparation for the Bill being passed into law at Westminster, and a constitution was drafted for this new shadow regime in the autumn of 1911. James Craig was at the centre of much of this activity, along with his ally Sir Edward Carson. Craig was the taciturn organiser, while Carson was the charismatic communicator and showman, and together they set about demonstrating to London that their threats of armed resistance were far from idle. While much of this involved private lobbying and larger set-piece speeches, both Craig and Carson realised they needed London to sit up and take notice. Some drama was required, and where better to provide it than the Ulster Hall.

The Ulster Hall became the emotional home of Ulster unionism when it provided the public centrepiece rally in their campaign against the Third

Home Rule Bill on 27 September 1912. The following day had been declared as 'Ulster Day' and featured a number of mass meetings across the province, ending in Belfast with the signing of the Solemn League and Covenant. Ten days earlier, Carson had reviewed a Protestant militia of up to 40,000 men in Fermanagh to show London that they had not just the intent but also the means to resist.

Ulster Day on 28 September 1912 was preceded by a highly theatrical gathering at the Ulster Hall, where Carson rallied support for the task of signing of the covenant the following day. On the one hand, this emphasised the loyalty of unionists to the Crown, while on the other it declared that their loyalty was conditional on a protection of the civil and religious liberty of Protestants in Ireland. The whole event was intended to tap into unionist nostalgia, energising the rank and file into believing their cause was just and that their survival as a community was at stake. This meeting in the Ulster Hall on 27 September was an intensely emotional event, unleashing a nostalgic defiance and creating headlines beyond Belfast – which was of course the intention. Ulster Day itself began in the Ulster Hall with a religious service, after which Carson, flanked by a personal guard of several hundred supporters, walked the short distance to Belfast City Hall where the covenant was to be signed. The atmosphere was appropriately solemn rather than triumphalist, the city's factories and shipyards quiet as all unionists gathered in the centre of the town to play their part.

It was a beautiful autumn day in Belfast on 28 September 1912 and the sun beamed upon Carson, Craig and the other dignitaries in the city hall as they solemnly undertook their duty to sign the covenant and distribute the pledge of resistance to their supporters. The covenant would become the template for unionism's conditional political loyalty for the next hundred years. Carson stepped up to sign on a table draped with an enormous Union flag, and following him came a who's who of Belfast's civic and religious dignitaries. Over 200,000 men signed the covenant in Belfast, with a similar number of women signing a 'Declaration' in the Ulster Hall that was similar in sentiment but did not commit them to the prospect of resisting by force. So around 470,000 unionists signed up to the undertaking to resist Home Rule, and it remains to this day one of the most impressive examples of collective political resistance in Belfast's illustrious history. Carson left for Liverpool later that evening, mobbed by a crowd of around 100,000 supporters and well-wishers. Ever the clever barrister working the jury, he milked the applause for effect, turning a ten-minute walk into a one-hour celebratory cavalcade.

The Ulster Hall unquestionably played a key role in unionist resistance to Home Rule, and it has since become a building with a cultural resonance for unionists in terms of their ongoing political disputes and insecurities. The Ulster Hall was thrust into the spotlight once again in the 1980s when unionists wanted to demonstrate opposition to the Anglo-Irish Agreement signed by British Prime Minister Margaret Thatcher in 1985.

Once their initial shock had abated, unionists set about trying to undermine and remove the hated Anglo-Irish 'Diktat', as they liked to call it. Their minds turned inevitably to Sir Edward Carson, to the covenant and to that Ulster Hall meeting in 1912. By this point, political unionism was being led by James Molyneaux of the Ulster Unionist Party (UUP) and Rev. Ian Paisley of the Democratic Unionist Party (DUP), and they were as different in personality as Craig and Carson before them. Molyneaux was a taciturn and dour man, an old-fashioned and understated politician who in his own words liked to take 'the long view' rather than engage in photo opportunities. Paisley was cut from a different cloth, a ruddy-faced preacher who saw himself as the reincarnation of Carson and the saviour of unionism. Actually he displayed a religious zealotry that owed more to Roaring Hugh Hanna than it did to the Dublin-born barrister. Like Hanna, Paisley founded his own Church in County Down, the Free Presbyterians, with himself as its Moderator, and he founded and led the DUP. Again, we can see that streak of radical individualism displayed by Hanna and many others before him over previous generations, an inclination to go against the grain and defy authority that is woven into the DNA of the city. Where Paisley did display a similarity to Carson was in his dalliance with political violence and his understanding that arguments would have more leverage if they had the backing of a wider alliance that included armed groups. While he frequently warned about the disintegration of law and order, many of his critics believed he was hell-bent on precipitating the sort of violence he claimed to be trying to prevent.

Paisley supplemented rhetorical invective with political dalliances which included some people who were close to loyalist paramilitary organisations. Channelling his inner Carson, Paisley helped set up a series of Ulster Clubs (which Carson had used in 1912 to marshal resistance to Home Rule). The Ulster Clubs were an attempt to bestow legitimacy on their actions and ensure broader solidarity across the unionist community. Alan Wright, the Chair of the Ulster Clubs in 1985, made the link back to Carson very clear when interviewed about their activities: '[We] need to have what Carson had which was a people's army to make this country totally ungovernable to bring this government to its knees.'[16]

A year into their campaign against the Anglo-Irish Agreement, neither the two big unionist parties nor the activities of the Ulster Clubs had made a dent in British government policy. Desperate to find a cutting edge over their opposition, unionists turned once again to the Ulster Hall, which became the venue for a rally on 10 November 1986. This 'by invitation only' event saw 2,000 unionists bussed to the Ulster Hall to form a new shadowy organisation which called itself 'Ulster Resistance'.

The Ulster Hall had once again become the venue where unionist politics intersected with armed paramilitary factions, as those organising it wanted to demonstrate there was some muscle behind the political rhetoric. The meeting consciously mimicked those that had taken place during the Home Rule crisis and was equally focused on engineering a campaign of civil disobedience. The high-profile politicians who attended the formation of Ulster Resistance walked a fine line between providing leadership to their supporters and inciting them to break the law. There was a tacit admission by several high-profile politicians that, while the actions of Ulster Resistance might break the law, that was only happening because the law was illegitimate and therefore they should not feel bound by it.[17]

Politicians including Ian Paisley and his deputy Peter Robinson were pictured inside the Ulster Hall wearing red berets, the favoured paramilitary chic of the Ulster Resistance movement, which placed a strain on the DUP's links to more moderate unionist opinion. There was a view at the time that Paisley wore his beret reluctantly, in an attempt to provide leadership to the paramilitary group and restrain its more violent urges. However, he seemed very happy to play to the gallery in the Ulster Hall at the group's launch, using its threat to gain political leverage, only disavowing the group when he was worried it would implicate him in its illegal activities. Over the next few years, Ulster Resistance joined forces with the UDA and the Ulster Volunteer Force (UVF) and imported weapons that were responsible for numerous murders, including the massacre at the Sean Graham bookmakers' shop in Belfast's Ormeau Road in 1992 which killed five Catholics, and the Loughinisland massacre in 1994 in which six Catholics were shot dead.

In recent years, the Ulster Hall has hosted less controversial events, as the peace process emerged in the 1990s and as other larger venues emerged for political conventions and meetings, notably the Waterfront Hall. The Ulster Hall will forever be linked to the high drama of unionist activism at key points in Belfast's turbulent history, but the political events held there will reflect the changing political geography of the city as unionists, nationalists and the non-aligned learn to share it with one another. A case in point came with the announcement in early October 2022 that the civic association Ireland's Future was to hold a public meeting in the Ulster Hall on 23 November 2022 under the banner of 'Planning and Preparing for a New and United Ireland'.

PARLIAMENT BUILDINGS

The first very noticeable thing about Stormont is its size. It is an enormous 365-foot-wide stone lump of a building, though incredibly it is smaller than originally planned as the political focal point for the recently minted Northern Ireland. An insecure unionist government that took over the fledgling provincial administration in 1921 was worried about its long-term viability due to passive and active opposition from nationalists in both parts of Ireland and from the British government in London. So what they needed was a civic statement in the shape of a massive parliamentary building on a hill in East Belfast that could be seen far across the city. Unionist politicians wanted an architectural statement, a large one that said Northern Ireland had prestige, stability and permanence – just like its parliament. In this sense, Parliament Buildings has as much to do with political psychology as it does with the administrative and bureaucratic needs of Northern Ireland. In essence, it was saying Northern Ireland was here to stay – its giant stone parliament as permanent as its in-built unionist majority.

The first meeting of the new Northern Ireland government took place in Belfast City Hall on 7 June 1921 – a historic day for the new fledgling regime called Northern Ireland as well as for Britain itself. The forty unionists elected turned up, but the six Sinn Féin MPs and six MPs from the more moderate Nationalist Party boycotted the meeting, objecting to partition and what they saw as an illegitimate political system. Sir James Craig had been appointed Northern Ireland's first Prime Minister the day before by the King's representative in Ireland as the more obvious candidate between him and Sir Edward Carson had become disillusioned and regarded partition as a political failure. Craig faced financial and organisational challenges, political opposition and resentment among the Catholic nationalist community in Northern Ireland and across the other twenty-six counties of Ireland and lukewarm support from the British government. Sectarian violence was the midwife at the birth of Northern Ireland, and public disorder added to the pervasive sense of crisis.

One of the initial tasks was to identify an institutional home for the new parliament, which had a lower House of Commons as well as a Senate, and this was an item of discussion at Craig's first cabinet meeting on 15 June. By the autumn, the Stormont Estate in East Belfast had been identified as the ideal home of the parliament, and the 230-acre site was purchased for the princely sum of £20,334. While plans were devised for Parliament Buildings at Stormont, the Northern Ireland government took up a lease at the Union Theological College in the university area of the city. This magnificent building was designed by Sir Charles Lanyon, who also built the even grander Queen's University that sits adjacent to the Theological College in South Belfast. Like many building projects, the construction of Parliament Buildings took longer than expected, and the government had to wait eleven years (instead of the anticipated three) before the Stormont parliament could be opened in 1932.

Arnold Thornley, the architect appointed to lead the project design, took his brief to produce an eye-catching building seriously, his first effort stretching both the ambition and the finances of his clients. It included a huge four-storey central building with a tower and a dome as its centrepiece and two smaller blocks either side for law courts and the civil service. The costs escalated to the point that by 1925 it was estimated that the design would require £1.25 million to build, a figure that was difficult to justify given the other pressing financial issues Northern Ireland had to deal with during the first decade of its existence. Eventually, the plans were adjusted to lower costs, which resulted in merging the three buildings into one and losing the central dome. The name 'Parliament Buildings' was kept even though the design was merged into one structure, building work finally getting underway in 1928.

Four years later it was complete, a 365-foot-wide building made from white Portland stone and opened with great fanfare by the Prince of Wales, the future Edward VIII, on 16 November 1932. Its white neo-classical structure was quite a statement, standing on a hill in East Belfast overlooking the city and claimed by Hugh Pollock, Northern Ireland's first Finance Minister, to be 'the outward and visible proof of the permanence of our institutions; that for all time we are bound indissolubly to the British crown'.[18] This was certainly the message that Craig's government wanted the building to convey, less than a decade after the Boundary Commission had finally confirmed the border between Northern Ireland and the Free State. By this point, unionists had replaced the proportional representation electoral system with the British first-past-the-post model, solidifying their hold on power and making it clear that nationalists would never be able to win an electoral majority and govern Northern Ireland from the gleaming new white building that had just been opened.

For Northern nationalists, the opening of Stormont was nothing to celebrate, as it represented to them the seat of unionist misrule and the physical manifestation of their permanent minority status. Former First Minister David Trimble remarked in his speech when accepting the Nobel Peace Prize alongside John Hume in 1998 that for many years Stormont had been a 'cold house' for Irish nationalists and that only the peace process of the 1990s had begun to rectify the situation: 'Ulster Unionists, fearful of being isolated on the island, built a solid house, but it was a cold house for Catholics. And northern nationalists, although they had a roof over their heads, seemed to us as if they meant to burn the house down.'[19]

During the Second World War, Stormont became a dark house for everyone as well as a cold one for Catholics as the government scrambled to do what it could at the last minute to protect the building from German bombs. Belfast was underprepared for the onslaught to come, its buildings and its people underprotected as a result of ambivalence in London and incompetence in Belfast. The stark reality was that the British government was unwilling to include Northern Ireland in the preparations being made in Great Britain. The view from the Home Office was that Stormont was responsible and it should get on with making its own plans. In 1937, as the likelihood of war with Germany grew stronger, Westminster introduced the Air Raid Precautions Acts. The new legislation mandated local authorities in Great Britain to step up defences, recruit local volunteers and provide air raid shelters in urban areas. When the Northern Ireland government pleaded to be included in this, they were rebuffed by London.[20] In truth, the Stormont government was chronically underprepared for air attacks, and it was only in the last few months before the outbreak of war that it woke up to the fact that Belfast was a prime target for German bombing due to its industrial capacity. Unfortunately, when the penny dropped in Belfast so did the bombs of the German Luftwaffe, with much greater severity than anyone had anticipated.

Even at the point that the UK declared war on Germany, the Northern Ireland government was still dithering about what precautions should be taken, with the cost implications of protecting public buildings and its citizens uppermost in its mind.[21] The amateurish nature of the Stormont government, less obvious in peacetime, was cruelly exposed by its preparations for war. Belfast had the lowest number of publicly available air raid shelters, and despite the Stormont government imposing a blackout like the rest of the UK, many pubs and other facilities remained open and lit up at night. Incredibly, even after Belfast was bombed in April 1941, lighthouses on Belfast Lough carried on functioning as normal, shining their lights after sirens warned that German bombers were approaching.[22] More attention was given to the prospect of Sir Edward Carson's statue at the base of

Parliament Buildings being destroyed by a bomb attack than to the homes of those who surrounded the estate. Carson's possible destruction was considered a step too far by the unionist government, and a plan was hatched to temporarily remove the great leader from his plinth and relocate him further down the hill in a less conspicuous site. This idea was abandoned when the sculptor assured the government that he had a substitute head for Carson, as he had planned for the eventuality that he might lose his first one.

In Parliament Buildings itself, meanwhile, the bright white Portland stone was considered too soft a target for the Luftwaffe searching for the Harland and Wolff shipyard, which was constructing ships for the war effort. As a result, its exterior was coated in a black paint that was a mixture of bitumen and cow manure (or shite, to use the Belfast vernacular). Unfortunately for the building and the politicians who occupied it, while this was effective in stopping the Nazis from bombing it, the substance seeped into the Portland stone over time and, like a bad make-up job, proved very difficult to remove afterwards. Despite seven years spent trying to take the paint off, the stone never fully returned to its former white splendour, and faint remnants of the mixture remain within the stonework to this day. In that sense, it is a fair (if crude) observation that there will always be a bit of shite inside Stormont – a fitting metaphor, some might argue, for the city's muddied political history: a permanently discoloured building for an endemically dysfunctional and tainted political system.

In its most recent political incarnation, Parliament Buildings has been the home of a devolved government since 1999 as a result of the Good Friday Agreement. This was based on power-sharing between unionists and nationalists, which has produced very brittle institutions that have collapsed on several occasions. However, it did demonstrate a capacity for political agreement and for the building to operate as a seat of local government for the people of Northern Ireland. There have been signs of the cold house warming up for the nationalist community, due in part to the changes in Northern Ireland's political demography and its knock-on impact on Parliament Buildings. In the Assembly election of 5 May 2022, Sinn Féin emerged as the largest party and now has the right to nominate a candidate to the position of First Minister, if power-sharing is restored. These changes in the power balance are also reflected visually, with a new permanent exhibition of paintings installed in 2022 entitled *Parliament Buildings: A Journey of People, Politics and Peacebuilding*, which includes nationalist politicians such as Eamon de Valera and Michael Collins as well as unionist leaders.[23]

For the last ninety years, Stormont has been more than just a building, representing a key site of historical, political and cultural significance in the city. Since its opening in 1932, it has represented the physical manifestation of division and disagreement within the city and within Northern Ireland more broadly. It would be a tragedy if Parliament Buildings were to be mothballed once again as the centre of democratic governance in Northern Ireland and another generation of children were to grow up using the lawns at Stormont as their football pitch due to the dearth of more important activities taking place on the estate.

BELFAST CITY HALL

Belfast City Hall is arguably the most recognisable public building in Belfast after Parliament Buildings at Stormont, and it is inextricably linked to the political, social and cultural history of the city. The building dominates the centre of Belfast in Donegall Square, its four sides being fully accessible to traffic and pedestrians and a focal point for buses picking up and dropping off shoppers, tourists and those going to and from work.

Originally, the city hall was the site of the White Linen Hall, designed by the accomplished architect Roger Mulholland, who was also the first President of the Belfast Reading Society (aka the Linen Hall Library). Following the granting of city status to Belfast by Queen Victoria in 1888, a new building was commissioned to mark its increased prominence. The new building was designed by Alfred Brumwell Thomas, and he produced a masterpiece in Portland stone that radiated civic pride, opulence and grandeur. The building was opened in August 1906 and made a bold statement signifying the industrial success of the new city and its engineering prowess.

The civic identity of the city hall was a British identity, sharpened after partition in 1921 but evident from its opening in 1906. Its grounds feature monuments and military memorials to Britain's imperial past, notably an impressive statue of Queen Victoria. The city hall was the natural venue for the opening of the new Northern Ireland parliament before Parliament Buildings at Stormont was constructed. King George V did the honours on 22 June 1921 when the city hall was still in its infancy, having been opened just fifteen years previously. Drawing up to the ornate new building in a horse-drawn carriage amid a throng of well-wishers, the King made a conciliatory speech inside what is now the council chamber. The lofty ideals and ambitions he expressed were sadly not reflected by the events beyond its walls in the years that followed, or by the politicians who shaped those events: 'I inaugurate it with deep-felt hope, and I feel assured that you will do your utmost to make it an instrument of happiness and good government for all parts of the community which you represent.'[24]

King George V's opening of the new parliament added to the sense that Belfast City Hall was a building firmly identified within the unionist and British tradition, an impression that was clear from its architecture as well as the events that took place inside it. The stained glass windows are reflective of the way in which the unionist political narrative dominated the architecture of the building until relatively recently. An RUC window was installed on the ground floor in tribute to the role of the Royal Ulster Constabulary during the Troubles. The window was installed in 1999 with the RUC coat of arms and a Latin inscription which includes the words 'honesty, impartiality, courtesy, compassion and courage'. This positive narrative would be contested by nationalists, who saw the RUC as anything but courteous and impartial.

A UDR window was installed in 1992 to commemorate those who served in the Ulster Defence Regiment from 1970 to 1992. The UDR was another contentious part of the British military apparatus in Northern Ireland that nationalists considered to be malign and antagonistic. The UDR was almost exclusively Protestant in its makeup and was seen by Catholics as a unionist militia, even though it was under the command of the British Army. There is extensive evidence of UDR soldiers doubling as loyalist paramilitaries or colluding with such paramilitaries in the murder of Catholics in Northern Ireland.[25] The window was commissioned for Belfast City Hall when unionists were in control of civic life in the city and because the UDR had been decommissioned by the UK government under pressure from nationalists in Northern Ireland and the Irish government.

There is also a British Army window on the ground floor of the city hall that pays tribute to all the regiments of the British Army who have served in Belfast since 1969. Again, this presents an uncontested narrative of a highly contested period in the city's history, when the British Army were fighting an undeclared war with many residents of the city whom they considered to be terrorists. Many of those republicans have now transitioned from paramilitaries into politicians, but for them and the voters who elect them, there is little love for the British Army whose memory adorns the building. This, of course, is reflective of the period in history that the architecture of the city hall represents and the unionist domination of politics in Belfast for most of the twentieth century.

Perhaps the most famous windows are in the Great Hall on the first floor of the city hall, which survived a direct hit on the building from a bomb dropped by the German Luftwaffe in the Belfast Blitz of 1941 that demolished the room. The windows depict the four provinces of Ireland, Ulster, Munster, Leinster and Connaught, and the three British monarchs who had visited Belfast before the city hall was built, William III, Victoria and Edward VII. Luckily, a forward-thinking Lord Mayor had the presence of mind to have the stained glass windows removed to the safety of a country estate in rural County Down, and they were restored to their previous position when repairs to the room were completed in 1952.[26]

The Cenotaph and Garden of Remembrance are also housed in the grounds of the city hall and are the location for ceremonies to mark Remembrance Sunday every year. In the past, these were exclusively unionist events, remembering members of the British military who died in the service of the Crown, though in more recent years nationalist politicians have also joined these ceremonies. This reflects the beginning of a post-conflict dynamic in the city where political nationalism and unionism have tried to move towards one another and extend leadership across the whole community. This has been sporadic rather than consistent but has seen conciliatory gestures made in both directions, including Social Democratic and Labour Party (SDLP), Sinn Féin and Irish government representatives attending Remembrance Sunday ceremonies at the Cenotaph at Belfast City Hall.

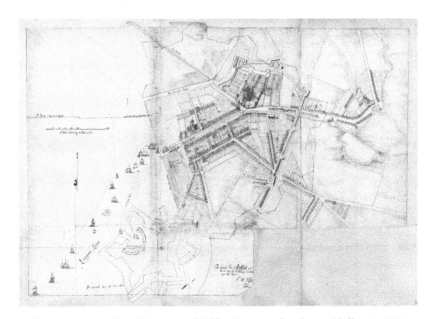

1. An early ground plan of the town of Belfast drawn up by Thomas Phillips in 1685 as part of his survey of Irish towns and fortifications. It shows existing landmarks including Belfast Castle, the Farset, Blackstaff and Lagan rivers, and his own ideas for future expansion.

2. Line engraving of Arthur Chichester, Baron Chichester, possibly by Charles Hall and dated to 1781. Soldier, politician and Lord Deputy of Ireland, Chichester was responsible for the expansion of Belfast, gaining a royal charter in 1613 that gave the town legal and political status, and new investment.

3. Queen Victoria first visited Belfast in 1849 and commissioned a number of commemorati paintings. This one shows her knighting the Mayor of Belfast, with the royal yacht in t foreground of Belfast Harbour. The triumphal arch bearing the inscription 'Céad Míle Fáil ('One Hundred Thousand Welcomes') was a temporary decoration.

4. Mary Ann McCracken w a Belfast Presbyterian radic feminist, philanthropist a a proud Irish republican. S was a passionate campaign for women's equality a for the abolition of the sla trade throughout her li A statue in her memory h been commissioned for t grounds of Belfast City Ha

5. The White Linen Hall, built in 1787, was designed by Roger Mulholland and dominated Donegall Square in the centre of Belfast. It was the physical embodiment of the linen boom and a business hub in the town. It was demolished in 1896 to make way for Belfast City Hall.

6. One of a set of four paintings by local artist Michael O'Neill commemorating the Society of United Irishmen, located in the Cathedral Quarter at the old Four Corners area. Here Thomas Russell and Edward Bunting meet Mary Ann McCracken. Today these paintings languish behind wheelie bins, litter and parked cars.

7. This 1875 statue of evangelical Presbyterian Rev. Henry Cooke stands defiantly in College Square East, his back to Inst (the Royal Belfast Academical Institution) in protest at the school's liberal teaching on religion. It is known locally as the 'Black Man', though its copper exterior has ironically turned green.

8. This photograph shows a heavily decorated Castle Junction looking towards Bank Buildings on Royal Avenue (now Primark). The picture dates from *c.* 1901.

9. This picture taken by Alexander Hogg from Gardiner Street over the rooftops shows Millfield and Boyd Street in 1912. It is close to the back of the area that in recent years has been known as CastleCourt Shopping Centre.

10. 28 September 1912, 'Ulster Day' in Belfast, showing huge crowds of unionists in Donegall Square North with Belfast City Hall on the right of the picture and the iconic Robinson & Cleaver building on the left. They had come to sign the Ulster Covenant in protest against the Third Home Rule Bill.

11. On Ulster Day 1912 booths had been set up inside Belfast City Hall to allow as man[y] men as possible to sign the covenant. (Women were confined to signing a separate declaratio[n] of support.) It shows the level of organisation that went into the event.

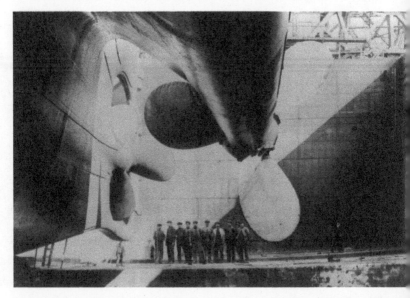

12. Harland and Wolff shipyard workers looking at the huge propellers of RMS *Titan[ic]* shortly before its launch in 1911. It was second to none in build quality and the opulence [of] its finish. Like so many others, these men could not have imagined the tragedy that woul[d] unfold when the 'unsinkable ship' did just that.

13. The White Star Line RMS *Titanic* looking majestic as it is escorted on its way out of Belfast Lough on 3 April 1912. It would never return. At 46,000 tonnes, 270 metres long and 53 metres tall, the largest ship in the world would also tragically become the most infamous.

14. When British troops arrived in Belfast in August 1969, their early fortifications were somewhat ad hoc and make do. The sandbags and barbed wire on display here at an army checkpoint at Bridge End on 27 September 1969 would soon look a lot more robust and permanent.

15. Royal Avenue in the commercial centre of the city suffered extensive damage following a Provisional IRA bomb attack in 1974. Here, fire brigades deal with the aftermath of the explosion.

16. View of Donegall Place from Belfast City Hall with the old Robinson & Cleaver building (Cleaver House) on the right and Cave Hill in the distance. The photograph was taken during the Ulster '71 festival, a largely unsuccessful attempt to mark the fiftieth anniversary of Northern Ireland's existence.

17. View of boats on the River Lagan during the Ulster '71 festival. The serene scene belies the mayhem taking place elsewhere in the city with the introduction of internment and rising levels of violence doing little to boost festival attendance over the summer months.

18. Belfast City Hall looking resplendent and unusually tidy with Queen Victoria front and centre. While it looks like it has been here forever, the City Hall was only finished in 1906. It was built to mark Queen Victoria's granting of city status to Belfast in 1888, replacing the White Linen Hall.

19. Parliament Buildings, known less formally as Stormont, was the centre of unionist political control in Northern Ireland for forty years and is now the centre for Northern Ireland's devolved power-sharing institutions. A statue of Sir Edward Carson stands defiantly at its base.

20. Leo Boyd's *Belfast Romances* Pop art-style mural is a collaboration involving DC Tours, the Bullitt Hotel and Jameson Irish Whiskey. It references several Belfast icons and landmarks including the DeLorean car, Belfast Zoo, a wind-up police Land Rover, City Hall, the Albert Clock and Titanic Belfast.

21. The two iconic gantry cranes of the Harland and Wolff shipyard, Goliath (1969) and Samson (1974), are synonymous with the Belfast skyline. They have become much more than cranes and now represent indispensable landmarks and cultural artefacts in the city.

22. Opened in 2012, Titanic Belfast tells the story of the city's rich maritime history, focusing on its most famous ship. Located on Queen's Island where the *Titanic* was built, the multi-award-winning visitor centre has become a leading tourist attraction. With typical Belfast humour, locals have dubbed it 'the iceberg'.

23. King Charles III meeting First Minister designate and Sinn Féin Vice President Michelle O'Neill and Speaker of the Northern Ireland Assembly Alex Maskey (also of Sinn Féin) a Hillsborough Castle ahead of the funeral of Queen Elizabeth II in September 2022.

24. Originally built in 1769 on the corner of North Street and Waring Street as the single storey Exchange, a second floor was added in 1776 with further modifications in 1845 The Assembly Rooms is one of the oldest and most important public buildings in Belfas but is currently derelict and at risk.

Despite some recent glimmers of cross-party consensus, Belfast City Hall has more predictably been the site of political demonstration and protests. In 1985 and 1986 a number of unionist rallies were held in protest against the Anglo-Irish Agreement, the city hall being a symbolic and geographically convenient rallying point for people to gather to listen to speeches and signal their opposition. In one of the rallies on 23 November, eight days after the agreement was signed, over 100,000 unionists thronged the front of the city hall and Donegall Square listening to speeches from their political leaders and venting their fury at the agreement. At another event some days later, the Secretary of State for Northern Ireland, Tom King, was attacked and verbally abused by unionist demonstrators at the city hall and condemned as a 'traitor' in a public melee that the police did little to stop.[27] Members of the DUP (including future deputy leader Nigel Dodds) climbed up the outside wall of the building trying to gain access through an iron gate, jabbing their fingers and snarling abuse at those they saw inside.

Unionists were back in numbers protesting at the city hall in December 2012 over a decision to limit the number of days the Union flag would be flown on the building. Since it was opened in 1906, the Union flag has flown on the building every day, but on 3 December 2012 Belfast City Council voted to bring the building into line with civic buildings in Great Britain by reducing the number of days the flag would be flown to eighteen. Nationalist councillors supported this move, while unionists opposed it, but the non-aligned Alliance Party also voted in favour, tipping the balance and demonstrating that Belfast's civic buildings were no longer the unionist citadel they once were. This led to months of protests from unionists who saw the decision as part of a culture war against their British identity and were not at all convinced by the argument that the change brought them into line with the practice in the rest of the UK.

The question that now presents itself is how can binary political traditions and the growing number of people who subscribe to neither share the building from this point forwards? There are examples of agreement being possible between unionists, nationalists and the non-aligned in terms of how to commemorate the heritage of the city in a more inclusive way. A statue of Mary Ann McCracken, Belfast radical, Presbyterian, Irish republican and dedicated campaigner against the slave trade, received cross-party support in June 2021 and will be erected in the grounds of the city hall in 2023. A statue of republican trade unionist Winifred Carney, County Down-born Sinn Féin activist and close ally of James Connolly in the 1916 Easter Rising, has also received council support.

It seems likely that Belfast City Hall will reflect a much wider array of political and cultural identities in future decades as the city continues to develop into a post-conflict space where binary perspectives of British and Irish identities are becoming more complex and nuanced. It is also the case that traditional identities are increasingly being complemented by a growing non-aligned community, especially among the young, while a burgeoning LGBTQ+ community also helps to provide a more diverse social profile to the city.

In addition to the new statues being planned for the grounds, the addition of a wider range of stained glass windows in recent years, covering more diverse events, such as the Great Famine, the 1907 Docks Strike and Belfast people's participation in the Spanish Civil War, reflects the more diverse political makeup of the city. There are also now windows commemorating the contribution of the National Health Service (NHS) to the city and celebrating the LGBTQ+ community. Interpreting the architecture and grounds of Belfast City Hall in line with the changing profile of those who live in the city in the twenty-first century has to be considered a positive development and suggests that the building will continue to play a role in defining the city in the future as it has done in the past.

THE CRUM AND THE KESH

Given Belfast's recent history, it should not be surprising that two of its prisons feature in this chapter on some of the city's historically important buildings. Crumlin Road Gaol is an older Victorian prison and is geographically located in North Belfast opposite the former Crumlin Road Courthouse. Designed by Sir Charles Lanyon, the architect behind several of Belfast's most celebrated buildings, Crumlin Road Gaol was the last word in Victorian incarceration, complete with a tunnel under the road so prisoners could be easily transported between the courthouse and the gaol, literally without seeing the light of day.

The gaol was opened in 1845 as the explosion of Belfast's population during the industrial age required a larger detention facility. Today a thriving tourist attraction, when it opened in the mid-nineteenth century this was a brutal and desolate building, where the criminal justice system enthusiastically extended its reach to children as young as six years of age, many of whom had been incarcerated for stealing food. The Crum played an important part in the justice system during the Troubles, but it was infamous long before then as a focal point for crime and punishment in the city. If the crime was deemed serious enough, inmates would be hanged inside or outside the gaol, and many others (including children) committed suicide within its walls due to the brutal conditions they had to endure.[28] Lanyon did not include a gallows in his original design, as the Victorians liked to do their executions in full public view in front of the gaol. After the Capital Punishment Act made public executions illegal in 1868, the Crum took the grisly business in-house and the condemned had the luxury of a relatively private death. Hangings continued at the gaol until 1961, when Robert McGladdery was executed after being convicted of murder. While we might look back at the Crum and think of it as being a cruel institution, it could be viewed as an example of progressive values if looked at in its historical context. A larger prison was needed because the population was rising but also due to the fact that the criminal justice system was becoming less brutal and capital punishment was increasingly seen as an inappropriate sentence for minor offences. With fewer executions, room was needed to incarcerate those who would previously have been put to death.[29]

At full capacity, the Crum had 640 cells available for inmates, and it was built by Lanyon to look and feel austere, with a design philosophy modelled on Jeremy Bentham's idea of the 'Panopticon'. The belief was that twenty-four-hour surveillance would destabilise inmates to the point where they would behave in a more compliant manner and conform to the prison system more readily.[30] Former prison officer Patrick Greg worked in the Crum for many years, and his account emphasises its forbidding atmosphere: 'Tragedy, death and despair are etched into the bricks and mortar of the landings and cells of all the wings, and cannot be confined to any specific area. All manner of unfortunate events took place throughout the jail, from D-wing punishment cells and the tunnel beneath the Crumlin Road linking the jail to the court-house, to the woodyard and the prison hospital.'[31]

The Crum closed in 1996, but in its 150 years it housed several notable political figures, including former Irish Taoiseach Eamon de Valera, who was jailed in 1924 for entering Northern Ireland illegally. Rev. Ian Paisley was given a three-month sentence in the Crum in 1966 for unlawful assembly, until he was quickly released after his fine was paid anonymously. This did Paisley no harm with unionist voters, as the arrest raised his public profile and gained political traction against the unionist establishment. Former leader of the Provisional IRA Martin McGuinness (who later went on to a distinguished political career as Deputy First Minister in the Northern Ireland Executive) also spent time in the Crum after being charged with IRA membership in 1976. McGuinness's colleague in the Executive Peter Robinson, who took over as leader of the DUP and First Minister of Northern Ireland in 2008, was also detained during the 1980s as a result of unionist protests against the Anglo-Irish Agreement. In an ironic twist, both men who had served time at Her Majesty's pleasure had the pleasure of welcoming Her Majesty to the gaol in 2014. The two former inmates were now marketing the Crum as one of the jewels in the crown of Belfast's tourist economy, aided and abetted by the Queen and the Duke of Edinburgh.

Amid all the violence, death and destruction, the Crum also played a significant political role in the post-1969 Troubles era that connected it to the even more infamous jail of that period, Long Kesh. As the civil rights movement was beaten off the streets by the police in the early 1970s, an increasingly reactionary unionist government brought in internment without trial in August 1971. By 1972 close to 1,000 people were being detained, and by Christmas 1975 nearly 2,000 internees were being held in jail without charge, 96 per cent of whom were Catholics.

Detaining such large numbers of people at short notice raised the issue of where they were going to be accommodated. The Crum quickly filled up, so the authorities resorted to a former Second World War airfield near Lisburn on the outskirts of Belfast, previously occupied by the RAF. The facility was known as the Long Kesh Detention Centre, and a series of Nissen huts (referred to as cages by the internees) were used to house the prisoners. The compounds were overcrowded, cold and uncomfortable, and there were frequent complaints about living conditions.[32]

The injustice associated with the internment policy led to the civil rights movement evolving into an anti-internment protest which also demanded that internees be recognised as being political prisoners rather than common criminals. This demand for political status was soon adopted by the Provisional IRA, who saw themselves as prisoners of war and demanded to be treated as such. By the summer of 1972 the security situation was dire, with more than one bomb attack taking place in Belfast every day. Amid this mayhem, Billy McKee, leader of the Provisional IRA in the Crum, was leading forty republicans on a hunger strike in pursuit of the right to be treated as prisoners of war. Concerned by the implications of McKee dying, Secretary of State William Whitelaw conceded special category status to prisoners in June 1972.

The Crum and Long Kesh had become the epicentre of the battle for legitimacy between the UK government on the one hand and militant republicanism on the other. Billy McKee's successful hunger strike in the Crum bled into Long Kesh to devastating effect, both in terms of its death toll as well as its lasting political impacts. Whitelaw quickly realised his mistake, but it would be another four years before the British government withdrew special category status on 1 March 1976, by which time Merlyn Rees had replaced Whitelaw as Secretary of State. By this point, Long Kesh had been renamed the Maze Prison, part of a rebrand to coincide with the introduction of the newly constructed H-Block complex (named after their shape) and the removal of special category status. The H-Blocks were constructed between 1975 and 1978, precipitated in part by the Provisional IRA, whose imprisoned members burned down some of the compounds in protest at the conditions they were living under. Those who were convicted of terrorism-related offences under the new rules were the very antithesis of the compliant prisoners that Sir Charles Lanyon and his Victorian colleagues had envisaged when they designed the Crum 150 years earlier.

The first person to be imprisoned under the new regime in September 1976 was Ciaran Nugent, who had been given a three-year sentence for possessing weapons and hijacking a car. When Nugent was ordered to wear normal prison clothes, he refused. The following day he was given a blanket and wore it to take exercise – the 'blanketmen' had been born, as subsequent prisoners arrived in the H-Blocks and also refused to wear prison clothes. By the end of the 1970s, more than 200 republicans had gone 'on the blanket', and the issue became a rallying point for support outside the jail. By 1978 the blanket protest had degenerated further, as prisoners refused to leave their cells to defecate as it would entail being forced to wear a prison uniform.

When prison officers refused to clear the excrement up, the prisoners spread it over the walls of their cells. Rotting food on the floor was attracting maggots so they mixed it into the excrement, diluting the foul mixture with urine to help it to spread. By the end of 1978, 300 republicans were on the 'No Wash/dirty protest', which brought international media attention to the issue of political status and made the physical fabric of the prison itself a site of resistance.

By 1980, the 'blanket' and 'dirty' protests had been going on for four years, and the prisoners were becoming demoralised as the British government, now led by Margaret Thatcher, showed no sign of compromise. Discussions began inside the jail about the possibility of a hunger strike, as this had been the tactic used by Billy McKee in the Crum to get special category status in the first place in 1972. On 27 October 1980, seven republicans led by Brendan Hughes refused breakfast. This act of defiance lit the fuse that eventually led to the political rise of Sinn Féin and ultimately the peace process itself.

The initial hunger strike lasted for fifty-three days, and while the British said there would be no concessions to the hunger strikers, discussions were held to look for a solution. A document was produced that seemed to indicate movement on the crucial issue of prison clothing, and the strike was called off with one of the prisoners, Sean McKenna, close to death. However, on closer examination it transpired that prisoners were to wear 'civilian-type' clothing issued by the prison, rather than their own clothes. The hunger strike had failed, utterly.

Bobby Sands, the new IRA leader in the H-Blocks, came to the conclusion that a more staggered hunger strike was required, which would be a fight to the death for everyone involved. The second hunger strike began on 1 March 1981 (the fifth anniversary of the ending of special category status), when Bobby Sands refused food. This fast went on from March to October 1981 and ended in the death of ten republican prisoners, two of whom – Bobby Sands and Kieran Doherty – had been elected to the Westminster and the Irish parliament, respectively. Over 100,000 people attended Sands' funeral, and the ripple effects were felt around the world. The deaths of the hunger strikers revitalised the political dynamism of republican politics and demonstrated that electoral growth could help to broaden their campaign for Irish reunification.

The H-Blocks are a physical manifestation of the Troubles, part of its conflict archaeology, which makes the buildings themselves more than just bricks and mortar. This is one reason why some of the H-Blocks, including H6, which contained the prison hospital where the hunger strikers died, have been listed in recognition of their historic importance. However, having preserved them, we have struggled to agree about what to do with them for the last two decades. There have been several attempts to convert the site into a facility that can contribute to the post-conflict economy of Northern Ireland, but so far these have failed to secure the cross-community political support required in the Northern Ireland Executive. The future of the Maze/Long Kesh site is a metaphor for the viability of the peace process itself, and the site is in every sense a political and cultural artefact of the Troubles.[33] Whether or not the conflicting narratives of the Maze/Long Kesh can ever be reconciled, its story is imprinted indelibly on the place and the people who lived through the political conflict from the 1970s until the present day. It is part of the region's political and cultural heritage, even though it represents a painful period in that story. As such, it should be sympathetically curated and developed at a pace that can secure consent across the community.

5

THE TROUBLES

One of the first times that I realised I was living in a divided society that was experiencing a violent conflict came when my church was bombed and the British Army put a fence around the perimeter to prevent further attacks. The small Catholic chapel that I attended on the Holywood Road had been blown up in an explosion by loyalist paramilitaries in September 1973, thankfully when no one was in the building. A short time later, following a petrol-bomb attack, the army put a barbed-wire security fence around it and provided an armed guard every Sunday protecting the parishioners as they prayed. I still remember the look of alarm on my dad's face when the bomb went off, the reverberation from the explosion knocking pictures off the living room wall.

The Christ the King chapel was originally built for Catholics in the British Army during the war and was mostly empty apart from Sunday mornings as it was a satellite of the larger St Colmcille's Church in Holywood. The original St Colmcille's was opened in 1874 but was itself destroyed by a fire in August 1989. Only the spire and bell tower escaped the blaze, with a new circular church being opened in 1995. St Colmcille's was the main church in my parish, where I dutifully went to do my First Holy Communion and the other rituals demanded of me, including the dreaded fortnightly confession session. We would be taken out of primary school to confess our sins, until mine became so heinous that I did not have the time to do the penance required. On the plus side, I was an altar boy at the church and sometimes had a great excuse to get out of lessons in school to do the odd wedding during the week.

However, on Sundays we would go to Mass at the much smaller Christ the King chapel on the Holywood Road, passing through its metal security gates and into the consecrated compound with its barbed-wire fencing, under the protective gaze of the British military police Red Caps. It was a miracle in retrospect, given its geography and the levels of sectarian violence during the 1970s, that there was not a significant massacre there, and without the attention of the Red Caps it is highly likely that there would have been. It was a vulnerable building down a leafy laneway to the church that was not visible from the road, and despite the fencing, minor attacks and vandalism were a regular occurrence.

Some years later, after one of these attacks, I came to realise that the protective bubble that I had grown up in was in the process of popping as I moved from childhood into my teenage years. I had the luxury of living in a street which, while mainly Protestant, also had some other Catholics living there, and as a kid religion was not an issue, though we used to feel sorry for our Protestant friends who would have to go to Sunday School on a Sunday afternoon having just been to church in the morning. This always seemed like overkill to me, even for Protestants, who seemed to hate having any fun at all on Sundays or allowing anyone else to have any either. We were all divided by our common Christianity – but we were devout while Protestants were staunch in the separate practice of our faiths. Keeping the Sabbath holy was a big priority for Protestants in Belfast in the 1970s, and as they were in charge, shops were closed, all the parks were closed, the swings were chained up and the streets were dead. But Sundays aside, we were in and out of each other's houses, we would call for them, they would call for us, and we just played in the street or in each other's gardens. Normally it was our garden (Gustav Wolff's old croquet lawn) getting a hammering in the summer with everyone playing football in it until it was too dark to see the ball. However, almost imperceptibly, as we got older, the sectarian conflict came closer to us, bicycles allowing us to roam beyond the protection of our own street and secondary school bringing with it a uniform and a tie that acted as a flag of religion and ethnicity. The tie of my secondary school was blue, white and black, but in the political and social context it may as well have been the green, white and gold of the Irish tricolour. Taking your tie off on the way home from school was little help either, as it was a signal to any would-be sectarian bullies that you were afraid to wear it and that a closer inspection was needed, with demands to take your tie out of your pocket followed inevitably by a beating.

This provides an example of the everyday social impacts that affected everyone in Belfast during the period known as the Troubles (Protestant and Catholic), and of course it was a very minor irritant compared to what many others were living through at the time.

If my own childhood is anything to go by, kids in Belfast had their own particular version of stranger-danger teaching, where we were schooled in making sure that we didn't expose our identities or where we lived to people we did not know. This was just an everyday mundane reality that was absorbed into the collective psyche, but as we grew older, met more people and became more mobile, it became increasingly difficult to sustain the pragmatic conceit.

THE TROUBLES IN CONTEXT[1]

The Troubles era from 1968 to 1998 cannot be understood properly unless it is located in its historical context. In that sense, the political violence that shot Belfast into the international media spotlight in the 1970s needs to be seen as a continuation of, rather than a departure from, the city's divided past.

While the Troubles are dated in the popular imagination as the period from 1968 to 1998, their roots can be found in the formation of Northern Ireland in 1921, and as previous chapters of this book have demonstrated, the city was built on a sea of troubles dating back to when English military rogue Sir Arthur Chichester put the royal stamp of approval on the town in the seventeenth century. Centuries of troubled history were crystallised into a generation of political violence from the 1960s until the 1990s. This helped fuse historical, political, cultural and social divisions into a heady cocktail of sectarian violence that grabbed international media attention, while dislocating the region and those who lived there.

While people in Britain and across the wider world woke up to sectarian conflict in Belfast and Derry in the late 1960s, those living there were well aware that the roots of this violence predated that by several generations. In truth, Northern Ireland has always been a divided society, since partition in 1921 created the region as a political unit. Partition itself was a symptom of a wider division between Northern unionists and Southern nationalists going back several centuries. Even when Northern Ireland looked peaceful from the outside, it was riddled with discrimination, insecurity, fatalistic nationalist anger and unionist arrogance laced with existential fear. It was a pressure cooker and it was only a matter of time before the lid blew off and violence erupted in Belfast and across Northern Ireland.

The partition of Ireland in 1921 led to a numerically dominant but hugely insecure unionist community and a marginalised, frustrated and angry nationalist population. Unionists craved political control of Northern Ireland and inherited a system that allowed the majority party to exert that control. Initial rules to protect the nationalist minority (such as proportional representation) were quickly eradicated by a unionist party which understood that electoral cohesion guaranteed political control.

Northern Ireland became a de facto one-party regime within the UK, with no rotation of power between the unionist and nationalist communities for over fifty years. The Unionist Party won every election between 1921 and 1969, while the Nationalist Party lost on every occasion. Belfast became the capital city of this majoritarian democracy and was defined by it for several generations.

From the outside (especially London), Northern Ireland seemed to be a stable part of the UK. However, appearances can be deceptive, and nationalist resentment and anger eventually began to bubble to the surface. While the unionists and then also the British government tried to keep the lid on these frustrations, through various combinations of repressive legislation, partial government, piecemeal political reform and harsh security policies, momentum grew during the 1960s to the point that it could not be contained. By the time Britain and the rest of the world woke up to the fact that Northern Ireland had been incubating a serious political illness, it was too late to cure it – at least until a significant amount of self-harm had taken place.

So while the Troubles started in 1968–69, it is important to understand that period as a symptom of more deep-seated causal factors rather than as a behavioural aberration by particularly violent people. There is also a tendency when looking back at the past to suppose that what took place was carefully planned or an intentional outcome of premeditated action. However, in many instances our past has been shaped by unintended consequences, coincidence, serendipity, accidents and mistakes. Irish history certainly has its fair share of these, the 1916 Easter Rising and 1981 republican hunger strikes being just two examples. In this sense, the outbreak of the Troubles was neither premeditated nor predetermined. It was rather the outcome of a series of miscalculations, short-term victories that led to long-term failures, at times bloody-minded ignorance, and a belief among some that violence was both legitimate and effective.

Belfast had never benefited from the Union to the same extent as people in 'mainland' cities, such as London, Manchester or Birmingham. Unemployment was nearly always higher than the UK national average, sometimes glaringly so: in 1961, unemployment in Northern Ireland as a whole stood at 7 per cent, compared with a UK average of 1.2 per cent. The nationalist community had no formal political outlet to seek redress for the fact that they had been excluded from political power since Northern Ireland was created in 1921, discriminated against in employment, denied public housing on the basis of their religion and harassed by the criminal justice system. As the political system was rigged against them, many nationalists sought out other avenues to make themselves heard – and they looked across to the emerging civil rights campaign in America as their inspiration.

THE ACCIDENTAL REVOLUTION

In essence, a civil rights movement was energised by the serendipitous emergence of civil rights protests in America and the arrival of an articulate and educated student movement. Ironically, the emergence of a cohort of young, well-educated Catholic graduates in the 1960s was a consequence of British rather than Irish politics, in particular the welfare reforms in postwar Britain, which resulted in the 1947 Northern Ireland Education Act. This extended free education to children regardless of social class, including the disadvantaged Catholic community in Northern Ireland. By the mid-1960s, this group had progressed through the educational pipeline and emerged with qualifications that equipped them with the intellectual tools and the confidence to challenge the political status quo. The civil rights campaign in Northern Ireland was not carefully programmed or thought through but developed incrementally, and it was shaped significantly by the defensive response of the unionist government to its demands for reform. The arrival of television in the 1960s as a means of mass communication was serendipitous timing for the civil rights movement, allowing them to broadcast their demands for fair treatment and peaceful protest as well as the heavy-handed and brutal response of the police and unionist government to a global audience.

The Troubles began, then, not as a separatist movement but as one that asked for equal access to the benefits of citizenship. It only morphed into a separatist and militant movement when those who could have extended nationalists equal rights and fair treatment refused to do so and attempted instead to repress and suppress demands for reform.

A pattern emerged at the end of the 1960s when civil rights marches would be announced and frequently declared illegal by the unionist government at Stormont, on public order grounds. The friction between peaceful protestors and an antagonistic police force often led to heavy-handed tactics by the overwhelmingly Protestant police, the RUC. Not every police officer was violent and not every civil rights marcher was non-violent, but in the main it was the police who were the aggressors, and, on the orders of the unionist government, they tried to baton peaceful protestors off the streets.

While civil rights campaigners and many external onlookers believed that their protests were about achieving equity and fairness within the political system, there was a strong feeling within unionism that this was just a convenient excuse for wider motives. The fear of some within the unionist community was that the civil rights movement was a Trojan horse for a political attack on the Northern Ireland government and an attempt to undermine its credibility in Britain.

By the end of the 1960s, nationalists were increasingly confident that the civil rights movement was providing a dynamic for change and that London would be forced to intervene. Unionists were becoming fearful that 'their' government was incapable of containing the volatile political situation and was caving in to unreasonable demands from nationalists.

It was a tinderbox, and sparks began to fly into it as the civil rights movement increasingly became a site of community friction with the police. Fires are notorious for spreading quickly, and the political disintegration of Belfast was similarly fast-paced, the latent tensions exploding into violent sectarian clashes in 1969. Renowned historian Professor Marianne Elliott recounts her surprise at the speed of events: 'No one then expected the Troubles. I had just finished my second year at Queen's when they erupted in 1969. I had left Belfast on a beautiful June morning to work for the summer in the United States. I returned in September to a war zone. The Belfast in which we had moved without inhibition, ranging freely with no sense of restricted zones, had gone. It has never returned.'[2] It became clear during that summer in 1969 that the unionist government could not contain the level of violence on the streets and had little option but to ask the British government for military support to restore order.

THE ARMY ARRIVES

Crowds came in off those side streets – off the Shankill Road. . . . They came up in hundreds and they were led by a character who was stripped to the waist he had nothing on him only his trousers he was stripped to the waist and he was shouting 'burn them out' and 'get the young ones, get the young ones, get the young ones'. . . . When I seen this character and all the crowds and they were throwing stones and petrol bombs I just grabbed the children and I ran with them.[3]

Rita Canavan was a resident of Bombay Street and describes the moment on 14 August 1969 when a loyalist mob attacked Catholics and burned them out of their homes. Belfast was on the brink of civil war, and for many of those caught up in the daily attacks by sectarian mobs it must have felt as though they were already at war.

By the summer of 1969, street rioting had become a nightly occurrence in Belfast between rival mobs of petrol bombers, the police unable to cope with the scale and ferocity of street disturbances. In the major urban centres, Catholics and Protestants existed in a tightly packed sectarian apartheid

– often living side by side in the lattice of streets and alleyways, but their paths rarely crossing. The incendiary atmosphere of August 1969 made life intolerable for anyone living at such an 'interface' between the two communities, and attempts were made to remove people physically or by simply burning them out of their homes. After one riot in mid-August, which lasted for several days in the network of streets between the mainly Protestant Shankill Road and the largely Catholic Falls Road in Belfast, eight people lay dead and over seven hundred were injured. Residential areas like Bombay Street became iconic emblems of sectarian hatred, as people were filmed being burned out of their homes. Many people fled to safer areas, before they were burned out, becoming refugees in their own country. British, Irish and international camera crews filmed homes being gutted and recorded the pitiful images of people loading their furniture and possessions onto trucks and vans before their homes were torched by their fellow citizens in the city.

In scenes reminiscent of wartime, large numbers of people in Belfast were becoming evacuees within the UK. By the end of August 1969, over 170 homes had been destroyed and nearly 500 more had been damaged by arson, most of them occupied by Catholics. The Scarman Tribunal,[4] which was established to investigate the violent events of that summer, estimated that in Belfast itself over 1,800 families had fled their homes, 1,500 of them Catholic.

On the same day that Rita Canavan and her neighbours were attacked, the British Army arrived on the streets of Belfast and Derry in an attempt to reduce sectarian attacks and restore order. At the time, their presence was seen as a temporary measure, and their role was defined as being a 'limited operation'; however, they were to remain in Northern Ireland for a generation.

Initially brought in as peacekeepers, the troops soon came to be regarded by the nationalist community as an army of occupation than one of liberation – and, of course, they became an obvious target for militants. 'Operation Banner' (as the military deployment was formally termed) would last until July 2007, and, as Northern Ireland's General Officer Commanding, Lieutenant-General Sir Ian Freeland, commented four days after their deployment on the streets, political failures in Belfast would inevitably result in the army being sucked into a confrontation with the population:

149

The honeymoon period cannot, I do not think, continue for ever obviously. We're perhaps at the peak now with everybody smiling and swapping cups of tea and all this sort of business and cracking jokes . . . but unless there is a solution or some hope for the future . . . and this is where the politicians have got to come in, the soldiers are not going to be welcome on the streets for ever and ever.[5]

This was to prove a prescient warning, as the British Army became bogged down in an undeclared war that it could not win, did not fully understand and could not bring to an end. For the British state, out of sight was very much out of mind and its inherent ignorance was cruelly exposed on the streets of Belfast and Derry after the army was sent in during the summer of 1969. While British politicians had frequently sought to portray themselves as being above the fray, they were not, as it was their responsibility to maintain political oversight of the region regardless of the powers devolved to Stormont.

At best politically detached from Northern Ireland, at worst callous in its colonial contempt for those who lived there, successive British governments were guilty of nothing less than criminal negligence in their governance of Northern Ireland at the end of the 1960s and into the 1970s. While the British government sent in soldiers to shore up the unionist government in August 1969, it did not take political responsibility for events or for the operational control of the troops it subcontracted to an increasingly desperate unionist government.

While politicians dithered, paramilitary groups that emerged on both sides of the political fence were taking security into their own hands, cordoning off large areas of Belfast, setting up impromptu roadblocks, with masked men scrutinising people's driving licences and home addresses, carrying out vigilante attacks and ignoring what might theoretically be called 'the rule of law'.

The dominant nationalist perspective believes that the police and army stood back and allowed Protestant mobs to burn Catholics out of their homes in places such as Bombay Street in what amounted to an anti-Catholic pogrom. The army and police undoubtedly sympathised with the unionist community and instinctively saw the nationalist population as the greater threat, developing a more relaxed relationship in unionist areas. An example of this is provided in Tony Macaulay's personal memoir of growing up on the Shankill Road in Belfast during the 1970s, when he recalls the close relationship with the troops on the streets: 'All the women in our street loved the soldiers. . . . The soldiers were here to protect us from the IRA, so during the day when the men were out at work, all the women in our street would invite them in for a cup of tea. . . . I don't know in fact how the soldiers made it up our street in a single day, because everyone wanted to give them tea and buns.'[6]

While the army were plied with cups of tea and sandwiches in nationalist areas too at the beginning, these quickly dried up when they began raiding people's homes in the early hours of the morning, breaking property and dragging the residents out of bed and into their armoured vehicles. British troops cut an unusual sight in the built-up streets of Belfast, their light khaki camouflage standing out like a beacon against the dull grey of the local area. It was like a moon landing – as much for the troops themselves as for the Northern Ireland locals they had been sent to deal with.

In truth, the British Army was deployed in Belfast with no idea of its mission (beyond quelling the immediate violence), no understanding of the politics of the region and no strategic political leadership from the British government. It demonstrated that Britain's tactical approach to Northern Ireland was to move reluctantly and slowly, muddling through and never quite dealing with problems at an early enough stage. When it was eventually moved to action, the government often made the situation worse rather than better, contributing to a cycle of violence that lasted for the next thirty years.

THE FALLS CURFEW

By the summer of 1970, Belfast was in turmoil, with street riots, bomb attacks and shootings part of the day-to-day abnormality of the city. It was the beginning of July, which is a tense time every year, as it is the run-up to Bonfire Night on 11 July, which is the start of the 12 July celebrations by the

Orange institutions of the Battle of the Boyne and King William of Orange's victory over Catholic King James II. July is traditionally a month when tensions between the unionist and nationalist community are at their highest and can easily explode into sectarian violence. The context to the Falls Curfew is that it came on the heels of other sectarian violence in the city at the end of June, as the tinderbox of sectarian tension, stoked by the imminent Orange celebrations, caught fire on the streets of the city. As the *Sunday Times* Insight Team wrote shortly afterwards: '[T]he scene was set for a bloody night – and also for a decisive one. For the first time, the Provisional IRA went into battle.'[7]

On 27 June, stone-throwing and fighting erupted between an Orange parade and nationalist residents in Ardoyne, during which three Protestants were shot dead. In response, loyalist gangs started burning nationalists out of their houses in the Short Strand district of East Belfast. Paddy Kennedy, the Stormont MP for the area, went to the nearby Mountpottinger RUC station and requested protection for those being attacked and for St Matthew's Church, which was also coming under arson attack from loyalist mobs. However, the response from the police was that the army were already overstretched and could not help.[8] In an effort to defend the area, the Provisional IRA, led by Billy McKee, took up a strategic position in St Matthew's Church and spent the night sniping at the loyalist arson attackers, killing another three people. This went down in nationalist folklore as the moment the Provos (as the Provisional IRA were colloquially known) stood up and defended them from loyalist mobs when the police and army were nowhere to be seen. It was a declaration of intent from the Provisionals that they were going to engage loyalist militants directly, and the British Army decided that it needed to quickly reassert its control and authority in the city.

While the British Army was struggling to control events on the ground, the government in London was, to put it bluntly, clueless about what was going on or what could be done about it. The Conservative Party had just come to power, and a new Home Secretary, Reginald Maudling, strode into his new responsibilities with all the vigour of a sloth. Maudling paid a visit to Belfast shortly after the riots on 30 June to see what all the fuss was about and to take the temperature, a visit that made headlines for the wrong reasons. The army seemed unimpressed by Maudling's failure to understand the situation or to provide any practical solutions, concluding that he just seemed to be out of his depth and amazed at the 'ghastly situation'. As Maudling got on his plane back to London, his comment went down in infamy as indicative of British political ignorance and callous disregard for a region of the UK it was responsible for governing. 'For God's sake bring me a large scotch. . . . What a bloody awful country.'[9]

On 3 July the British Army moved into the Lower Falls to search houses for weapons and bomb-making equipment. By this point, the army had long outlived its honeymoon period and was reviled by the nationalist community, who saw it as the cutting edge of a malign unionist government at Stormont. The operation was led by the RUC and the Royal Scots Regiment of the British Army. As they finished their house searches, the troops came under sustained attack from a group of rioters throwing stones and petrol bombs, and the soldiers responded by firing volleys of CS gas. As the fighting became entrenched, paramilitaries took over from the rioters, and both the Provisional and Official IRA engaged the British Army directly in a gun battle. Militant republicans had split from the Officials six months earlier, frustrated by their socialist idealism and lack of action. The Provisionals favoured a more militant engagement with the British state, and the aggressive tactics of the army provided them with the perfect opportunity to recruit support. Both factions took up arms against the British Army in July 1970, and in fact it was the Officials who took the lead, as they were more numerous in the Lower Falls at the time.

For several hours, volleys of shots were exchanged between soldiers and the IRA while residents in the Lower Falls took cover wherever they could and tried to avoid being hit by stray bullets. Hundreds of residents were evacuated from their homes overnight and housed in communal shelters while sporadic shooting continued. Eventually, the army sealed off an area of over 3,000 homes and imposed a curfew while they tried to root out the gunmen and re-establish control. The place was in ferment by this stage, as the soldiers had been unwelcome to begin with but had now enraged the local community and were imprisoning them by force. Army helicopters flew over the Lower Falls area with their searchlights piercing the gloom and loudhailers announcing that the area was under lockdown.

Any vestige of peacekeeping had long since gone by this stage, and the troops were not shy in enforcing their will on the local population – often in a brutal fashion. Homes were raided one at a time, and residents who resisted were beaten by the army, their property destroyed as the soldiers broke ornaments, ransacked cupboards and snarled their way from one house to the next in their search for elusive weapons.

After twenty-four hours of this brutal treatment, the army announced (through its loudhailers) that residents would be allowed out for one hour in order to get vital supplies. The imagery of British oppression was classic and could hardly have been improved upon, even if the newly created Provisional IRA had had access to its own public relations department. The personal testimony of a local bar owner in the Lower Falls that evening illustrates the way normality was being pierced by emergency and how everyone on all sides was quickly adapting to their new reality with a combination of fear, resentment and weary pragmatism:

> I went over to the soldier and told him to fuck off because my window might be broken. He told me to 'get back in or I'll shoot your fucking head off'. I was aghast at that. The curate from St Peter's pro-cathedral told me later that they weren't ordinary soldiers, they were Paras. My brother took me back into the pub and I started to shout 'Time!' The next thing there was a bang. The soldiers had disappeared and there was a hole in the ground. Somebody had thrown a hand-grenade. Everybody ordered carry-outs and headed for home. I locked the bar that night and took the TV set home with me.[10]

Those inside the curfew zone were eventually saved when a group of women from the neighbouring Andersonstown district travelled to the Lower Falls and walked through the curfew area with food for those inside. When the curfew was lifted on 5 July, four civilians had been killed by the British Army with over seventy people injured, including eighteen soldiers. One of the civilians killed, Charles O'Neill, was run over by an army Saracen and (according to eye witnesses) deliberately crushed, an exhibition of callous cruelty from British soldiers that incensed the nationalist community and helped the Provos to win the argument against the Officials that a more muscular militant approach was needed. Ironically, O'Neill was an invalided British ex-serviceman, run over and killed by the very army he had served. A greater example of the cruel ignorance of the British soldiers imposing the Falls Curfew would be hard to find.

As might be expected in a fast-moving and violent episode, when mindsets on all sides are programmed to expect the worst, rumours circulated as fast as the CS gas. Suggestions that the army removed the lid of a child's coffin during a wake while searching a house for weapons were not substantiated, though other urban myths from the episode have persisted. Journalist Malachi O'Doherty relates the tale that a close relative of Gerry Adams, who would later become President of Sinn Féin, wheeled guns out of the area in her pram during the curfew, and that a soldier even unwittingly helped her to carry the pram over a kerbstone despite it being unusually heavy.[11]

Nearly 400 arrests were made, and a large number of weapons, explosives, ammunition and two-way radios were captured in the operation, but it left a lasting scar across the nationalist community in Belfast that undoubtedly bolstered the Provisional IRA. While the army tried to play down the scale of the operation at the time and claimed, ludicrously, that just 15 rounds had been fired by soldiers, it later emerged that the figure was closer to 14,000 rounds.[12] While the army had imposed its will on the Lower Falls, it had lost the wider battle for hearts and minds which was essential for its counter-insurgency campaign against the Provisional IRA. While army helicopters toured overhead when people came out of their houses at the end of the curfew, their message to those on the ground – 'we are your friends, we are here to help'[13] – just rubbed salt into an open wound. The sting was not helped when the army escorted two grinning unionist politicians around the area, which nationalists saw as unnecessary gloating at their expense.[14] According to the *Sunday Times* Insight Team and other records of the period, the Falls Curfew drove people into the arms of the Provisionals: 'the movement grew from fewer than a hundred activists in May–June to nearly 800 by December.'[15]

ROUND UP THE USUAL SUSPECTS

Relationships had broken down across multiple fronts in Belfast by 1970, and these declined further over the next two years as an undeclared war took hold and all sides bedded down for the fight. The Provisionals had quickly usurped the Officials, had gained willing recruits, and were focused on scaling up their campaign of violence. This included an intensive and relentless bombing campaign in the centre of Belfast, as well as targeting members of the Crown Forces, which involved murdering members of the police and army, judges, lawyers and prison officers, as well as any civilians who assisted them or even gave information to the 'security forces'.

Loyalist paramilitaries had also recruited, especially into the UDA, which was still legal, and the UVF, which was not, along with their murderous sister groups the Ulster Freedom Fighters (UFF) and Red Hand Commandos (RHC). The British Army was also evolving, improving its surveillance and intelligence-gathering operation and its local knowledge of the area. However, it remained an army of occupation for half of the community, and increasingly harsh security policies introduced by a desperate unionist government only served to demonise it further and bolster the very security problem it was trying to mitigate.

Perhaps most controversially, the drive for better intelligence, allied with the permissive legal apparatus, led to the lengthy detention of suspects, coercive and abusive questioning and a perilous lack of accountability or political oversight of the security agencies. The legal apparatus was the bedrock for security policies in Northern Ireland during this period. The Special Powers Act provided wide-ranging and draconian powers to the police and other security agencies, including the right to arrest people without a warrant, intern people without trial, issue curfews and prohibit inquests into allegations of illegal killings.[16] These 'emergency' powers were made permanent in 1933, until the Emergency Provisions Act (EPA) in 1973 supplemented this legislation with the introduction of Diplock courts (trial without jury) for a range of 'scheduled' offences. This notion of 'scheduling' packaged certain offences with mandatory prison sentences, such as membership of a proscribed organisation or possession of firearms, required a low burden of proof (for example, uncorroborated confessions were considered acceptable) and were processed through the courts by individual judges in non-jury trials. This led to fast and efficient prosecutions but also allegations of injustice and maltreatment.

The Prevention of Terrorism Act (PTA) was introduced in Great Britain in 1974 following the Birmingham pub bombings, which killed twenty-one people and was similar in nature to the EPA in Northern Ireland. Both the EPA and the PTA were defined as unfortunate but necessary temporary legal arrangements required to cope with an extraordinary situation, though in practice they became permanent fixtures in the UK's legal portfolio as a means of pursuing its counter-insurgency strategy in Northern Ireland. The legal academic Fionnuala Ní Aoláin has highlighted the fact that when the emergency becomes the norm, the criminal justice system inevitably becomes politicised as a consequence: 'ordinary law has been bent out of shape and beyond all recognition in Northern Ireland. Its surgical remoulding has been both responsive to the conflict and defining of it. This tells us that legality is not a neutral actor in a situation of conflict. Law defines and takes sides and it has done so in Northern Ireland.'[17]

This point was conceded by the leadership of the British Army itself at the time, with Brigadier Frank Kitson becoming one of the central architects of Britain's counter-insurgency effort as head of the army in Northern Ireland. Kitson had been a counter-insurgency practitioner in Kenya and South East Asia before pitching up in Belfast in 1970, and he even wrote a classic text on the subject in 1971, in which he stated: 'The law should be used as just another weapon in the government's arsenal . . . For this to happen efficiently, the activities of the legal services have to be tied to the war effort in as discreet a way as possible.'[18] While the legal framework provided a cloak of respectability, the brutality that accompanied the implementation of these policies further alienated the nationalist community from the rule of law. While Kitson has since been lauded as a military strategist and counter-insurgency guru (and his book was undeniably influential within the British Army), this reputation seems unwarranted. In truth, his ideas and his period in control of the army in Belfast from 1970 to 1972 were disastrous and led to an escalation rather than reduction of what the

British now called 'terrorism'. His approach only served to inflame violence and help to legitimise those resorting to it, and he set back any prospect of political agreement by several years.

Interning the enemy without evidence of wrongdoing, using and abusing the legal system, running propaganda campaigns to try to delegitimise the Provisional IRA and even targeting key paramilitaries for assassination was Kitson's modus operandi during this period. However, he succeeded only in driving people towards the Provos rather than away from them. The IRA did not have to work hard to paint the British Army as bogeymen, as Kitson was sitting in his headquarters in Palace Barracks on the outskirts of Holywood with buckets of paint and a full set of brushes doing it for them. Kitson wanted intelligence on the Provos and was prepared to use harsh tactics to get it, including the coercive questioning of suspects, or what most people would think of as torture.

> A hood was pulled over my head and I was handcuffed and subjected to verbal and personal abuse, which included the threat of being dropped from a helicopter which was in the air, being kicked and struck about the body with batons on the way. . . . After this all my clothes were taken from me and I was given a boiler suit to wear which had no buttons and which was several sizes too big for me. . . . I was then taken into what I can only guess was another room and was made to stand with my feet wide apart and my hands pressed against a wall. . . . My brain seemed ready to burst. What was going to happen to me? Was I alone? Are they coming to kill me? I wished to God they would, to end it.[19]

The above quote does not refer to the treatment of someone incarcerated in the notorious Abu Ghraib Prison in Iraq, but to a suspect held without charge in Magilligan army base in Belfast in 1972. Paddy Joe MacLean, a school teacher from County Tyrone (who had no paramilitary involvement), was one of a group of fourteen detainees since referred to as the 'guineapigs' or 'hooded men', who were subjected to the 'five techniques' of sensory deprivation during coercive questioning in 1971. These techniques involved a pattern of physical and mental ill-treatment combined with attempts to confuse and disorientate suspects to make them more suggestible, through hooding, sleep and food deprivation, repetitive questioning, subjugation to white noise and a range of more petty harassments over a period of days. This was carried out by the British Army's Force Research Unit (FRU) and RUC Special Branch at a number of army centres, chiefly Palace Barracks and Girdwood Barracks, together with Magilligan and Ballykilner army camps.

Unionist politicians such as Brian Faulkner, who became the Prime Minister of Northern Ireland in the summer of 1971, were attracted by Kitson's commitment to 'going in hard' against the Provos in an effort to quell the daily mayhem taking place on the streets of Belfast. Faulkner was a physically lean and weedy figure with a rasping nasal drawl of a voice, but he was considered at the time to be a hard man. Faulkner is one of the most interesting political leaders of unionism, as he rose to the top on the back of an uncompromising law-and-order message but ended his career as someone willing to take risks for peace, attempting to lead his party into a power-sharing executive with nationalists in 1974. He would not be the last unionist leader to make the journey away from hard-line positions towards political compromise, but those who followed him suffered a similar fate, their careers fatally damaged due to the loss of support they experienced.

However, back in 1971, Faulkner was still to make his journey towards political accommodation and had got the top job in Northern Ireland because he claimed to know what to do to end the violence, especially the bombing campaign of the IRA. His key policy was to introduce stronger measures to crack down on the violence and those perpetrating it.

Internment was formally known as Operation Demetrius, and it refers to the practice of arresting and detaining without trial people suspected of being members of illegal paramilitary groups. The legal basis was the Special Powers Act, which allowed for the indefinite detention of anyone considered to be a threat to public order. Suspects were 'lifted' for interrogation and either charged or simply detained without legal representation after questioning for as long as was thought necessary. Internment was introduced on 9 August 1971 and continued in use until 5 December 1975. During this period, a total of 1,981 people were detained: 1,874 were Catholics, and only 107 were Protestants.

If this all sounds a bit dry and statistical, the reality was a lot more colourful, as it amounted to the brutalisation of the nationalist community in parts of Belfast by the British Army that had been supposedly deployed to protect them. That fallacy had long since dissappeared by August 1971, as it was clear from the army's behaviour as it imposed internment that it saw nationalists as the enemy. In practical terms, its soldiers forced their way into people's homes during dawn raids, smashed furniture and dragged men out of their beds at gunpoint, before loading them into army vehicles and taking them away for questioning and incarceration.

The following account of army behaviour during these raids, published by authors on behalf of the Independent Labour Party in 1971, is consistent with many other contemporary reports.

> Mrs. C., of Glenalena Road, who is four months pregnant, told us how she had been awakened during the early hours of the morning by the noise of breaking glass. When the soldiers entered the house she and her husband were upstairs. Her husband, partly dressed by now, was holding their ten-month-old baby. The troops smashed their way in, shouting something about 'Fenian Bastards'. They came up the stairs shouting and creating a general commotion – the child was knocked out of the husband's arms and when Mrs. C. attempted to go towards him, she was knocked through a bedroom door and fell over her nine year old daughter. The husband was told to get outside and when he asked if he could put his shoes on a soldier replied 'can you fucking hell'. He was hit on the head with a rifle butt, which caused him to fall downstairs. At the foot of the stairs he was made to walk through the broken glass in his bare feet. A soldier, cursing and swearing and rushing about in the kitchen, kicked and smashed the kitchen table legs.[20]

What might have seemed like a good idea to Brian Faulkner on paper fell apart when it collided with reality on 9 August 1971. The introduction of internment was chaotic and rushed, initially being planned for September but suddenly being triggered on 9 August 1971, before the army had finished preparing its plans for what to do with all the detainees it lifted. The army and the police were involved in turf wars over access to intelligence information, and even different regiments were bickering among themselves about who was in charge. One of the leaders of the Ulster Defence Regiment (UDR) in Ballykinlar army base (20 miles outside Belfast) was ordered back from his annual leave early to find that a Royal Artillery regiment had arrived to build an interrogation centre for prospective detainees and were demanding the keys to buildings on the site. When the UDR adjutant refused to hand them over, the invading regiment just broke in and took the facilities over by force.[21] Such chaotic behaviour was indicative of the way the army and the politicians behind them were responding to events and were to some extent just making policy up as they went along.

Internment failed to catch the main paramilitary actors due to the poor intelligence available to an army that was still trying to understand the region and that had advised against the use of internment in the first place. The selection of targets was based on old RUC Special Branch intelligence on around 450 republican activists and their last known addresses. These lists were hopelessly out of date – in one case, the army spent some time in Armagh trying to find and detain a man who had been dead for four years.[22]

In hindsight, internment probably did more to entrench and inflame the Troubles than any other British government policy in Northern Ireland after partition. The people who were lifted were for the most part unconnected with paramilitary organisations, the policy was overwhelmingly targeted at the Catholic community, and instead of being reduced, the level of violence escalated dramatically afterwards.[23] In political terms, internment cast the army as an aggressive malevolent force and presented Northern Ireland as being in a state of emergency, a narrative which suited the Provisional IRA perfectly.

BLOODY FRIDAY

Belfast and the rest of Northern Ireland experienced many bloody days during the period known as the Troubles, and while Derry suffered the trauma of Bloody Sunday on 30 January 1972, Belfast was torn apart by Bloody Friday on 21 July 1972. The context of the period was that the

Provisionals – emboldened by the brutality meted out to the nationalist community by the British Army through policies like internment – were in the ascendency by the summer of 1972. By this point, the Provos had wiped out the Officials and were in control of militant activities in Belfast, their membership and arsenal of weapons bloated by internment and by Bloody Sunday in Derry the previous January. By the spring of 1972, the Stormont government had been prorogued by the British government, which was greeted with a mixture of triumph and relief among the nationalist population (and anger and dismay across the unionist community). Faulkner's hard-nosed 'root out the terrorists' policy and Frank Kitson's counter-insurgency approach had made things worse rather than better, and the British government lost faith that the unionist government was capable of dealing with the situation.

Violence escalated dramatically in Belfast after internment, with bomb attacks and fatal shootings a daily occurrence. By the end of 1972, 467 people had been killed and there was mayhem on the streets, with over 10,000 shooting incidents and 1,800 bombings across the city.

It was clear by 1972 that the security situation was untenable and something radical would have to be done to curb the disintegration of law and order. By the spring, the British government had decided that there was nothing for it but to take back political responsibility for a part of the UK it had spent the previous fifty years trying to forget about. On 1 April 1972, fifty years of majority-rule devolved government came crashing down around unionist ears and direct rule from London was imposed on Northern Ireland.

A bitter statement released by Brian Faulkner and his Cabinet colleagues in March 1972, following their political emasculation, emphasised their view that the sword was actually mightier than the pen: 'I fear . . . that many people will draw a sinister and depressing message from these events: that violence can pay; that violence does pay; that those who shout, lie, denigrate and even destroy earn for themselves an attention that responsible conduct and honourable behaviour do not.'[24]

However, the British government's mind was made up, and Faulkner became the last Prime Minister of Northern Ireland to hold office within a majoritarian political system. Unionist political domination at Stormont had come to an end, and there was an eerie silence at Stormont in the days that followed, punctuated only by the sound of bombs exploding across Belfast as the paramilitaries sought to provide a military answer to their collective political problem.

Militant republicans felt confident that they had the British on the run and that their bombing campaign was sapping the will of the government to remain in Northern Ireland. This was a huge misreading by the Provos, caused in part by a total lack of understanding of British thinking, combined with delusions of grandeur about their own significance.

The Provos exploded any chance they had of moving the British towards them politically, as surely as severed limbs were scattered over the streets in the centre of Belfast on Bloody Friday. The word 'atrocity' has been so over-used by the media in their coverage of the Troubles that its impact has been dulled. The word should have been reserved for days like Bloody Friday, as in the space of an hour, on the afternoon of Friday 21 July 1972, nineteen bombs exploded in various parts of Belfast city centre.

There were no effective warnings given by the IRA to prevent the mayhem and carnage that followed from the series of car bombs and explosions at bus and railway stations, hotels, shops and offices. The bombs were planted with the intention of killing as many people as possible, and men, women and children were literally blown to pieces on the streets of the city. In scenes reminiscent of the Belfast Blitz in 1941, plumes of smoke could be seen rising all over the city, accompanied by a cacophony of sirens from the emergency services and fire alarms from burning buildings.

Deafened by the noise, dazed and frightened, Friday afternoon shoppers wandered around looking for a route out of the chaos. My own mother was one of them, and she recalls walking home from the city as the buses had stopped running and the roads in the centre of town were clogged with emergency vehicles ferrying the dead to the morgue and the wounded to hospital. The footage of the clean-up operation at Oxford Street bus station, where six people died, is still too graphic to be shown on mainstream television. The grainy pictures of firemen shovelling the charred remains of bodies into plastic bags and lifting severed limbs and other unrecognisable parts of the victims off the pavement are difficult to stomach. In Malachi O'Doherty's

163

account of the period, he describes how one of the fire engines going to another bomb attack had to swerve to avoid a woman's head that was lying in the middle of the road outside the bus station.[25] These are among the most shocking visual images of the Troubles, and I used to show them to my undergraduate students every year to remind them of the reality behind the statistics of violence, as they all sat in awkward silence watching the footage. While they, hopefully, never saw it, I often had a tear in my eye when I turned the lights back on, even though I was familiar with the footage and knew what was coming.

Peter Taylor, a British journalist whose first story in Northern Ireland was Bloody Sunday, related the recollections of a police officer a quarter of a century after he witnessed the event: 'One of the most horrendous memories for me was seeing a head stuck to the wall. A couple of days later, we found vertebrae and a rib cage on the roof of a nearby building. The reason we found it was because the seagulls were diving onto it. I've tried to put it at the back of my mind for twenty-five years.'[26] Miraculously, given the number and force of the explosions, only nine people died, though over a hundred were injured.

In Britain and across the world, the reaction to Bloody Friday was one of revulsion. In Ireland it was also condemned, including by many nationalists and republicans who were shocked at the scale and severity of the attacks. The *Irish Times* compared the IRA to Nazis and questioned the moral compass of a nation that could harbour such violent intent. The Provisional IRA admitted responsibility for the attacks but accepted no moral culpability. IRA Chief of Staff Seán MacStíofáin looked metaphorically through the debris and concluded that five of those killed were 'innocent civilians' adding that 'our attitude was that it was five too many'. But for MacStíofáin and his colleagues in the IRA, the underlying cause was the continued British presence in Ireland and the failure of the British Crown Forces to pass on the warnings that had been given.

In political terms, Bloody Friday was a huge setback for the IRA in the way that Bloody Sunday was for the British Army. It was a propaganda disaster that cast the Provos as the perpetrators of violence, the killers of innocent women and children who were clearly nothing to do with the

British war machine. Beyond this damage to their reputation as 'freedom fighters', Bloody Friday presented William Whitelaw with a tactical opportunity to hit back. Public revulsion opened the way for him to pursue a more robust security response. British public opinion demanded it and Irish opinion accepted it – in the short term, at least. Whitelaw now had the pretext he needed to send the army into the so-called no-go areas of Belfast. Here, semi-permanent barricades had been set up by the IRA (and to a lesser extent by the UDA) and armed paramilitaries stood around openly checking cars and people's driving licences while the police and army looked on helplessly. The British government had effectively ceded control of these parts of the UK to armed republican and loyalist militias.

The weekend after Bloody Friday, seven more battalions of British soldiers arrived in Northern Ireland, raising troop levels to 22,000, the highest since 1922. The largest British military exercise since Suez in 1956 was launched by the army at dawn on Monday 31 July 1972, codenamed Operation Motorman. Serious military hardware accompanied the arrival of the troops, including a planeload of riot shields and a hundred armoured personnel carriers and tanks. The operation involved 38 army battalions, as 22,000 British troops saturated the no-go areas and used tanks and bulldozers to smash through the barricades that had been set up to keep them out. Though Prime Minister Edward Heath had been bracing himself for up to 1,000 casualties, the operation in fact met with little resistance. Unlike the disastrous internment policy, Operation Motorman was well planned, properly resourced and effectively led by the army, in close harmony with Whitelaw and Heath. Just as importantly, the timing of this military initiative was unusually deft, coming at a point when all but the most ardent supporters of the republican 'armed struggle' accepted that there was a need for some restoration of law and order to ensure that the carnage of Bloody Friday was never repeated.

THE PEACE PEOPLE

Most of this chapter has focused on several of the more notorious incidents of the Troubles era, but there were also iconic community-driven initiatives that emerged out of the violence that attempted to bring it to an end. By the mid-1970s, Belfast had settled in for a long war, as paramilitary groups on republican and loyalist sides became more proficient at killing and the police, army and rest of the British security apparatus built up its armed presence and settled into the realisation that the best it could hope for was to contain the paramilitaries rather than defeat them.

1972 turned out to be the most violent year of the Troubles, but at the time, every year in the 1970s seemed to be chock-full of bombings, shootings, sectarian riots and bellicose politicians ranting on the television about who was to blame for it all. To say that violent events such as Bloody Friday and the other less notorious shootings and bombings traumatised the people of Belfast (and Northern Ireland more generally) would be an understatement. While their physical impact in terms of death and injury was quantifiable, the indirect effect on the mental health of those who lived through them is more difficult to assess.

Some people responded to the violence by getting involved in it directly, either by joining a paramilitary group or the police, the RUC, or the British Army as a reserve member of the UDR. People on all sides were motivated to defend their communities from attack, while many others left Belfast (such as actor Kenneth Branagh's family, thus providing the premise for his Oscar-winning film named after the city). Everyone was caught up in the violence of the 1970s and 1980s one way or another, though some of those unlucky enough to get caught in the crossfire attempted to do something about it.

One episode from the 1970s epitomises both the pain and the courage of those who became victims of the violence, and it was a story that would reverberate around the world. On 10 August 1976 there was a car chase in West Belfast involving a vehicle being driven by a member of the Provisional IRA and a British Army Land Rover. Along the road, Anne Maguire was wheeling a pram containing her six-week-old baby and with her three other children (aged from two to eight years) in close attendance. The soldiers shot the car driver, killing him instantly but causing the vehicle to career off the road and into the Maguire family, killing the baby and two of the other children and severely injuring the mother. Though she recovered from her physical injuries, Anne Maguire never got over the mental trauma of losing her three children and took her own life several years later. Even by the standards of the time, this tragedy shocked the community. In solidarity, some women set up a shrine at the scene of the incident and held a walk through the housing estate where it had occurred. Anne's sister, Mairead Corrigan, went on television to appeal for an end to the violence, and women across Northern Ireland started a door-to-door petition calling for paramilitary ceasefires. This spontaneous activism, sparked by the human cost of the conflict, was typical of many of the NGOs that emerged at the time. It was also the type of story that the media found easy to cover, as it focused on the anguish caused by violence without the need for any further context or complex political analysis. Who was responsible? The IRA driver for hijacking a car and robbing a bank, or the British soldiers for recklessly shooting the driver dead? For most of those caught up in the human tragedy, the answer did not matter very much. As the British and international media interest in the 'human angle' grew, more energy flowed into the wider community and the parades and vigils increased, until Mairead Corrigan joined with two other activists (Betty Williams and Ciaran McKeown) to form the Peace People.

Over the next twelve months the Peace People grew into a mass movement, with peace rallies across the island of Ireland, as well as in the US and Britain, where a vigil in Trafalgar Square drew a crowd of over 10,000 people. The three leaders of the Peace People were awarded the Nobel Peace Prize in 1976 but gradually faded into the background as public enthusiasm waned and as paramilitary violence continued unabated into the 1980s. The Peace People movement was also viewed with suspicion by the republican community, many of whom saw it as part of the British propaganda machine, while the simplistic emotional demands for an end to violence offered little to those who were victims of the British security forces.

I remember a piece of graffiti daubed on the walls around the city at the time which said '7 years is too many, don't make it 8'. But despite the efforts of citizen activists such as the Peace People, eight years became nine, then ten, and it would be another eighteen years before long-lasting paramilitary ceasefires would be agreed in combination with a demilitarisation phase by the British security forces.

THE SHANKILL BOMBING

Eamonn Ferguson was a paramedic and one of the first to arrive at the scene of the Shankill Road bombing in October 1993. Recalling the event in 2018, he vividly describes the carnage that confronted him.

> I sort of moved a stone away and that's when I saw a child's face looking at me through the rubble . . . I could tell the child was dead but, for some reason, I just thought if we could somehow manage to free this child then we might be able to resuscitate them. . . . We were digging and digging, trying to free the child . . . then I saw another arm underneath the child, which was another child.[27]

As the Peace People episode demonstrated, one of the unusual by-products of political conflict is that violent incidents can produce positive dynamics as well as negative ones. While it might seem paradoxical, there are occasions when a violent event can result in unintended consequences, producing a sense of collective threat or looming catastrophe that focuses minds and redoubles efforts to find non-violent alternatives. Northern Ireland is no different in that respect to other conflicts in which turning points were reached not through progressive initiatives but as a result of collective revulsion and a desire to step back from the abyss of violence.

Another case in point was provided by the Shankill bombing in 1993, an attack that would go down in infamy as one of the worst sectarian incidents of the Troubles. This attack triggered a wave of violent reprisals but at the same time provided a catalyst for dialogue between the political parties. The Shankill Road in West Belfast is an almost exclusively Protestant and unionist/loyalist area, which parallels the Falls Road, which is an almost exclusively Catholic and nationalist/republican area.

Tensions had been rising in the city during the early 1990s as targeted assassinations were increasing between loyalist and republican paramilitary groups spurred on by the whiff of political change that was in the air. Secret talks between the SDLP leader John Hume and Sinn Féin President Gerry Adams had recently been made public, and loyalists felt that moderate nationalists were in cahoots with armed republicans in what they condemned as a 'Pan-Nationalist Front'. Mainstream unionist politicians doubled down on the use of this phrase – which potentially widened the number of Catholics deemed 'legitimate targets' by loyalist paramilitaries. The Provisionals issued statements denouncing this and claiming that 'there would be no hiding place'[28] for what they liked to refer to as loyalist 'death squads'.

Saturday 23 October 1993 was a beautiful, sunny autumn morning in Belfast, punctured when two IRA bombers – Sean Kelly and Thomas Begley – left a bomb in Jimmy Frizzell's fish shop on the Shankill. It exploded prematurely and without warning, killing nine shoppers and one of the bombers (Begley). The IRA had believed a meeting of the commanders of the West Belfast UDA was scheduled for that morning above the fish shop, but the information was wrong and the loyalist targets were not present. The IRA had been aiming to assassinate UFF leader Johnny 'Mad Dog' Adair, but they missed their target and killed nine Saturday shoppers instead, including several women and children. The television footage of the after-math, with passers-by and relatives of the dead and injured pulling victims from the debris, was so graphic that it had to be carefully edited.

Michelle Baird, who was just seven years of age, and thirteen-year-old Leanne Murray were among the dead. Leanne's mother gave an interview the following day that provides a stark reminder of the fragility of life in conflict and the impact of violence on its victims, both those who are killed and those left bereaved:

Leanne had just left me to go in to the fish shop. Suddenly there was this huge bang. We ran screaming for Leanne. We couldn't find her. No-one had seen her. There were people lying in the street covered in blood. My little girl was underneath all that rubble. We started clawing at it with our bare hands. I was screaming her name. But it was no use. My little daughter was dead – just for a tub of whelks.[29]

Begley was given a full republican funeral, and his coffin, draped in the Irish flag and IRA standard-issue black beret and gloves, was carried by Sinn Féin President Gerry Adams amid a storm of media criticism. The *Sun* newspaper was predictably the most hyperbolic: 'Gerry Adams – the two most disgusting words in the English language'.[30] The other bomber, Sean Kelly, received nine life sentences for his part in the attack. He was released from jail on licence along with other paramilitary prisoners in July 2000, under the terms of the Good Friday Agreement prisoner release scheme.

The Provisional IRA claimed that the Shankill bombing was an operation that went 'tragically wrong', but this was ridiculed, given that the attack had taken place on a Saturday morning, at the busiest shopping time of the week. On the twenty-fifth anniversary of the attack, the BBC's former Security Correspondent Brian Rowan reinforced the point that, far from being an accident, the operation would have been known by the IRA to have inevitably resulted in civilian casualties:

> As part of my work at the BBC, I had visited that office on occasions to speak with UDA leaders. Any warning was never going to be sufficient to clear the area. This is the lie in the IRA statement of that day. They must have known they were going to kill and injure civilians. Indeed, many years later, one of the IRA's most-senior leaders in that period accepted that the nature of the attack meant there would be 'collateral damage'.[31]

Loyalist paramilitary retaliation was not long in coming. On 30 October, the crowded Rising Sun pub in the village of Greysteel, County Derry, was attacked by three members of the UFF, who killed eight people. The gunmen yelled 'trick or treat' as they opened fire on patrons celebrating Halloween. Some of the victims pleaded for mercy as the killers reloaded their weapons and opened fire on them. The UDA later claimed that the attack had been a reprisal for the previous weekend's Shankill bombing. Over twenty people had been killed in the space of a week, and the news was filled with condemnations, funerals, grieving relatives and a pervading sense of dread across Northern Ireland that things were getting worse rather than better.

One of the lasting images of the period was of SDLP leader John Hume breaking down in tears at the funeral of one of the victims of the Greysteel shootings, an enduring image of the embryonic peace process that seemed at that moment to be consumed by the spiral of violence. If the darkest hour is before the dawn, then this was it, in the context of the Troubles, as fear of violence running out of control jump-started the formal political process. Politicians across Ireland and Britain recognised the responsibility they shouldered and the human cost that would result if they failed. More deaths, more funerals, more tears, more grieving families and no political solutions.

The initial result of talks between the two governments came with the publication of the Downing Street Declaration on 15 December 1993. The document was publicly unveiled, by British Prime Minister John Major and Irish Taoiseach Albert Reynolds on the steps of Downing Street, and amounted to a carefully worded balancing act by the two governments in an attempt to establish the basis for political dialogue and agreement in Northern Ireland.

It underlined two key principles that became foundation stones for the subsequent negotiations that led to the Good Friday Agreement in 1998 and everything that came after. First, that Britain had no selfish strategic or economic interest in remaining in Northern Ireland against the wishes of a majority of the people living there. If and when the majority wanted to end the Union and integrate with the rest of the island of Ireland then Britain would enact the necessary legislation to facilitate this transfer of sovereignty. Second, the Irish government recognised that the consent of the people in Northern Ireland to any such change was a prerequisite for Irish reunification.

The Downing Street Declaration was a masterpiece of ambiguity and became the cornerstone of the peace process, upon which everything else was subsequently built. The British and Irish governments presented themselves as facilitators (rather than advocates) of political change and as neutral in relation to the constitutional fault line that ran through the conflict: was Northern Ireland to remain within the UK or to become united with the rest of Ireland? The declaration also made clear that the engine of political change was the democratic process and that all those with a political mandate who committed themselves to exclusively peaceful methods had a right to participate.

While it is important not to interpret complex political relationships and events as clear linear steps, it is reasonable to make an indirect connection between the Shankill Road bombing and the Greysteel shootings in the autumn of 1993 and the renewed political impetus for dialogue and agreement in Northern Ireland that followed. Out of the rubble of the Shankill bomb a peace process slowly emerged that brought the Troubles to an end. It remains fragile and incomplete, but hopefully some among the bereaved, whose loved ones were killed or maimed in these violent events and the many other tragedies of the Troubles, can find some comfort in that thought.

6

THE TOURISM

One Friday afternoon during the early 1990s, before the republican and loyalist paramilitary ceasefires had been announced, I parked my car in a high-rise car park on the appropriately named High Street in Belfast city centre (the road that the River Farset runs silently beneath). I spent the next few hours enthusiastically doing research for my PhD at the Linen Hall Library, returning towards the end of the afternoon to find the street cordoned off by the British Army due to a bomb scare in the car park. As I stood pondering how I was going to get home and whether my precious car was going to be blown up, a North American voice beside me asked what was going on. I explained that there was a bomb scare in the car park and that the army was sending in a robot to take a look at the suspicious vehicle. Before I had finished briefing her about this bad news, she exclaimed: 'Oh that is simply wonderful! We are on holiday from Canada and didn't think we would be lucky enough to see a real-life bomb scare!' She turned to her young son and said, 'Aren't we lucky to see this? I mean what were the chances we would get to see an actual bomb scare?' A little irked by her attitude and by the unexpected impounding of my wheels, I told her that the Northern Ireland Tourist Board put on a mock bomb scare every Friday teatime in the summer as part of an attempt to attract international visitors to Belfast. For several minutes I think she believed me, until I mentioned that most of the rest of the crowd were extras made up of people on income support who were forced to turn up or have their benefits cut by the vicious Tory government. At that point she laughed a bit nervously, realising I was having her on, and she shooed her child away from the overly sarcastic local.

In the end, the car park was closed all night, so I got a lift home from my dad and told him about all the excitement – of seeing a real-life Canadian tourist in Belfast. At times during the 1970s, bomb scares had been almost more numerous than tourists in the city, but my meeting on High Street twenty years later was a harbinger of what was to come, as the peace process began to develop into what would gradually transform into a post-conflict tourist economy. While I was not to know it at the time, the trickle of external visitors was to become a flood a few years after this encounter, facilitated by paramilitary ceasefires in 1994, a dramatic reduction in violence and eventually multi-party talks that resulted in the Belfast/Good Friday Agreement in April 1998.

TOURISM AND THE PEACE PROCESS

Over the last twenty-five years, Belfast has gradually been discovered by increasing numbers of external visitors, attracted by its virtues rather than by its violence. The city has a lot going for it as a tourist destination, and the arrival of relative stability has resulted in new investment in visitor attractions and infrastructure, which has helped the city to showcase its history, culture and natural environment. While I am biased, Belfast is a breathtakingly beautiful place, especially if you arrive by ferry and sail into the city up Belfast Lough. If you stand out on deck (and if it is not pelting down with rain) it can be a magical way to arrive and to see the way that Belfast is nestled between the sea on one side and Cave Hill on the other. We have an incredible history, a vibrant cultural scene and spectacular scenery, and while we did a great job in scaring visitors from coming in the second half of the twentieth century, those days are now hopefully behind us. Belfast is also renowned (rightly) for being an incredibly friendly city – and while we might hate one another, we love visitors.

We've certainly had a makeover, largely thanks to the peace process, the investment that followed and a collective sense that the future was going to be more upbeat than the past. Belfast is now defined geographically by historical and cultural reference points such as the Linen Quarter, the Titanic Quarter, the Cathedral Quarter and the Gaeltacht Quarter – which packages the city neatly for visitors. There are now shiny new hotels to stay in (if you can afford to), new attractions such as Titanic Belfast, a vibrant nightlife and any number of high-end restaurants in the centre of town or in the nearby suburb of Ballyhackamore – recently dubbed 'Ballysnackamore'.

We now have public art illuminated at night, such as the *Beacon of Hope*, a 20-metre-high metal figure overlooking the River Lagan and towering over Queen's Bridge as you enter the city. Nicknamed Nula with the Hula, it is quite striking at night, when it is illuminated in blue. The largest piece of public art in the city is *RISE*, formed of two huge spheres at Broadway roundabout on the M1, which are unmissable, especially when they are illuminated at night – actually, they are quite distracting when you are battling with the traffic. Belfast humour being what it is, they have been variously dubbed the 'Balls on the Falls' and the 'Westicles', as they sit at the entrance to West Belfast and the Falls Road area. But the point here is that at least we now have public art and it is not getting blown up, and while the blue light can be distracting, it is certainly much nicer than the army helicopter searchlights that used to strafe the cityscape during the Troubles.

Street art has also evolved in the city from a marker of community identity into a tourist attraction and has recently seen the emergence of a new wave of wall murals that are reflecting more complex identities. In the past, wall murals functioned as carefully codified artistic message boards for the community and as signs of political resistance and resilience. Wall murals have traditionally been highly political and were designed to defend and validate particular narratives of the conflict. They still play this role, as shown by graffiti in loyalist parts of Belfast relating to community opposition to the implementation of Brexit and the Northern Ireland Protocol that came into effect in January 2021, imposing a trade border in the Irish Sea between Great Britain and Northern Ireland.

However, street art in Belfast has moved with political developments in the city, and there has been a new wave of murals, especially in the cultural centre of the city, in what has become known as the Cathedral Quarter. Some of this street art has itself been political, facilitating a conscious cultural rebranding of the city, with images of the Harland and Wolff cranes (Samson and Goliath) and the *Titanic* moving from wall murals into museum gift shops and purveyors of tourist merchandise. The commodification and sanitisation of Belfast street art has connected directly into debates over the legitimacy of the conflict itself, the iconography of what is being depicted in the murals and the political narrative that surrounds such messaging.[1]

The political dimension here is one faced by all deeply divided societies that have experienced longstanding violent conflict; namely, the extent to which such street art retains a political and cultural authenticity, or whether it morphs into an attempt to dilute the past through more anodyne imagery, with inclusive murals of football legend George Best and legendary writer C.S. Lewis replacing the more militant imagery of paramilitary factions and threats of violent resistance. Tourists certainly want to see the latter, but the picture is a much more mixed one today than it was twenty years ago. As well as local artists, international street artists like MTO have descended on the city and painted it – magnificently. You can, of course, now take street art walking tours of the city, and you should, if you visit. You can also take historical walking tours, music tours, political conflict tours, black taxi tours and open-top bus tours, as our past is gradually morphing into our heritage.

None of this is unproblematic or has taken place without criticism, but it has only been possible because of the peace process and what followed it in the 1990s. The political agreement reached on 10 April 1998 placed tourism on an entirely different level, in terms of both the number of people who wanted to visit Belfast and other parts of Northern Ireland and how it was organised. The devolved institutions were finally established in 1999, and tourism was at the centre of the new power-sharing executive's economic policy, as well being as a key component of cross-border cooperation and the newly formed North–South bodies.

Tourism and its 'promotion, marketing, research and product development' was identified within the Good Friday Agreement as one of six areas for cross-border cooperation between Northern Ireland and the Irish Republic.[2] This provides a good illustration of the way tourism can play a direct role in building joint initiatives for communities after violent conflict has ended and a political agreement has been reached. While we might think of tourism as part of an economic strategy (and of course it is) or even as an aspect of cultural policy (which it also is), political institutions are integral to tourism development in the aftermath of conflict. Tourism was identified within the Good Friday Agreement as an area of mutual interest for the people within both political jurisdictions, where the tourist product could be developed to the benefit of everyone on the island. It was hoped that this would be a classic win–win scenario, where cooperation for mutual advantage would benefit everyone on the island without threatening established political allegiances.

In the wake of the Good Friday Agreement, new structures were established to more effectively integrate the marketing of Irish tourism (North and South). Tourism Ireland was established in 2002 to connect the Southern-based Bord Fáilte and the Northern Ireland Tourist Board, now rebadged as Tourism Northern Ireland. Despite complicated lines of communication across several departments and two political jurisdictions, all parties recognised the capacity of tourism to provide significant economic benefits on both sides of the border, to the point that tourism has become a flagship for 'place-branding' in Ireland.

It is a key aspect of foreign policy in the Irish Republic and a major element of economic policy in both parts of the island, driving employment and foreign direct-investment initiatives. *People, Place and Policy – Growing Tourism to 2025*, released in March 2015, has been a key plank of Irish government economic policy over the last decade, aiming to create an extra 50,000 jobs over the 10-year period, bringing the total of tourism-related jobs in Ireland to 250,000. The link between tourism, economic development and peace and stability was made explicit here, and the follow-up Tourism Action Plan 2019–2021 suggested that the income generated from overseas tourism to Ireland had reached almost €5 billion in 2017.

While Northern Ireland only gets a fraction of this overseas tourism and the income that comes with it, inevitably, as the overall number of visitors increases, more tourists venture north. The increased political stability after the Good Friday Agreement has encouraged tourists to discover the landscape, leisure and cultural offerings in the north of the island, as well as the legacy of its violent conflict.

TURNING SWORDS INTO PLOUGHSHARES

Belfast is no different in benefiting from post-conflict tourism initiatives to many other places that have used their new-found stability to help navigate their way out of conflict. Tourism can play a number of important roles in transforming conflict relationships that go beyond just reviving the economies of fractured societies. While there is an understandable focus on the money that such tourism generates, it is also inherently political in nature. 'Conflict tourism' packages the narrative of the past in a way that frames issues of causality, victimhood and suffering. At a very basic level, it deals with issues of legitimacy and responsibility for the events that are being remembered and prioritised as artefacts or places of interest. Equally, tourist operators are influential mediators in decisions over what tourists *do not* get to see and what gets left off the tour itinerary. Tourism can also promote personal change and help to reduce negative stereotypes about places that have been written off by international media coverage as being mad, bad or dangerous to visit. Increasing the exposure of overseas tourists to such 'war zones' can help to change the image of such places with their personal testimony that the reality is more complex – assuming the experience is a positive one. This process has been helped by the proliferation of social media sites such as Facebook, Instagram, TikTok and Twitter, as well as travel review sites such as Tripadvisor and Airbnb, where visitors share positive experiences and photographs of where they have been.

While tourism cannot *bring* peace to a violent conflict, there may be scope for believing that it is capable of *helping* a peace-building process gain traction, once a political agreement has been established. It is certainly the case that violence in Northern Ireland during the Troubles resulted in a drastic reduction in tourist numbers. The most violent year in the post-1969 era of the Northern Ireland conflict was 1972, and this was reflected in its lowest figure for tourist visitors (435,000) – a 53 per cent decrease from 1967.[3] Tourism went up by 20 per cent in 1995 (the year after the initial paramilitary ceasefires), with tourist-related spending up by 17 per cent and visitor enquiries up 59 per cent on 1994 levels.[4]

In more recent years the tourism market in Northern Ireland, and Belfast in particular, has continued to expand at pace, notwithstanding the challenges of the Covid-19 pandemic and the lockdowns that prevented travel and tourism activity. Belfast developed a cruise-ship industry once the peace process had brought stability to the city, and in 2012 this resulted in over 70,000 visitors coming into Belfast port. By 2019 this figure had grown to over 270,000. Tourists are also flying into Belfast in increasing numbers, and in the twelve months from June 2018 to June 2019, approximately nine million visitors travelled through Belfast International and Belfast City airports. Staggeringly, for a city of under 400,000 people, in the eight-year period between 2011 and 2018, Belfast had over 32 million visitors to the city.[5]

Following the adage that if you build it, they will come, to accommodate the surge in tourism over the last decade, a number of landmark hotels have sprung up in the city centre, evidence not just of the demand for overnight stays in Belfast but also that major hotel chains have sufficient confidence in its stability to invest their money. This has influenced the urban landscape of the city skyline as well as driving its economy, with the £53 million 23-storey Hastings Grand Central Hotel boasting a top-floor cocktail bar where patrons can sip their expensive drinks with a panoramic view across the city.

In addition to the Grand Central Hotel, a number of other prestigious landmark developments have appeared, offering high-end visitor accommodation, including the Hilton, the AC Hotel owned by the Marriott US chain, the five-star Merchant Hotel and the Titanic Hotel, conveniently situated next to Titanic Belfast and themed accordingly. Belfast has therefore seen the opening of a swathe of prestigious hotels, and these have been filled with tourists and other customers at an impressive rate, at least prior to the Covid-19 pandemic in 2020. In 2018 it was reported that occupancy rates across Belfast's hotel accommodation had been running at a very healthy 75 per cent and above since 2012.[6]

The caveat to all of these statistics is that tourism is a complex multi-dimensional industry, which makes it difficult to provide easily quantifiable numbers – but the general trend and pattern seems relatively clear and provides an overall picture that the peace process has been a massive stimulus for tourism in Belfast and across Northern Ireland more broadly. Increased political stability and enhanced visibility has produced a peace dividend, where swords are slowly being hammered into ploughshares.

THE DARK SIDE

Today, despite the political tensions that remain, Belfast has a thriving tourist economy that is mediating the difficult space between a divided history, heritage and the new opportunities presented for economic recovery. Belfast is no different from any other city seeking to present its history as a driver for tourism and other forms of economic development. Cities that have experienced difficult periods, including famines, plagues, wars or other infamous episodes of violence, may at some point seek to construct a tourist narrative around that notorious past. Belfast is in that sense no different from Sarajevo in former Yugoslavia, which suffered terrible damage during the Bosnian war in the early 1990s, or more recently New York City, which perversely now gets more tourists at the site of the 9/11 attacks on the World Trade Center than visited the Twin Towers when they were actually there.

This phenomenon is often referred to as 'dark tourism' or 'conflict tourism', and, although it may be an uncomfortable thought, the reality is that violence sells, and, as tourists, we seem drawn more to tragedy than to triumph. There has been a fertile debate surrounding the nature of dark tourism and the boundaries of the term, first coined by academics Malcolm Foley and John Lennon.[7] We are often drawn as tourists to former war zones and sites of conflict, hopefully because we seek to learn more about the history of places we may have seen on television or read about.

This is relatively easy to do with violent conflicts that took place centuries ago, but it becomes more delicate when we engage with conflicts within living memory, or where the outcome remains contested and thus the narrative of legitimacy that is framed for tourists can be disputed. Where memories remain vivid, the tourist trail is strewn with historical, political, religious, economic and cultural landmines. What is included in the tour and what is excluded, where you visit and where you do not and the narrative provided on what took place can be highly contentious. At times, the lines between the conflict experience and the post-conflict economy can become very blurred, and the tourist can be confronted with uncomfortable questions about whether it is really appropriate for them to be crawling through tunnels, looking at sites of massacres or firing blanks out of machine guns used in guerrilla fighting.

In her ground-breaking book *Holidays in the Danger Zone*, Debbie Lisle maps the intersections of the war–tourism relationship, pointing out how inextricably entangled the two have become.[8] While once war time and leisure time seemed like different worlds, Lisle's message is that they occupy a mutually interdependent and integrated space where battlefields have become tourist landscapes and post-conflict commemoration has infused the battlefield into the mainstream tourist industry.

Creating a tourist product out of the ashes of violent conflict presents some tension between providers and consumers that needs to be considered. How can a positive experience be provided out of such a negative context without the tourist becoming traumatised in the process, or being unable to avoid squarely eyeballing the horror that is inherent in the subject matter? In this sense, dark tourism can be both enabling and disabling. It can provide attention, reputational benefits and much-needed economic dividends to shattered societies after violent conflicts, but there is a price to be paid for the attention and resources that arrive, as the consumption of the experience by the tourist can require some level of adjustment and accommodation. This might relate to simplifying or sanitising the reality of what happened in a manner suitable for tourist consumption.

Regardless of the motivation, we do seem inexorably drawn to sites of political violence and large-scale human suffering in our recreation time. Belfast has seen a burgeoning of dark tourism initiatives, and a proliferation of what can loosely be termed 'Troubles tours' have developed since the conflict began to wind down at the end of the 1990s. There are multiple 'black taxi' tours vying for business in Belfast and numerous bus tours, in addition to walking tours from a variety of operators. The smaller tours are often rooted within a republican or loyalist narrative and are staffed by ex-prisoners for additional 'authenticity'. Other tour providers are consciously designed to cross over conflict divisions in their itineraries, narratives and management structures in order to provide balance and access to conflict sites.

Northern Ireland Black Taxi Tours has become a mainstay for visitors to Northern Ireland, offering bespoke trips around the city with explanatory commentaries. Its website offers itineraries that focus on the republican and loyalist wall murals of the Falls and Shankill Roads, as well as other iconic buildings and monuments, including the 'Peace Wall'. There are also broader tours that focus on the *Titanic* and the landscape of Belfast and beyond, including the north coast's Giant's Causeway and Bushmills Distillery.

While some of these tours certainly make an effort to cover both sides of Belfast's divided history, others are more rooted within specific communities and single-narrative experiences of the past. Coiste Irish Political Tours is located firmly within a nationalist/republican narrative of the conflict but stresses the local authenticity of the tourist experience, linked to the personal reflections of the former prisoners who are now tour guides: 'Coiste guides are Republican ex-prisoners and members of the republican community whose narrative comes from their experience of our recent history, political activism and political imprisonment. Our story is the story of our communities and their struggles.'[9]

There is an inevitable tension within conflict tourism involving ex-prisoners from one side of the community. It divides opinion between those who see such initiatives as part of post-conflict peace-building and economic regeneration, and others who view it as a cynical exercise in rewriting history and rewarding the guilty. In 2017, victims' campaigner Raymond McCord made this point when he complained about the Belfast Free Walking Tour's 'Conflicting Stories' tour, which was being run with the cooperation of loyalist and republican ex-prisoners. The advertising blurb stated: 'We invite you to walk the streets of the city on both sides of the peace line with the men and women who risked life and liberty and served time in prison for standing up for their beliefs.'[10] McCord claimed that such marketing spiel was 'warped' in that it presented the ex-prisoners as the victims – rather than the many who suffered at the hands of the illegal organisations to which those very ex-prisoners previously belonged. McCord, whose son had been murdered by the loyalist UVF in 2007, condemned the tour and the logic behind it: 'I would never pay to go on a tour like that, and don't understand anyone who would, especially not if it was hosted by ex-terrorists. It is just profiting from misery and death.'[11]

Despite such opposition, these forms of tourism *can* provide economic regeneration and political commemoration to places like Belfast with violently divided pasts. However, clearly disagreement remains as to whether these examples of local entrepreneurship amount to educational forms of tourism or are merely exploitative business enterprises that use the conflict as their unique selling point. A community worker from East Belfast pointed to the fact that people living with the aftermath of the conflict had themselves become a commodity for those who sought to make economic gain from their situation.

> Buses drive into the heart of inner city Belfast to allow tourists to gape at the massive walls dividing Belfast's communities – murals depicting violence. Tourists take photos of the division lines that are not consigned to history, but are a part of living Belfast . . . The places and the people themselves have become a spectacle, an attraction. If this were history perhaps it would be more acceptable – but it's not.[12]

From this critical perspective, those who continue to live in the city have become part of the spectacle, extras in a packaged attraction, for the benefit of external visitors. All of this is sold for internal consumption as a healthy form of conflict transformation, where tourists are educated in the context of 'The Troubles' while helping to provide economic benefits, including local employment. This begs a question: Do these visitors learn anything worthwhile from the experience? Undoubtedly, some do, coming away with a more nuanced understanding of Belfast's past and the degree to which the peace process has changed the city. Others may just be happy to have a selfie with the mural of Bobby Sands on the Falls Road. Whether we see this as something to worry about or that needs to be 'fixed' depends very much on our tolerance for tourism and perhaps, more cynically, whether we are profiting from it or not.

Another potential criticism of this depiction of Belfast's past is that highlighting the visual symbols of violent conflict and keeping the physical geography of the conflict alive by marking the sites of explosions and massacres perpetuates the sectarian culture on which it is based. The numerous republican and loyalist wall murals, walking tours and taxi/bus tours thus provide a political economy for division rather than for conflict transformation, keeping the wounds of the past open rather than allowing them to heal and disappear over time.[13]

The political sensitivities of connecting conflict transformation with tourism and heritage were brought together in 2012 with the abortive plan to convert the Maze Prison (Long Kesh) into an international conflict transformation centre and museum. It had taken over ten years for the political parties to agree on moving forward with the Maze-Long Kesh project, its hyphenated title demonstrating that the name itself divides, as the Maze was the rebranded name given to the prison after special category status was removed in 1976.[14] Before he backed away from the initiative, First Minister Peter Robinson suggested in 2012 that the site could become 'a Mecca for tourists'.[15] This prompted critics such as Traditional Unionist Voice leader Jim Allister to condemn the First Minister for supporting a 'shrine to terrorists' which was an insult to the victims and a reward to the 'victim makers'.[16] Official papers released since suggest that the conflict transformation centre would have featured the hospital wing as a key feature of the 'attraction', where ten republicans, including Bobby Sands, starved to death on hunger strike in 1981, their memory remaining a central part of Irish republican political identity today.

While the Maze-Long Kesh project failed to get off the ground due to a lack of support from the DUP, another Belfast prison did make it through to become one of the top tourist attractions in Belfast. As explained in chapter 4, Crumlin Road Gaol was a working prison for 150 years until its closure in 1996. Tourists are able to visit the condemned prisoner's cell and the execution chamber, which remains the only one of its type within the UK. Over 900,000 people have visited the 'Crum' since it reopened in 2012, making it one of Belfast's most visited tourist attractions.[17] Its Co-Director Kieran Quinn commented in 2015 that the notoriety of the location and its role in the conflict was the key hook for its popularity as a tourist destination: 'Really, I think it's the curiosity factor . . . People have been hearing about Crumlin Road Gaol in the news for 40 years and they just want to know what it's like. Many of the people that come in here have had relations or friends that were held here.'[18]

THE ART OF TOURISM

Key stops for any self-respecting tourist visiting a city for the first time are its museums and galleries. If you visit Paris, you go to the Louvre; you go to

London, you visit the British Museum, the V&A or the Tate Modern; you go to Madrid, you visit the Prado – and if you visit Belfast, you go to the Ulster Museum. It is in the museums and galleries that the past is curated and can be consumed before you exit through the gift shop laden with mementos. In stable societies, the narrative of *what* past has been curated and the way it has been framed goes largely uncontested. However, unsurprisingly, in places like Belfast where that narrative remains contested, museums and galleries can be very political spaces.

The pull to visit 'dark' tourist destinations like Belfast inevitably distorts and refracts the physical geography of such sites and converts them into something else entirely. A prison building and its infrastructure, the void where a building once stood, a plastic bullet casing or even a dustbin lid[19] can morph from what was once a mundane item into a site of emotive significance, or an object with subliminal cultural resonance.[20] Dustbin lids were frequently banged on the pavements by women in republican areas of West Belfast during the conflict as an early warning device to signal the arrival of British Army patrols into the area, especially during the republican hunger strikes in the summer of 1981. The sound of banging in the streets would signal the death of another hunger striker, and the significance of the noise would be understood by everyone who heard it. Thus, such objects are more than objects, and dustbin lids among other ephemera have become *artefacts* of the conflict, to be consumed by tourists viewing art exhibitions such as *Everyday Objects Transformed through the Conflict*, created in 2008 as a result of the Healing through Remembering project. One of the most valuable aspects of this exhibition was the way it showed how ordinary items gained a cultural significance and could trigger memories for those who lived in Belfast during the Troubles, while being presented in a way that eschewed a hierarchical narrative and allowed everyone's stories to be heard.

The Art of the Troubles exhibition, hosted by the Ulster Museum in partnership with Wolverhampton Art Gallery, brought together the work of fifty artists with pieces exploring the legacy of the Troubles, including an evocative piece by Locky Morris titled *An Bhearna Bhaoil – The Gap of Danger*. This was comprised of seven burnt dustbin lids arranged in a horizontal line across the wall, each one daubed with tar (as were suspected informers during the 1970s by the Provisional IRA). Another piece, *Veil* by Belfast artist Rita Duffy, was composed of six doors taken from Armagh women's prison that formed an enclosed cube. This was an interactive piece where the viewer is invited to look through the eye-holes in the doors that prison officers would have used to see a blood-red interior and a collection of eighty glass teardrops within. On the outside, the doors were surrounded by a layer of salt on the ground to represent tears.[21]

In this sense, the location and region itself, and the everyday objects we take for granted around us, can be transformed into artefacts for consumption with a significant back story and pathos.[22] More recently, the Ulster Museum included an exhibit as part of the Decade of Centenaries programme supported by the Department of Culture, Arts and Leisure at Stormont and the National Lottery Heritage Fund of Northern Ireland. A programme of principles for remembering had been developed which emphasised the need to understand the past beyond a purely black-and-white context using the idea of 'multi-perspectivity'. One of the displays in a new gallery in the Ulster Museum juxtaposed two iconic documents (which are of course more than just documents) – the Ulster Covenant of 1912 opposing Irish Home Rule (see chapter 3) and the Declaration of the Irish Republic read at the 1916 Easter Rising in Dublin. Here, visitors were confronted with symbols of identity full of facts that had the capability to undermine and challenge what Dr Paul Mullan, Director of the Northern Ireland Lottery Heritage Fund and Chair of the regional Decade of Centenaries roundtable, calls those 'single narrative approaches within which traditional unionism and nationalism were rooted. The point was not to destroy people's beliefs but to open their minds to other perspectives, and more plural readings of what happened.'[23] This is the essence of the conflict transformation approach, adding complexity rather than reducing issues to binary choices, getting past either/or to both/and.

TIME FOR TOURISM?

As Belfast's history demonstrates, cities are frequently carved out of dreadful carnage in one way or another, either through invasion, war and internal revolt, or as a result of violent episodes that were endured and resisted, with survivors rebuilding and over time developing an official narrative that is packaged as heritage. Tourism inevitably collides with the legacy of violent conflict and frames its narrative, while providing new resources that are likely to be much needed but also contested. The danger is that tourism can construct, legitimise and authenticate one particular narrative through what it includes and what it excludes, or airbrush out the inconvenient or unpleasant dimensions of the violence that took place.

No tourism product can fully replicate the violent events, physical suffering or emotional dislocation experienced by those who lived through the conflict – nor would it seek to. Instead, what is often sought is a safe space for commemoration via various representations, from physical artefacts, tours and public monuments, educational materials and a vast array of merchandise. However, it remains the case that any museum or memorial of violent conflict is innately political in nature and infused with highly sensitive issues. *Whose* heritage is being commemorated and how? Which actors in the conflict or victims of it are being downgraded or written out of the narrative that tourists are given access to? These are highly charged issues and can often be a stimulus for further conflict, especially if issues of legitimacy and economic resources are connected to it. Put more bluntly – this form of tourism allows those in control to rewrite the story of political conflict, select specific aspects of it and shape perceptions of causality and responsibility.

Time is often a factor in this process, with more longstanding violence having longer to become decoupled from contemporary political allegiances so it can exist in a less contested cultural space. This process is more difficult with conflicts that are more recent, as they are still inextricably linked to ongoing political disputes and narratives of legitimacy.

Belfast today sits in the middle of this contested space, between some who feel that our divided past should be remembered and explained to those who visit the city, while others worry that we are marketing and monetising the experience of political violence in a way that exploits the suffering of victims and survivors. From this perspective, tourism is a beneficiary of the conflict transformation process rather than acting as a catalyst for it to take place.[24] This has created a political economy based on the exploitation of 'Troubles hot-spots', rather than grass-roots conflict transformation approaches that will benefit the post-conflict society that Belfast aspires to become. Critics of the new wave of Troubles tourism in Belfast argue that the profit motive has resulted in some of the most vulnerable people in Belfast, who are still living with the aftermath of the conflict, being transformed into a commodity for consumption by visitors to the city, in a dystopian zoo of enduring sectarian division. The degree to which this form of conflict tourism is regarded as being a legitimate and authentic reflection of people's lived experience, rather than a theme-park exploitation of such suffering, might itself reflect unresolved tensions from the conflict and expose new conflicts over legitimacy and identity.[25]

This was brought home to me personally when I took a walking tour of the city during research I was doing for the book with DC Tours, one of the longest-standing and most respected operators in the city, which provides tourists with an informed and non-partisan tour of some of the main sites of violence in Belfast during the Troubles. As we walked around the city during an informative and entertaining two-hour experience, it struck me that most of the sites we walked to were related to violent incidents that had occurred during the 1970s. I thought it would have been good for the tour to have spanned the timeline of the conflict, as there was no shortage of bomb attacks and sectarian murders in the 1990s, the sites of which were within easy walking distance of the route. However, when I spoke to DC Tours afterwards it became clear that this was not a simple omission and that a lot of thought had gone into the selection of incidents covered on the tour.

DC Tours (which stands for Dead Centre Tours) was started in February 2013 by Mark Wylie and Paul Donnelly, who identified a space for a tour of Belfast that went beyond a sightseeing experience and included an informed commentary on the post-1969 period of political conflict in the city. Wylie, with a background in anthropology and archaeology, explained that the initial idea that led to the creation of DC Tours had come from an article he had read on dark tourism following the opening of the Titanic Centre in Belfast in 2012, which highlighted the tension between the tragedy of the *Titanic*'s sinking and public fascination about the disaster a century later: 'The building would never have been built if the ship hadn't sunk and that expanded into looking at dark tourism around the world. How many people were interested in dark tourism without knowing that they were dark tourists? And that kind of sparked something in me.'[26] While there were initial efforts at conflict tourism in Belfast stretching back to 1993, the year before the paramilitary ceasefires, this was run by one of the large bus companies, and while it transported visitors around the main sites, there was little attempt made to provide a detailed history of the conflict or engage with the conflicting narrative of events. While the black taxi companies embraced the concept of 'Troubles tourism', this evolved organically within the republican and loyalist communities in the city, rather than as part of a strategic plan by the Northern Ireland Tourist Board or private sector investment. In fact, there was an initial hesitancy from statutory agencies to develop conflict tourism due to the sensitivities involved and because it was just safer to market the magnificent landscape, sporting activities and museums in terms of building a tourist brand at the time. As Wylie argued: 'To be honest they were happy if [Troubles tourism] was kept in the districts and they didn't want it sullying the main tourist presentations at that time: golf, the Giant's Causeway and the new Titanic building.'[27]

Wylie went on to say that he had felt there was nothing available for the growing number of people coming to Belfast wanting a balanced and historically accurate tour of the Troubles, so he had approached his friend Paul Donnelly, who he knew from their days at Queen's University, with an idea to develop a tour. Donnelly had a background in community education, mediation and conflict studies, and both had an intimate knowledge of the political geography of the city. 'I thought there was room in Belfast for a tour which explained the history of the Troubles from a neutral and unbiased perspective and a non-partisan perspective. . . . [Prior to this, tourists] were getting a really insincere product, they were getting the "misery Olympics" and they were getting no guarantee of historical accuracy.'[28]

While some tourists inevitably have preconceived ideas and know what they want to hear about the conflict, Paul Donnelly, DC Tours' co-founder and lead guide, suggested that these are very much a minority. He has found that even American participants, who might be thought to be the most likely to harbour a romantic Irish nationalist perspective, were more eclectic in their outlook than he had envisaged. 'That's not to say we haven't had those people. But the vast majority of Americans we get . . . would be by and large reasonably well read, or if they are not particularly well read they're quite open-minded.'[29]

When I asked about the choice of sites on the tour and why most were clustered around the 1970s, it became clear that their experience was that any more recent events were too traumatic and sensitive to include without potentially risking upsetting victims of those events or surviving family members of those who had died. When they piloted the Troubles Tour and the sites they had chosen, feedback from test groups was that a post-2000 event was too recent; this was duly removed. Another event, from 1992, remained, but following a critical article in a local newspaper in 2013, which mentioned the 1980s incident and framed it as an example of exploitation rather than education, a relative of the victim wrote a complaint to Belfast City Council, as a result of which DC Tours had its accreditation as a tour operator cancelled. In effect, this meant that, while they could still trade, their tours could not be sold in the Visit Belfast shop, and if tourists walked in and asked about DC Tours, they were not recommended.[30] Four years later in 2017, after nine months working with a business mentor provided through Belfast City Council, they were able to become fully accredited again and promoted via the city council and other statutory tourist outlets in Belfast.[31]

This was clearly a difficult moment in the early development of DC Tours, but it provides a good example of the sensitivities surrounding the itineraries of these types of tours, as well as the reputational and business risks that relate to them. Unlike most war tourism, where the events are in the distant past and are relatively disconnected from today's political sensitivities, tourism in more recent conflicts, such as that in Northern Ireland, has a time-related tipping point, after which it becomes highly problematic to include events as they are within the living memory of its victims. Precisely where that tipping point lies will depend on the individual, as well as the nature of the tourist experience concerned and those who participate in it.

Despite its initial difficulties, DC Tours is now one of the best-known walking tours in Belfast, providing an informed and non-partisan guide to the city. They have found an appetite across a very wide range of clients for their 'History of Terror' tour and other guided tours around the city, including a 'Best of Belfast' tour. 'We've had people from Boris's Cabinet Office, MEPs, and members of the German Bundestag,' said Donnelly.[32] DC Tours has also provided private tailored tours for parliamentarians and international human rights lawyers on fact-finding missions. So, in this case at least, it seems clear that the tourist product on offer is about educating as well as entertaining external visitors who want to learn more about the city in general and the Troubles era in particular.

BELFAST'S INVISIBLE TOURIST SITES

There is much more to tourism in Belfast today than just the Troubles, and as we wind back the years it becomes slightly easier to decouple the heritage of the city from contemporary political and cultural divisions. The imprint of our divided past remains, but there is much more space to breathe when dealing with events from two hundred years ago than twenty years ago. A fascinating example of this is presented by the way in which Belfast's radical past is being slowly hauled back from near obscurity into the mainstream narrative of the city's heritage. Tours that focus on the early political geography of the city, such as the 1798 United Irishmen Walking Tour, provide a way of complicating the narrative of the past, allowing us to see it from a different angle in its greater complexity. This type of tourism moves away from the binary reductionism of us versus them into a space of complexity and potential empathy driven by greater understanding.

This idea of commemorating our past in a way that expands the complexity of events rather than reducing them down to a zero-sum equation is a key element recognised by practitioner academics such as Dr Paul Mullan. He explained that there is a tendency to understand the past through our contemporary political perspective, which can easily warp the meaning of events and relationships out of their historical context. Mullan cited as a case in point the graveyard tours run by celebrated public historian and former Sinn Féin politician Tom Hartley, which frequently concluded with the grave of Rev. Rutledge Kane, a Church of Ireland minister in Belfast at the end of the nineteenth century. Kane was an enthusiastic opponent of Irish Home Rule and a committed member of the Orange Order but epitomised the complexity that can easily get written out of the narrative of the past. 'The Rev. Rutledge Kane was a Hell and brimstone Protestant preacher, who was also a member of the Gaelic League, spoke Irish and his gravestone describes him as being an Irish patriot. What's going on there? Well, when you look at that time actually it is all quite clear . . . [because] they don't think with our contemporary political prism. We've really pushed these binary perspectives on people.'[33] Of course, during the period in which Kane was politically active, Ireland had not been partitioned and there seemed nothing incompatible, as far as he was concerned, about being an Irish unionist, an enthusiastic Irish language speaker and an Orangeman all at the same time.[34] This connects us back once again to Guy Beiner's *Forgetful Remembrance* and reflections on how Presbyterians refracted the memory of the 1798 Rebellion and the way in which collective acts of remembering and disremembering can change over time.[35] Our past is complicated, but that complexity has been chipped away at because the political meaning we give to it has required a simplification into binary polarities.

The tourist narrative often requires people and events to be painted in primary colours rather than pastel shades, so examples of nuance and complexity where the detail is syringed back in are to be welcomed. The 1798 United Irishmen Walking Tour of Belfast provides an excellent example of how this can be done, combining a detailed historical narrative with an entertaining delivery and infectious enthusiasm.[36] The 1798 Tour is run by Seán Napier and Colm Dore and is a celebration of the importance of the United Irishmen to Belfast and to the emergence of liberal democratic values across the whole island. This tour is an homage to the people, places and empty spaces that were at the centre of politics, commerce and culture at the end of the eighteenth century. It brings to life a hidden history that is slowly being airbrushed back into the public narrative of the city.

One of the striking things that occurred to me when I took this tour was the disconnect between public spaces in the centre of Belfast and the dramatic past that sits behind them. Most tourism sites are about tangible places, buildings, memorials and statues that at least hint at the narrative of events, but what is striking about the 1798 United Irishmen Tour is how much of it is about the invisible history of the city. The crowning glory of this hidden heritage must be the Assembly Rooms (formerly the Exchange) on the corner of Waring Street, as explained in chapter 4, now a derelict eyesore of a building that is home to pigeons and largely ignored by the citizens of the city who walk past it every day. It was here that United Irishman Henry Joy McCracken was tried for treason and sentenced to death, yet there is no public commemoration of that event or the importance of the building. Just across the road, roughly where a set of nondescript traffic lights now stands, was the house of Thomas McCabe, the man credited with preventing Belfast from becoming a slaving port by denouncing the scheme and invoking a celestial curse on anyone who signed up for it. The tour finishes at the point of Henry Joy McCracken's public hanging, at the market-house on High Street, and we stand looking at nothing in particular, no monument, no plaque or statue, no street named after him. Here, the tourist is presented with the invisible history of the city, defined by a narrative that found the story of the United Irishmen incompatible with the needs of political unionism that controlled the city after partition. A history of liberal Protestant radicalism dedicated to political independence from Britain and eventually to armed insurrection to achieve it was an unwanted complication for civic leaders who wanted to express the loyalty of the city to the Union and to what was left of the British Empire. There is a blue plaque above the archway in Joy's Entry claiming that he was born in a house near the site – but it is a subtle and rather vague marker, and given that we know *precisely* where he was executed, the lack of a marker or memorial there does seem like a chronic omission.

The 1798 Tour also brings visitors to some of Belfast's old entries that were at the centre of mercantile commerce and the life of the Presbyterian radicals in the 1790s. We stood in the physical space where legendary liberal Protestant revolutionaries lived and worked, people like Samuel Neilson, William Drennan, Samuel McTier and his wife Martha McTier, Mary Ann McCracken and the aforementioned Thomas McCabe. But if we had not been told, we would scarcely have known, as the entries, while revamped and beautified in recent redevelopment schemes funded by Belfast City Council among others, contain little reference to their illustrious past. Yes, they look nicer and safer to walk through, but their history remains largely hidden to the uninitiated. Again, the tour focuses as much on the unseen as the visible – which is part of its fascination – so we look at a blank brick wall painted white, which is the site of the old *Northern Star* newspaper, but there is little other evidence of this historically significant publication unless you look very closely: above head height, in a corner of the entry near a drainpipe, there is a tiny quill painting, which is an oblique reference to the use of the written word. The *Northern Star* was the publication of the United Irishmen, its main propaganda outlet which grew in popularity as the interest in political independence grew during the early 1790s. The entries during this period were full of life and fierce political debate that led eventually to a doomed armed insurrection in 1798. Arguably, it was these entries in Belfast in the 1790s that provided the catalyst for the political institutions that exist in both parts of Ireland today. Perhaps someday there will be an unmissable plaque, statue or a big eye-catching mural to mark the spot where revolutionary ideas leading to political independence were published in Belfast. For now, visitors will have to make do with looking at a blank wall while informed guides such as Seán Napier and Colm Dore fill in the blanks for them.

Arguably, this connects back to Dr Paul Mullan's 'principles for remembering' in terms of how our heritage is reimagined in Belfast today and how that is constructed into a public narrative for those new to the subject or the city. These 'principles for remembering' advocate for a more detailed evidence base for the period and presentation of historical facts; an appreciation of the context behind events and greater understanding of the causes and consequences behind such incidents and behaviour; an awareness of different perspectives rather than a simple linear narrative; and a passionate commitment to telling the stories of those involved in a way that deepens and broadens our understanding of the period.

The 1798 United Irishmen tour complicates the binary 'two communities' narrative which is literally visible in Belfast today along the Peace Wall and the murals that reflect 'bonding' rather than 'bridging' social capital across the city. It is a story of Protestant not Catholic separatism, middle-class rather than working-class revolution, religious tolerance and progressiveness rather than dogmatic spiritual prejudice; and, ironically, it is a story of European ideas and cosmopolitanism rather than an inward-facing Gaelic irredentism.

This invisible history represents a fascinating parallel universe to the official narrative that has been framed over a hundred years of mostly unionist control of the city that is only beginning to be rediscovered. So we have a tour of derelict buildings, blank walls, traffic lights where important houses used to stand and sites of public execution that are unmarked and unremarkable in terms of present-day signage. The high-water mark of this invisible history has to be in Warehouse Lane between Waring Street and Exchange Place, under a nondescript concrete archway behind a hotel. This was one of the highlights of the 1798 United Irishmen tour for me, as, if you can squeeze past the parked cars, step over the rubbish and debris and look behind the wheelie bins, you will see the most amazing artworks commemorating the United Irishmen. A series of four large framed oil paintings, one of which portrays Henry Joy McCracken saying farewell to his sister before being led off to the gallows, are framed and positioned where hardly anyone will see them. Another piece depicts Edward Bunting and Thomas Russell meeting Mary Ann McCracken at the Belfast Society for Promoting Knowledge (now the Linen Hall Library).[37]

This artwork was commissioned from local artist Michael O'Neill and went on public display in 2008 as part of the regeneration of the old historic Four Corners area in the centre of the city, but today (like the Assembly Rooms building) they sit largely unloved, partially vandalised and forgotten, hanging forlornly as a backdrop to parked cars, a row of wheelie bins and discarded litter at the back of the Premier Inn hotel.[38] In fact, the counterpoint between the beauty, skill and importance of these paintings and the now dilapidated and virtually abandoned space they occupy could almost be an artistic installation in its own right.

The paintings do provide a perfect embodiment of the point that *how* we remember and *whether* we remember at all is an inherently contextual and political project – defined as much by what we do not see, hear or experience as what we do. To be fair to the Social Development Minister at the time, Margaret Ritchie, who was responsible for the initiative that put the paintings there in the first place, the original intention was to showcase the theme of the United Irishmen as part of an urban regeneration scheme. When she unveiled the paintings in 2008, Ritchie indicated that the intention was to provide public art and to help improve the aesthetics of the area:

The regeneration of this historic Four Corners site and the commissioning of this art is another excellent example of how the private sector can work with government to deliver top quality development in a very important part of Belfast's city centre. . . . This art, Warehouse Lane, the Premier Inn hotel and the 4 Corners Bar and Restaurant that will open on this site in the coming weeks, are a further sign that the heart of this city can once again be vibrant and dynamic, not just during the day, but in the evenings also.[39]

However, while the initial intention may have been to showcase artwork highlighting the United Irishmen and their importance to the city, the reality is that this has not happened and the paintings have been abandoned, forgotten and left to rot. The obvious question this poses is: Why has a city with such a rich heritage and that spends so much time marketing its past avoided one of the most obvious unique selling points available to it? Of course, the *Titanic* is important, and the scenery around Belfast is breathtaking, and, yes, the golf courses are epic, and the street murals are colourful and vivid. However, there is a powerful history of romantic political ideals, inspirational leaders and heroic (if doomed) resistance that remains largely hidden within the bricks and mortar of the city. The story of the United Irishmen, who took Thomas Paine's ideas and built them into a liberal democratic revolution, while demonstrating that Protestants and Catholics *could* actually get on with one another, remains the poor relation of tourist offerings in Belfast today.

There was a time when a liberal Protestant separatist narrative was a politically uncomfortable one for unionists to embrace, but the peace process has helped open up space for them to do so. There are tangible signs of change, and figures such as Mary Ann McCracken are being rediscovered and given public representation in civic spaces, with a major new statue planned for Belfast City Hall, for example, as well as in the work of Clifton House, where she was a prominent activist. While this change is evolutionary rather than revolutionary, Belfast City Council has embarked on a progressive new strategy to 'relocate, rebalance and re-represent' how the past is remembered in the contemporary civic space.[40] Instead of ripping out and neutralising the politically loaded symbols of the past that gave a single-narrative understanding rather than pluralist representation of the city, the council has sought to transform the context in which symbols of our divided past are presented. Instead of taking flags away, they were moved to an exhibition space and given explanation and context, and other items were brought in to sit alongside them and broaden single-narrative representations to allow for greater cultural diversity and complexity. New stained glass windows were commissioned for Belfast City Hall, for instance, with one reflecting Irish Gaelic mythology, featuring Cú Chulainn (a mighty mythical Gaelic warrior in Ulster renowned for his strength and bravery), and another featuring the Spanish Civil War. There are also windows paying tribute to the role of working-class women and the trade union movement, which adds complexity to the more traditional civic narrative of Belfast's historic luminaries being male factory owners rather than female factory workers.[41]

In addition to the statue planned for outside the building, there is also a bust of Mary Ann McCracken displayed inside the city hall. However, the emphasis tends to be on her significance as an abolitionist, champion of the poor and pioneering feminist, not on the fact that she was a militant, Protestant, Irish nationalist revolutionary. This brings us back to the point that even though the passage of time has made it easier to construct tourism around events and political divisions of the 1790s than those of the 1990s, this remains an area of some sensitivity. Rebranding streets such as those named after Sir Arthur Chichester, a rogue feted as a statesman, with people such as Henry Joy McCracken, a statesman condemned as a rogue, might be popular with some but could easily bring such tensions to the boil.

The approach being taken by organisations like Belfast City Council, the National Lottery Heritage Fund and the Department of Culture, Arts and Leisure would seem to be a sensible one. This focuses on augmenting binary single-narrative approaches with alternative readings and perspectives and transforming zero-sum equations with looser alternatives that contain the capacity for greater inclusiveness. In other words, we share a divided past and need to buy into a mutual respect within that uncomfortable reality.

REIMAGINING BELFAST

> Shouldered by hills and both challenged and sustained by waterways, Belfast has been characterised by forces of endurance and determination since ancient times. Archaeologists have documented at least 9,000 years of human settlement in the mountains and high ground around modern-day Belfast. The importance of geography – both its tests and opportunities – has been evident through the long and compelling story of the city's development.[42]

This is taken from the beginning of Belfast City Council's latest cultural strategy document, 'A City Imagining', which sets out plans for a twelve-month cultural celebration of Belfast's heritage. This provides a good example of how far we have come since the peace process took hold in the mid-1990s, as prior to the paramilitary ceasefires in 1994 such inspirational language would have seemed rather far-fetched. The peace process has certainly allowed Belfast to blossom as a city and to build a new tourist product that was not available during the Troubles for obvious reasons. This treads a careful line in terms of how that conflict is remembered and represented and has replaced some of the more divisive and painful narratives of violence with more inclusive and positive messages that brand Belfast as a being a modern, progressive society with a rich, if divided, heritage. As Dr Paul Mullan explained: 'there's no one agreed version of what happened that we can refer to.'[43] Belfast City Council's cultural strategy is also careful to tiptoe through the political minefield of defining culture – by not defining it: 'We have decided that we don't want to define what culture means too closely because we know what it feels like to be defined. And definitions have held us back for too long.'[44] Belfast City Council's cultural strategy reflects this approach in highlighting the importance of local community involvement as co-creators of the stories that visitors to the city are presented with, because those authentic narratives rooted in experience are what tourists value more highly. There is a recognition here that the route to authenticity is to allow the people of Belfast to speak for themselves rather than to attempt to speak for them and that this, in turn, will shape the city.[45]

It has to be a good thing that the peace process has unlocked Belfast's tourism industry in a way that at least allows the city to reposition itself in the twenty-first century as a post-conflict space. There will inevitably be arguments about how that is done, who is benefiting from it and the political and cultural direction of travel. However, like the peace process itself, we are just at the beginning of that journey rather than at the end of it, and this seems set to be an exciting and vibrant next stage in the cultural development of the city.

FILM PILGRIMS

One of the key ways in which Belfast is being reimagined, and attracting tourists as a result, is through its growing reputation as a venue for major television and film production. Belfast is appearing more on screens around the world for the right reasons, and this is stimulating a tourist market that wants to see the locations where these shows were made.

Sir Kenneth Branagh's multi-Oscar-nominated film *Belfast* is perhaps the high point of this trend, a lovingly nostalgic semi-fictional biopic of his childhood and the outbreak of the Troubles that led his family to move to England. The violence is the backdrop to a story about ordinary people and ordinary lives, but the story is told in a way that draws you into the city rather than repelling you from it. It is a story of survival, lovingly told, and aside from its cinematic attributes, it was a positive global advertisement for the city. While the film was very well received, there were some more critical perspectives from those who felt that its black-and-white framing went beyond the cinematography and reflected an overly simplistic two-dimensional storyline. As one reviewer noted: 'The characters are given little psychological complexity; they each seem either inspirationally good and wise, or malicious and repugnant. . . . There are no conversations that surprise or delight, only set pieces in which nothing is hidden or confused.'[46]

I am not ashamed to say that I went to see it at the cinema equally prepared to nit-pick at the lack of historical accuracy, the occasionally dodgy accents or the romantic folksy dialogue of the main characters, and I could have done so. However, it was a love letter to a city that I love, and the final sign off, 'for those who stayed, those who left and all those who were lost', left me blubbing in my seat. In that sense, Branagh's *Belfast* provides an antidote to the bleakly tragic films that have portrayed Belfast as a city of violent division and religious hatred. Branagh's previous work depicted a much harsher dimension of life in the city during the 1970s, before the peace process or the tourists that followed it were even a figment of our imaginations. He could scarcely have imagined the city's contemporary renaissance when he played the lead role in Graham Reid's 'Billy Trilogy', a series of three gritty BBC plays dramatising urban life in Belfast in the late 1970s.

Apart from Branagh's Oscar-winning film, Belfast's tourism industry has been boosted in recent years by the growth of film-making in the city, as well as the city's depiction in key television series such as *Game of Thrones*. It is difficult to overstate the significance of *Game of Thrones* to Belfast's tourist economy and Northern Ireland's international profile as an attractive destination to visit.

The impact of *Game of Thrones* was brought home to me one morning when I took a family trip to the Giant's Causeway, just over an hour outside the city on the north coast of Northern Ireland. It was a typical bleak, windswept summer's day, and we had to park in the overflow car park before walking across to the visitor centre and on to the causeway's unique hexagonal rocks for the obligatory photographs. Just as we were getting out of the car, a big grey *Game of Thrones* tour bus parked up, and out jumped some twenty to thirty very excited Japanese tourists. I was pleased that Northern Ireland's geological heritage was so popular with international tourists but became increasingly perplexed as they ignored the signs for the visitor centre and walked in the opposite direction to the rocks, disappearing down to the bottom of the car park, where they stood looking at a nondescript wall of gravel and dirt and started posing for photos in front of it. On closer inspection, it turned out that this was a site on the *Game of Thrones* tour, a venue for a particular scene in the series that had become a tourist attraction in its own right. While I shook my head in disbelief that tourists could literally turn their backs on the UNESCO World Heritage site and place higher value on an otherwise unremarkable wall in a car park, it was nonetheless symbolic of the power of the multi-award-winning HBO series over the global tourist market.

The scale and longevity of *Game of Thrones* (running for 8 seasons, shown in 200 countries and watched by an estimated 18 million people) resulted not just in a steady flow of tourists on secular pilgrimages to visit the locations that featured in the series, but in actual new infrastructure in the city. HBO, the film company that made *Game of Thrones*, was the main tenant of Titanic Studios in the centre of Belfast for a decade – and the studios are now being used for other major film and television projects, including *Dungeons and Dragons* from Paramount Pictures. The growth of the film and television industry in Belfast mirrors a wider growth elsewhere in Northern Ireland, the global acclaim of *Derry Girls* being an obvious high point. This in turn has built on the expansion of film-making on the island of Ireland led by financial and tax incentives offered by the Irish government in the 1990s that made the country so attractive to film and television production companies it was given the nickname 'Paddywood'. Belfast's more recent success as a film location, and the tourism that has flowed from it, stands on the shoulders of initiatives that have been taking place for over thirty years, as well as the increased stability ushered in by the peace process in the 1990s.

Titanic Belfast's Chief Executive Judith Owens explained that the global exposure of James Cameron's *Titanic* film probably provided a considerable boost to tourist numbers: 'At Titanic Belfast, we highly value the importance of screen tourism for the city and often benefit from this ourselves with many visitors coming through our doors due to the popularity of the Titanic movie, particularly from international markets.'[47] With *Game of Thrones* expected to be a similar draw for tourists, in 2021 a Game of Thrones Studio Tour was opened at the Linen Mill Studios in Banbridge on the outskirts of Belfast. This €48 million facility features original props and sets from the show, as well as thousands of weapons and costumes and other memorabilia.

In this sense, the arrival of 'screen tourism' in Belfast is building virtuous circles that are driving the arts, tourism and economic regeneration of the city forwards with a positive brand, which is superseding the stereotype of the city as a centre of violent instability and religious intolerance. Belfast is unlikely to get away completely from the Troubles in terms of how it is perceived, and, arguably, it should not even try to do so. The key is to recognise that how the city defines its past is inherently political in nature and needs to be recognised as such. There is no agreed narrative on the past and it is unlikely that there ever will be, but developing some degree of empathy that understands that there are conflicting perspectives on the heritage of the city seems a sensible approach.

Dr Paul Mullan suggests that there are examples of this already happening within the heritage sector. For him, how we contextualise and frame the past is what matters – not chasing some illusory neutral space that will satisfy no one, but rather recognising and managing those disagreements as sympathetically and sensitively as we can. Key to this was getting past zero-sum binary depictions of the past and putting the complexity back into the picture, adding the awkward details back into simplified mythologies of our collective identity, which Mullan suggests Belfast City Council has been attempting to do since the peace process in the 1990s and the institutions that resulted from the Good Friday Agreement in 1998. The council started to reimagine the city and how it could begin to reflect the equality ambitions inherent within the Good Friday Agreement. 'But it is not taking things out,' he explained. 'Flags were moved from the Rotunda, but put into an exhibition space. So the repository of all the difficult stuff was put into an exhibition space – but cared for. Carson's Table used to sit in the Council Chamber and people would throw their coats on it. . . . Now it's pride of place in the exhibition and contextualised.'[48]

This provides an example of how Belfast is beginning to work out mechanisms and strategies for dealing with its divided past which are based on transforming the context in which it is presented, framed and understood. Tourism will always be part of how we frame and understand our divided past, and we should perhaps move forwards in a way that recognises its limitations while being open to the exciting opportunities tourism presents for cultural initiatives and economic regeneration in the decades that lie ahead.

7

THE POETRY

It was once remarked by the celebrated Irish poet and novelist Patrick Kavanagh that, at any given moment, Ireland had a standing army of up to 10,000 poets. The acerbic plain-speaking Kavanagh meant it as a jibe rather than a compliment, aimed in the mid-twentieth century at the romanticised vision of the land of saints and scholars associated with De Valera's Ireland. However, if you grew up in Belfast during the 1980s, you probably either were a poet yourself, had a poet in the family or knew one who lived on your street.

At a personal level, my wider family was mostly spread between East and North Belfast, and due to the difficulties of moving around the city in the 1970s we would only gather together collectively for special occasions such as First Holy Communions and confirmations, though once a year, just after Christmas, we would all meet up for a musical evening – usually at our house on the Holywood Road. I valued these events mainly for the food, because as soon as the turkey was finally destroyed my mother would begin a two-day marathon of industrial-scale baking of multiple pavlovas, lemon meringue pies, sherry trifles and a multitude of other sweet treats for the uncles, aunts and cousins who would descend on the house with their guitars, mandolins, banjos, harmonicas, tin whistles and sheet music. Given that it was the 1970s, a Dubreq Stylophone also made an appearance, though it struggled to be heard through the thrashing cacophony made by the rest of us.

This was my earliest exposure to Irish culture and songs, which they all knew and I gradually learned. Singers like Liam Clancy and Tommy Makem, the Dubliners and Phil Coulter were all debuted for me in my living room during these annual cultural evenings, along with more international fare such as Sinatra, ABBA and, of course, the Beatles. This is also where I first sang 'The Sash My Father Wore', an Orange loyalist song which was given an ironic if enthusiastic airing in the spirit of Christmas, which if nothing else confused our Protestant neighbours about what was going on. Everyone had a 'turn', sang a song, recited a poem or told a story, and we gradually got better at singing and storytelling ourselves.

I was lucky to grow up in a very literate and culturally rich family of teachers, musicians, amateur poets and writers, and from an early age I was exposed to adult conversations which ranged from whimsical tall tales and hilarious embroidered anecdotes to serious discussion and debate about the deteriorating political situation, the rise in violence and the performance of the government. Many others who grew up in Belfast in the 1970s will have had similar experiences, as when someone came for a visit, the tea and biscuits would appear as if by magic in the living room and everyone would gather around to listen. It was an event, and we expected to be entertained by the stories and anecdotes that were sure to follow.

No one in my family was more cultured, literate or better at telling stories than Grampa Dynan. My maternal grandfather was a formidable Cork man who moved to Belfast in the early 1930s having secured a job as a radiographer in a local hospital in the city. In fact, it was the only hospital in Ireland at the time that was employing radiographers, so he had little choice but to move to Belfast. He was also a teacher and had a series of other jobs, some professional, others voluntary. He eventually opted for the teaching profession, choosing speech and drama, in which he had always had an interest. More importantly, he was a poet and a storyteller, and he produced and directed a number of plays in local theatres in Belfast in the 1940s and 1950s. This led him to travel throughout Ireland as an adjudicator, something which he enjoyed very much.

He suffered from ill health and died when I was quite young, but I can still remember the days when he would babysit me and my older brother in his house on the Old Park Road in North Belfast. On dark winter mornings he would bring us to the local shop and buy us a magazine to occupy our time, or more likely to stop us fighting. I was always at him to buy me a comic called the *Beano*, but he never would, saying that it would rot my brains, and instead provided me with material that he claimed would improve me, like the *Look and Learn* magazine, which I found no fun at all. But it was his own stories that were the most memorable, and far superior to anything that the *Beano* could have provided. These were imaginative, detailed and usually dark, in fact almost always frightening and sinister, some of them made up on the spot, others versions of well-known Irish folk tales. We would sit in the parlour listening to his stories of 'the good people' better known as fairies, banshees, clurichauns and, of course, leprechauns. He played all the parts, did all the accents and drew us into the mystic, our only sanctuary being when our Nana came in to offer us snacks, make our lunch or to tell him off for scaring the daylights out of us.

He was a stern figure, with a rasping voice and a precise, clipped, almost military delivery. The lilt of his Cork accent had been dulled by several decades of living in the 'black North' but was musical nonetheless, and he was a master of timing and accents. In fact, if the horror movie actor Vincent Price had been born in Cork he would have sounded a bit like Grampa Dynan. He was a poet – culture was in his bones, and he had more stories to tell than most, many of them coming out of his adopted city.

Belfast is a city full of stories, and cultural vehicles such as poetry, music, drama and film have provided plenty of opportunities for those tales to be told. Everyone in Belfast will have at least one great storyteller in their family, and perhaps one of the reasons we speak so quickly is that you often had to fight for the right to be heard as relatives and friends pinged stories and anecdotes around the living room like verbal buckshot. History and politics, poetry, music, ghost stories and Gaelic mythology were passed down through families this way, before the age when everyone sat quietly in the house atomised into separate spaces by various electronic devices. Before Netflix, mobile phones, Xbox, Nintendo and PS5s got in the way, stories were told and songs were sung as evening entertainment, because there were few other options. In this sense, culture was a participation sport, and it was often a collective intergenerational space where the young learned how to tell a story, recite a poem or sing a song.

The moral of this story is that everyone in Belfast has a tale to tell, and that is obvious when two or more people from Belfast meet up. There will be stories, family connections and recollections related to the geography of the city – all, of course, with the shadow of political conflict and religious division ever present in the background. This is a part of the cultural stew, the common reference points, the vernacular and the heartbeat of Belfast that is carried by everyone who comes from the city.

A city with a history as rich as Belfast's inevitably has a cultural heritage that is equally impressive.[1] The fact that history is remembered (and misremembered) has provided an almost limitless range of opportunities for skilful storytellers to use cultural forms such as art, music, film and poetry to reflect on who we are, where we have come from, what has happened to us – and who is to blame for it. At times, culture has acted as a reservoir which we periodically dip into for refreshment, nourishment or for assurances that either confirm or challenge our sense of self and community. The key message here is that our identities are constantly being shaped by our exposure to cultural forms, which can help to cement our self-image as individuals and as members of a preferred imagined community. Belfast's history of religious and political division has driven cultural expression forwards as a means of explaining events or expressing emotions that were not adequately addressed by other means. In this sense, we have come to use cultural expression as a crutch to lean on when we need support or a cudgel to wield when we feel under existential attack.

THE PLAY'S THE THING

Poets, playwrights, film-makers, artists and singer-songwriters from Belfast have helped those living in the city to understand (or exorcise) the frustrations, anger and hope underpinning the political and cultural divisions that have shaped their lives. While poetry is the central focus here, playwrights have arguably used the theatre and television to critique notorious episodes of political and cultural bigotry in Belfast or to show how hope and tolerance can rise from the ashes of discrimination. Plays such as *Over the Bridge* by Sam Thompson in the 1950s and the 'Billy Plays' by Graham Reid in the 1980s hit a zeitgeist by connecting dramatised fiction to the realities of a city where bigotry, intolerance and division were incubated.[2]

In tune with a theme that runs through the book, these playwrights, poets and artists are radicals, who use their cultural vehicles to take risks with their audiences and cut through the banalities to get to realities that are not always comfortable to contemplate.

Sam Thompson was a radical, just like many of those who went before him in previous generations. In the 1950s, before the Troubles had erupted, he famously intervened to shine a light on the endemic sectarianism within the city when few people were ready to listen. His stage play *Over the Bridge* focused on anti-Catholic bigotry and violence in the Belfast shipyard. It is a nuanced play that deals with the realities of sectarian bigotry in the shipyard (and by extension across Belfast) and the challenges that it presented to the labour movement in terms of its belief in working-class solidarity. The main character, Davy Mitchell, is a shop steward who faces a Protestant mob that tries to intimidate a Catholic worker out of the yard. Mitchell, who is also a Protestant, stands with his Catholic co-worker and defends him on the principle that every man should have the right to work. As emotions run high between Mitchell and the mob, trouble predictably ensues. It is unmistakably a play about the shipyard and about Belfast, but it also speaks to more universal themes relating to integrity, courage and doing the right thing in the face of unpopularity and personal danger. It is also about those who turn a blind eye to bullying and whose inaction facilitates it, those whom the poet John Hewitt would refer to as the 'Coasters' in his poem about the middle class's denial of their own sectarian urges in Belfast in the 1960s.

The story of *Over the Bridge* is as much about what happened to the play before and after it was staged as it is about the plot itself. Life indeed imitated art as Thompson, his play and others associated with it came into conflict with powerful unionist politicians who had themselves made an art form out of the very same sectarianism and discrimination that sat at the heart of the play. Thompson offered it to the Group Theatre in 1958, and it was accepted and put into production by then artistic director Jimmy Ellis – later to become one of Northern Ireland's best-loved actors. However, the directors of the Group Theatre realised its political sensitivity. The Chairman of the Group Theatre was a personal friend of the leader of the Unionist Party and Northern Ireland Prime Minister Lord Brookeborough, and he demanded that cuts be made to the script. When Thompson refused to bow to the thinly veiled attempt to censor his play, the theatre cancelled production and released a statement condemning it as offensive and an 'affront' to everyone in Northern Ireland. This led to a split in the Group Theatre, with Ellis and a number of actors resigning to form their own company.

Typically, once something is banned, interest soars and everybody wants to see it, and so it proved with *Over the Bridge*: the Group Theatre could not have done a better job to sell tickets for the production if it had tried to. The play was eventually staged in Belfast's Empire Theatre in 1960 and was enormously successful both commercially and critically. Renowned poet Louis MacNeice attended the opening night and proclaimed it to be a 'red letter day' for theatre in Belfast, and when it was taken down to Dublin it became the hottest ticket in town, with Thompson himself being invited to meet the Irish Taoiseach Seán Lemass.

The play remains a formative moment in the cultural history of Belfast, when the arts were able to convey what politicians could not. Sectarian bigotry and discrimination lay, like a chronic sickness, at the core of society. *Over the Bridge* let that genie out of the bottle: within a decade, the civil rights movement had emerged and British troops had arrived on the streets in an attempt to quell disorder, rioting and political mayhem.

A generation after Sam Thompson's *Over the Bridge* gave Northern Ireland a collective cultural spasm, the Billy Plays written by playwright Graham Reid took a different approach to ingrained sectarianism in the city. Jimmy Ellis was again involved, playing one of the main characters, a taciturn father with a drink problem and fondness for domestic violence. And a new acting talent, Kenneth Branagh – born in Belfast, so not cursed by outsiders' mangled efforts at the local accent – gave his debut performance as Billy. The Billy Plays were made by the BBC as part of its long-running *Play for Today* series. In *Too Late to Talk to Billy* and *A Matter of Choice for Billy*,[3] broadcast in 1982 and 1983 respectively, Branagh's Billy Martin is a working-class Protestant struggling with life and relationships. These included the impending death of his mother and a cantankerous and inebriated father (played by Jimmy Ellis) in the first instalment, and love across the sectarian divide with his 'Fenian nurse' girlfriend in the second. The plays had a local authenticity and reality that lifted the vision of the people of Belfast beyond the stereotype of religious bigotry, political intransigence and the incessant depiction of Belfast as defined by the violence of the Troubles. It was a vision of Belfast from the inside out, rather than the other way around, which was more common. The Billy Plays unveiled a cultural truth within a politically divided society – namely that violence was a mundane normality for everyone and that life still went on around it. Here, the Troubles was the back story, not the centrepiece, and the play provided a reminder that normal life was also taking place for people in Belfast despite the abnormal political situation.

Viewed now, some of the scenes and dialogue seem archaic, inappropriate, even horrific – but at the time, the Billy Plays resonated across the whole community in Belfast, even though they were predominantly focused on one dysfunctional working-class Protestant family living on the Donegal Road in Belfast.[4]

WHATEVER YOU SAY, SAY NOTHING

The subtitle above alludes to a poem by Seamus Heaney which contemplates the complexities of identity and the difficulty of talking about political violence in Northern Ireland without lapsing into banal platitudes. The last generation of political violence in Northern Ireland has heightened cultural sensitivities on all sides over flags, anthems, language and symbols to the point where it has been difficult not to become sucked into the reductionist sectarian cultural vortex. There are certainly organisations and individuals who work hard to promote cultural pluralism in sport, music and the arts more broadly, but these are outliers rather than dominant forces in Belfast and elsewhere in Northern Ireland.

One cultural form that has largely managed to avoid this is poetry, which flourished in Belfast at the same time as political institutions were breaking down and sectarian violence was increasing in the late 1960s. The catalyst for this poetic renaissance was actually provided by an Englishman rather than an Irishman when the poet, critic and academic Philip Hobsbaum started up the Belfast Group at Queen's University in the early 1960s. It was here that key members of those who would become Belfast's literary glitterati over the next half-century honed their poetic skills. Seamus Heaney, James Simmons, Michael Longley, Derek Mahon and Seamus Deane were among the most active participants. In 1966, when Hobsbaum left Queen's for a job at Glasgow University, Heaney published his breakthrough anthology *Death of a Naturalist* with Faber, which established his reputation as a new literary talent. Heaney in turn nurtured and mentored new, internationally recognised poets including Medbh McGuckian and Paul Muldoon when he joined the staff at Queen's University. James Simmons founded the *Honest Ulsterman* magazine, which continued this poetic revival into the 1970s, allowing new poets to publish their work, as well as promoting renewed interest in the work of established poets such as John Hewitt, Robert Greacen and Louis MacNeice. Many of these poets were writing about themes related to poverty, sectarian conflict, existential identity crises and religious intolerance long before Belfast disintegrated at the end of the 1960s. MacNeice's masterful long-form poem *Autumn Journal* was written just before the outbreak of the Second World War and published in 1939 but was just as relevant to Belfast and the island of Ireland in the 1960s, and arguably it remains so to the present day.

Cultural activity is frequently stimulated and sharpened by grievance, anger and suffering, which might have something to do with the sheer volume of cultural excellence that has come out of Belfast over the last half-century.[5] These poets have inevitably interpreted the society around them and their work has reflected, refracted and challenged the political and cultural divisions within and beyond the city. At the same time, there was an ambiguity over the role of the poet at a time when politics was breaking down and sectarian violence was tearing Belfast apart. With rioting on the streets, the British Army turning the city into a militarised zone and bombings and shootings a daily occurrence, what could poets possibly contribute?

This concern about being relevant sat alongside a frustration that poets were being expected to explain the chaos and unpredictable events unfolding around them. They were caught in a catch-22 situation whereby if they wrote about the violence taking place around them they were vulnerable to the accusation that they were producing 'poetry of the latest atrocity', while if they did not they were criticised for evading their responsibility. Heaney's fellow poet Ciaran Carson when reviewing Heaney's *North* collection in the mid-1970s was critical of the way his much-esteemed colleague had become transfigured 'from being a writer with the gift of precision, to become the laureate of violence – a mythmaker, an anthropologist of ritual killing, and apologist for "the situation", in the last resort, a mystifier'.[6] For Carson, not everything could be explained away by using the mythology of the past as a metaphor for the violence of the present, and by making such corollaries Heaney was refusing to tackle the immediacy of the political situation right under his nose in the here and now, on the streets of Belfast and Derry and elsewhere across Northern Ireland.

However, Michael Longley pointed out that poets needed time to 'allow the raw material of experience to settle to an imaginative depth'.[7] Longley took a longer view, suggesting that poets were not journalists sent to record or react in real time to the events that surrounded them. Their task was rather to process and synthesise what was happening, make sense of it in the round and provide a wider lens through which to view and understand the world.

A fellow poet once remarked that Seamus Heaney's breakthrough collection, *Death of a Naturalist*, first published in 1966, with its 'bursting mortars' and similes comparing nature and violence, was not an account of what was happening in Northern Ireland but rather a predictive voice about *what was going to happen* in the future. And so it proved in the generation that was to follow, with Heaney himself becoming emblematic of the conflict that surrounded him, but able nonetheless to retain an optimism about the potential for peaceful change. At a very basic level, leaving his literary genius to one side, Heaney's work gave us all hope in a seemingly hopeless situation that better times lay ahead. Speaking in 2008 about the connections between his work and the Troubles, Heaney argued that good poetry displays the sort of ambition and honesty that politics could aspire to:

> All of us, Protestant poets, Catholic poets – and don't those terms fairly put the wind up you? – all of us probably had some notion that a good poem was 'a paradigm of good politics', a site of energy and tension and possibility, a truth-telling arena but not a killing field. And without being

explicit about it, either to ourselves or to one another, we probably felt that if we as poets couldn't do something transformative or creative with all that we were a part of, then it was a poor lookout for everybody.[8]

Heaney became an internationally recognised cultural figure – 'famous Seamus', who everyone wanted (and still wants, despite his death in 2013) a part of, as an interpreter of their narrative of historical and political legitimacy in Northern Ireland. This is not a uniquely Irish phenomenon, which again points to the way in which poets and other cultural icons – whether they like it or not – are woven into the political contexts that provided the backdrop to their artistic contribution. Heaney's work has been quoted by presidents including Bill Clinton during the peace process of the 1990s and President Joe Biden in more recent times, who is fond of saying: 'My colleagues always kid me about quoting Irish poets all the time ... They think I do it because I'm Irish. I do it because they're the best poets.'[9] At a much more minuscule level, some years ago when I was searching for a title for my Inaugural Professorial Lecture at the University of Kent, Heaney's work was a natural source of inspiration. The poem 'Digging' had stayed with me since my school days and encapsulated my journey through academia using my pen (and then my keyboard) to dig up evidence about Northern Ireland's fertile political history.

There has always been a useful ambivalence in Heaney's work in terms of the intersection of culture and politics that I have felt helps to capture the fluid and contested nature of identity in conflict relationships. As my professional life has been dominated by the study of conflict, political violence, peacebuilding and reconciliation, Heaney has been a reliable companion on that journey. He published 'Requiem for the Croppies' to mark the fiftieth anniversary of the 1916 Easter Rising, a poem commemorating the 1798 Rebellion of the doomed United Irishmen. This poem epitomised the tension between eulogising the sacrifice of Irish republicans who fought a guerrilla war against the British in the past and avoiding justifying the armed campaign of republicans during the Troubles.

In addition to commemorating a key event in Irish history and the martyrdom of Irish nationalists who died in the fight for political independence from Britain, the subliminal message here was that ultimately their cause would be reborn and persevere. Heaney tried to steer a course in this poem and in much of his other work somewhere between recognition and celebration, commenting some years later that the point was to have the right to speak rather than necessarily to be listened to – 'you don't have to love it, you just have to permit it.'[10] The edginess in the space between saying who you are and being told who you are by someone else, who might be in a position to enforce it, will resonate with many who live in conflict contexts. This came to the surface when Heaney was included in the Penguin anthology of British poets, which he objected to with a caustic literary jibe that referred to the colour of his (Irish) passport and a customary reluctance of his community to toast the Queen. This was seen by unionists and others as being indicative of an anti-British sentiment once the veneer of erudite tolerance was stripped away.

Heaney later reflected on this, making the point that cultural identity was fluid and contextual and that by the 1980s the Troubles (and the role of the British state as a protagonist in them) had reduced the capacity he had felt in the 1960s to comfortably occupy both a British and an Irish sense of identity:

> I didn't want to fly Margaret Thatcher's union flag for her. As far as I was concerned, there was a political as well as a cultural context to be taken into account. Things had changed since the 60s, when my work did indeed appear in an anthology called *The Young British Poets*, although even then 'silent things' were accumulating within me ... By 1983, I badly needed to serve notice that the British term was a misnomer.[11]

Even after his death in 2013, Heaney became embroiled in controversy at the intersection of culture, history, politics and identity, demonstrating not just the sensitive edges between these disciplines but also that there was no escaping their reach. In December 2020 a disagreement emerged when a painting of Heaney was used by the Northern Ireland Office (NIO) to promote the centenary of Northern Ireland without their having gained permission for its use, which was perceived by some to be using his image to legitimise partition. The painting, which was located in the Seamus Heaney

Centre at Queen's University, was part of a marketing campaign by the NIO and carried the slogan 'A Brand for Northern Ireland in 2021: Sharing Stories As We Go Beyond 100'. While the NIO defended his inclusion on the grounds that the intention was to embrace perspectives from all communities as a commitment to inclusivity, nationalist politicians criticised what looked like an act of cultural and political appropriation. SDLP leader Colum Eastwood argued that the use of the Heaney painting was at best misguided, as it presented a mono-cultural impression of a poet whose work focused on the struggle and complexity of identity and belonging: 'It is his account of life in a place struggling with its own identity and it would be wrong, therefore, to attempt to associate his image with a particular political narrative.'[12] He claimed it looked like a 'cynical attempt' to use Heaney's memory as a 'branding tool to promote that narrative about partition'.[13] Predictably, this led to accusations from unionist politicians such as the DUP's Gavin Robinson, MP, that such a response demonstrated a 'lack of generosity' and commitment to the principles of inclusivity.

Initially, the NIO claimed that it had received permission from the Seamus Heaney Centre at Queen's to include the painting, but this was quickly refuted by the Director of the centre, Professor Glenn Patterson. Patterson (a celebrated writer himself) made clear in a letter published in the *Irish Times* newspaper that while the centre did not own the painting and had not been consulted about its use, it would not have given permission in any case unless the family had explicitly agreed to it doing so: 'The centre could not have given permission for its use and even if it could have, would not have done so – nor would it do anything that involved Seamus Heaney's name – without first consulting the Heaney family.'[14] An awkward silence followed from Queen's until it admitted three months later in March 2021 that it had not consulted or sought permission from the Heaney family for the painting to be included in the campaign to commemorate Northern Ireland's centenary. The episode demonstrates the way in which political tension is often nested within cultural practice in Northern Ireland and that despite the generation that has passed since the Troubles abated in 1998, sensitivities can easily be triggered by the conflicting narratives of identity that persist.

PASSION, COMPASSION AND ADMONITION

While Heaney is without question the most decorated and celebrated poetic voice to come out of Ireland since Yeats, he was in the vanguard of a creative surge in the mid-1960s that included a swathe of internationally recognised voices. Perhaps the closest to Heaney in terms of his sheer quality of work and what might portentously be termed his civic importance, is Michael Longley. A native of Belfast, Longley was a contemporary of Heaney's and, after gaining a degree in English Literature at Trinity College Dublin, joined the Hobsbaum writing group at Queen's, which included Heaney, publishing his first collection, *No Continuing City: Poems 1963–1968,* in 1969. He has been a prolific writer ever since and has accumulated a swathe of prizes and awards, including the T.S. Eliot Prize and the Whitbread Poetry Award. Longley was awarded the Queen's Gold Medal for Poetry in 2001 and won the Griffin Poetry Prize in 2015 for his collection *The Stairwell,* published the previous year.

Longley's poetry is extremely diverse in terms of its subject matter, including work focusing on the First World War, human relationships and the natural world, but one of his enduring themes has been the city of Belfast and the political conflict in Northern Ireland since the late 1960s. Like Ciaran Carson, though more lyrical, meditative and gentle in style, Longley is a quintessentially Belfast poet whose work reflects the dynamics, quirks and political fault lines of the society itself. He is a very public poet and his work seeks to communicate moral complexity without intellectual game-playing or some of the deliberate obfuscation that some other poets appear to revel in. He is conscious of his public role as a voice within civic society and does not shy away from engaging with the sectarianism, violence and political division that has been the backdrop for most of the period in which he has been publishing his work. When asked if there was any tension between being a poet and also taking a position on wider political and social issues, including the impact of the Troubles, Longley responded: 'Though the poet's first duty must be to his imagination, he has other obligations – and not just as a citizen. He would be inhuman if he did not respond to tragic events in his own community, and a poor artist if he did not seek to endorse that response imaginatively.'[15] Interviewed in 2022 about his latest collection *The Slain Birds*[16] and the recent award of the prestigious 2022 Feltrinelli Prize worth €250,000, Longley was asked which one law he would pass or abolish if he had the power to do so. He replied, 'I would erase Brexit: a monumental disaster promoted by barefaced lies and frivolous politics.'[17]

In recognition of his body of work and cultural significance, Longley was appointed to the role of Professor of Poetry for Ireland in 2007, and the comments of Northern Ireland's Deputy First Minister Martin McGuinness at his inauguration referred to the importance of poets for the health and wellbeing of society more generally: 'He is an outstanding poet whose work is enjoyed today and will be enjoyed by generations to come. I believe that Michael, like previous holders of the chair, recognises the responsibility that comes with having such a gift. The impact that poetry and literature have on people and society should never be underestimated.'[18]

Much of Longley's work focuses on the human dimension of the Troubles, the pain inflicted, the victims who suffered and the mundane but desolate aftermath of the violence that had become part of the city's everyday reality. His work tends to focus on the outcome and impact of violence rather than searching for causal dynamics or fitting it into a wider analytical context. 'Wounds', published in 1972, connects the futility of the deaths at the Battle of the Somme in the First World War with murders during the Troubles in Northern Ireland. Here Longley conveys the fear experienced by those about to kill and be killed within a framing that is mundane and unremarkable. The emphasis here is on the way that lives are wasted for causes that are some distance away from the victims killed in such conflicts. Longley also opens up a broader issue here as to whether the perpetrators of violence are also victims themselves, drawn into conflict as a result of wider political circumstances over which they have little control.

'Wreaths', written in a similar style, is a trio of poems about the aftermath of sectarian murder, with a focus on the violence committed and the impact it had on the surviving victims, with very little attention given to who was responsible, what side they were on or any rationale for why they did what they did. The first of these, 'The Civil Servant', emphasises the mundane regularity of political assassination, when someone is killed in their kitchen while cooking an Ulster fry for breakfast. His killers come in and shoot him, the police come to the house and investigate, and his body is rolled up like a carpet and removed. The normalising of the violence is almost as shocking as the act itself, which at a wider level was how many people living in Northern Ireland felt when they turned on the morning news every day and were numbed while they ate their cornflakes.

While Longley's work was characterised by compassion for the victims of violence, some of his contemporaries were more condemnatory in style and focused more directly on the inequities of the political system prior to and during the Troubles. One of the most trenchant poetic voices in this regard during the 1970s and 1980s was that of Tom Paulin, who was brought up in Belfast and wanted to connect his work much more consciously with the political dysfunction that surrounded him. Paulin used the poetic form to engage directly with political issues, initially in an Irish context and later relating to abuses perpetrated by the government of Israel against the Palestinian people. So, for Paulin, culture and politics were inextricably linked and part of the same continuum rather than separate disciplines that could easily be disentangled. 'I do think culture is an argument',[19] was Paulin's way of explaining that his poetry and critical essays were part of a wider conversation in which ideas and beliefs 'should be flying about and banging into each other. It is a kind of energy. If you occupy static positions then things sort of ossify.'[20] One of the dominant themes in Paulin's work has been an attempt to reassert the voice of radical liberal Protestantism and critique the narrow-minded shrill invective of political unionism that had been in control of Belfast and the rest of Northern Ireland since partition at the beginning of the 1920s. His work railed against injustice, intolerance and the dissonance between the gritty Belfast vernacular and the more polished reservations and evasions he identified with Britain. His first full collection, *A State of Justice*, was published in 1977 by Faber to critical acclaim, winning the Somerset Maugham Award and pulling few punches in terms of his critique of events in Northern Ireland.

'A Partial State', published in 1980, looks back to the political disintegration of Northern Ireland in 1969 and focuses on the inability of unionists and the British government to reform the injustices suffered by the nationalist community that energised the civil rights movement. Here, the violence that erupted is cast as the inevitable outcome of the structural inequalities within Northern Ireland that neither unionists nor the British government remedied effectively. The final two lines allude to the point that violence was the symptom, not the cause, of the problem and that trying to keep the lid on the security situation by using the army could not ultimately redress a political system based on inequality.

Paulin's 'Desertmartin' is an even more pointed critique of political unionism, with a particular focus on the role of shrill religious intolerance. Here, again, he rails against the way in which Protestantism has been corrupted from a radical enlightenment individualist spirit and reduced to a desiccated husk of bitter certainties. It is an angry, disappointed poem, lamenting the way in which his own community has become a caricature of Britishness, reduced to cursing the very country that it professed loyalty towards. It takes a particular swipe at the then leader of the DUP, Rev. Ian Paisley, the firebrand Free Presbyterian unionist politician (the 'Big Man') leading a gullible electorate towards prison and a hopeless future.

Paulin's poetry has been criticised by some for being consumed by its own anger as he rages against a British government's callous ignorance towards the Protestant unionist community in Northern Ireland. This was combined with a deep despair at the Protestant unionist community's inability to present itself to people in Great Britain in a manner that would encourage them *not* to display such a callous ignorance towards them.[21] Paulin's poetry is often sardonic and withering, while at the same time yearning for the regeneration of the liberal enlightenment he sees embodied in the Presbyterian radicals of the late eighteenth century.

A TROUBLED ANTHOLOGY

During the 1980s, Paulin and Heaney combined with other Irish poets and playwrights, notably Seamus Deane and Brian Friel, along with actor Stephen Rea, to form the Field Day initiative. This was intended as a vehicle to produce plays, poetry and other work connecting the arts in Derry and Belfast to themes surrounding the political conflict in Northern Ireland. The mission of the Field Day collective was to combine cultural outputs with critical examinations of Irish history, politics and culture, specifically within the field of Irish Studies, and to produce literary criticism based heavily on promoting postcolonial theory within Irish cultural studies. The Field Day pamphlet series in the 1980s resulted in fifteen essays written by leading scholars, led by Seamus Deane and including Terry Eagleton, Tom Paulin and American-Palestinian writer Edward Said, with a focus on a postcolonial reading of Irish cultural studies and its relevance to the political conflict in Northern Ireland.

Field Day was not without its critics, seen by many as being a throwback recidivist form of Irish nationalism rather than providing a progressive or cosmopolitan agenda for action or even for scholarly inquiry. The centrepiece of the collective was the three-volume *Field Day Anthology of Irish Writing*, launched in Dublin in 1991 by former Taoiseach Charles Haughey in the presence of Deane, Heaney and Friel. At the time, Haughey was the most high-profile of Irish politicians, serving Taoiseach and with a reputation as a committed Irish nationalist, so his endorsement of the anthology mattered. Haughey was a divisive figure even then, with his critics viewing him as an unprincipled opportunist, a reputation that grew further in the decades that followed as his business and personal affairs came under greater scrutiny after he left public office.

The Field Day anthology came in for sustained criticism both for its political stance on Irish nationalism and for its lack of inclusion of female authors and important feminist writing. In her newspaper column, journalist and writer Nuala O'Faolain hoisted Deane with his own ideological petard: 'While this book was demolishing the patriarchy of Britain on a grand front, its own, native, patriarchy was sitting there. Smug as ever.'[22] To be fair to Deane, he had already issued a full and frank mea culpa having been confronted by this glaring anomaly, admitting that, ironically, he himself was guilty of precisely the sins of omission he was laying at the door of the erstwhile colonial overlords: 'To my astonishment and dismay, I have found that I myself have been subject to the same kind of critique to which I have subjected colonialism . . . I find that I exemplify some of the faults and erasures which I analyze and characterize in the earlier period.'[23] In 2002 two new volumes were published that focused on the contribution of female writers.[24]

The prominent Irish novelist Colm Tóibín, reviewing the Field Day anthology in the *Sunday Independent* newspaper,[25] argued that the assumptions made by nationalists in Northern Ireland were out of synch with the popular mood of those living in the Republic of Ireland. Tóibín suggested that the people there were much less enamoured by the project for political reunification than Deane and his colleagues in Belfast and Derry: 'Unreconstructed Irish nationalists have always had real difficulty with the 26 Counties. The 26 Counties are in limbo, they believe, waiting for the day when our island will be united and the British will leave. This leaves out any idea that Southern Ireland has been forming its own habits and going its own way.'[26]

This tension within Irish nationalism over the pace and even the direction of constitutional change coloured responses to the Field Day project and the *Anthology of Irish Writing* in particular. While the project was culturally rich, it was also politically controversial within the broad spectrum of Irish nationalism across the island. Unionists were for the most part even less enamoured, viewing it in the early 1990s as a cultural wing of what was disparagingly referred to as the pan-nationalist front.

Field Day progressed to a formal link between 2004 and 2014 with the Keough-Naughton Institute for Irish Studies at the University of Notre Dame, which co-published the *Field Day Review*, an annual journal of Irish political and literary studies.[27] Despite its critics, Field Day played a hugely important role in providing a platform for cultural outputs that engaged with politics and history in Belfast, Derry and Northern Ireland as a whole. The role played by the Northern Ireland Arts Council in funding many of these initiatives also deserves recognition, along with local publishers in Belfast that nurtured and mentored writers from the city. Blackstaff Press, in particular, has played an important role since the 1980s, as have smaller publishing houses such as Lagan Press, Abbey Press and Lapwing Publications and journals such as the *Honest Ulsterman*, which, from its establishment in 1968, showcased the best poetic talent emerging from Belfast and Northern Ireland. Frank Ormsby was elected to the Ireland Chair of Poetry in 2019 and fittingly gave his inaugural lecture in association with the Seamus Heaney Centre at Queen's University entitled 'The Honest Ulsterman Revisited'. Ormsby was editor of the *Honest Ulsterman* for twenty years and reflected in his lecture about the importance of the magazine for fostering (and criticising) local poetry. Over the years, it published work by John Hewitt, Roy MacFadden, Robert Grechan, Paul Muldoon, James Simmons, Carol Rumens and many others. In addition to helping emerging poets to get published and hone their creative skills, Ormsby suggests that the *Honest Ulsterman* played a wider social role during the Troubles: 'The fact that the magazine's life coincides with the Northern Ireland Troubles gave it the significance that all creative work has in time of conflict. It preserved peace-time values and kept them warm, as it were, during the most destructive phases, and acted as a foundation for the aftermath of the Troubles.'[28]

BELFAST'S MOST URBAN POET

Another of the poets published in the *Honest Ulsterman* was Ciaran Carson, who worked for many years as Traditional Arts Officer in the Northern Ireland Arts Council, eventually moving into academia as Professor of English at Queen's University Belfast and the founding Director of the Seamus Heaney Centre at the university. Carson was a native Irish speaker and a quintessentially Belfast urban poet. He also represents a generational shift from the Heaney, Longley and Paulin era into one where poetry was plugged directly into the Troubles period. His first collection, *The Irish for No*, was published in 1987, closely followed by his critically acclaimed *Belfast Confetti* in 1990. Among other awards for his work, Carson was awarded the T.S. Eliot Prize in 1993 for his *First Language: Poems* collection and the Forward Prize for *Breaking News* in 2003. While primarily a poet, Carson was also a prolific writer of prose titles, including *The Star Factory*. First published in 1997, this was a personal *tour-de-force* memoir of growing up in Belfast and one of the best books ever to have been written about the city. Little effort was made here to connect themes or chapters into any recognisable chronology, as the narrative flows across Carson's childhood in the Falls area of West Belfast to address wider historical and political themes driven and connected by his own personal odyssey and sense of place.

Carson's poetry is pared back and sparse in form, direct, even blunt, its apparent simplicity often masking an intense complexity. He engaged directly with the experience of living in Belfast during the Troubles, several of his poems focusing on the confusion, physical as well as existential, of what people were living through. It may be a personal reflection rather than one shared by his broader audience, but I have always found his poetry to have a strong narrative with an almost claustrophobic quality, where you feel trapped by circumstances, in a political and cultural cul-de-sac with no clear exits available. While Carson's poems are rooted in broad, sweeping political, historical and cultural themes, the narrative is often contained at the micro level, as if he was as much an urban geographer or a war correspondent as he was a poet. This is no more evident than in the poem 'Belfast Confetti', which takes us to the aftermath of a riot between Protestant shipyard workers and Catholic residents on the streets of Belfast. The poem is presented as a first-person account, an almost real-time eye witness to the violence and the questions such conflict poses. The poem suggests a chaotic turbulence both on the street but also in the protagonist's mind about what was happening to him personally, to his community, his city and his identity. It is a sharply written, direct, uncompromising poem where the reader is pitched head first into the melee. The spikey form and structure of the poem adds to the sense of disorientation, confusion, jangling emotions and sense of imminent danger that are its central themes. The poem has no answers to the many questions it poses, and even though the poem's speaker knows the city well, he feels trapped, with no way out – a predicament that is as much political and cultural as it is physical.

Much of Carson's poetry is rooted in the urban landscape of Belfast during the Troubles and its aftermath, containing shades of MacNeice and other poets such as W.R. Rogers in its literal directness. Words are sparse but coded, and he constantly plays with the imagery of language and maps, like a crazed cartographer charting the micro-level geography of the city. Places are both familiar and foreign, what was once a comfortable landscape now a hostile environment of machines, military hardware and aggressive, unanswerable questions. His poem 'Last Orders' is again pared back to the bone, and we are instantly transported into a city bar in the Troubles period, when few people could relax completely while they were socialising, given the possibility of attack by paramilitary gangs.

'Last Orders' is a claustrophobic masterpiece that anyone who grew up in the city during the Troubles period and who went through the steel security gates to get into bars in the city will instantly recognise and remember. The metallic click of the gates made it feel like you were going in and out of a cage – which essentially is what we were all living in, and to this day I am unable to sit in a bar or restaurant with my back to the door and will always choose a seat where I can see who is coming and going and what they are carrying with them. Police stations, prisons, courthouses and even pubs were often entombed within these metal cages, like a post-apocalypse human aviary. The Sunflower pub in the centre of Belfast has retained its metal cage at the entrance as an homage to this peculiar form of urban architecture. Formerly the Tavern Bar, on the corner of Kent Street and Union Street in the city, the Sunflower is now one of the city's best-known pubs and its wire mesh cage stands as a relic of Belfast's social history.

A NEW WAVE RISING

Beyond Carson's substantial contribution, Patrick Kavanagh's metaphorical standing army of 10,000 poets has strength and depth, and the top brass of Heaney, Mahon, Longley, Muldoon, Paulin, Carson and McGuckian have been joined by more recent Belfast recruits during and after the peace process in the 1990s. Medbh McGuckian was one of the most original and gifted poets to come through in the generation after Heaney, and while her work is only obliquely focused on the Troubles, or on Belfast, for that matter, it occasionally resonates in her poetry nonetheless. Frank Ormsby remarks on her epigraph to her *Captain Lavender* collection in 1994, which quotes Pablo Picasso's statement in 1944 about the relationship of his own work to war: 'I have not painted the war . . . but I have no doubt that the war is in the paintings I have done.'[29] McGuckian's focus was much more centred on the personal than the political, notwithstanding the caveat that these could be deemed indivisible in certain respects. Her first two collections, *The Flower Master* in 1982 and *Venus and the Rain* in 1984, were critically acclaimed and established her international reputation as a highly original poet whose work was rich in imagery if a little obscure and inaccessible for some readers.

Seamus Heaney taught McGuckian at Queen's and recognised her talent in a predominantly male literary environment and society in Northern Ireland. Ormsby quotes Heaney saying that McGuckian's poetry moved 'amphibiously between the dreamlife and her actual domestic and historical experience as a woman in late twentieth-century Ireland'.[30]

More recently, Dr Sinéad Morrissey is one of the most notable of this new generation of Belfast poets. Like many others, Morrissey combines academic teaching with her role as a professional poet. Morrissey was the youngest-ever recipient of the Patrick Kavanagh Poetry Award at the youthful age of eighteen in 1990 (though it now grates on her a little due to its constant repetition) and has a list of other literary achievements, including being awarded the prestigious T.S. Eliot Prize in 2013 for her critically acclaimed *Parallax* collection.

Morrissey grew up in North Belfast during some of the worst years of the Troubles but spent long periods outside Northern Ireland, including in Canada and New Zealand, before returning to the city in 1999 as the peace process struggled to bed in. She was appointed as Belfast's inaugural Poet Laureate in 2014 and was a Reader in Creative Writing at the Seamus Heaney Centre for Poetry at Queen's University before her appointment as Professor of Creative Writing at Newcastle University in 2016. Like that of many of her predecessors, Morrissey's poetry continues to mediate the difficult space between literature and politics, and her consciously anti-sectarian, anti-racist and anti-homophobic starting point sets her work in tension with some of the more conservative and antediluvian instincts within Northern Ireland's society. Interviewed about her upbringing, Morrissey referred to how anti-sectarian values were instilled by her parents from a young age: 'When things get very tribal and divided between two groups of people, much of reality is predetermined by which side of the divide you stand on and where your values were formed. It was very liberating not to be on either side and to feel quite apart from those two dynamics.'[31]

Her first collection, *There Was Fire in Vancouver*, was published in 1996 and focuses on the poet's journey, physical as well as intellectual, away from Belfast, family and the conviction of her Marxist upbringing to a more independent but uncertain future. The anthology contains poems such as 'Double

Vision', 'Europa Hotel' and 'Belfast Storm' that reference the natural and man-made infrastructure of Belfast as well as its historical, political and cultural peculiarities.

Morrissey represents a more modern profile within Belfast society, one which does not conform to the binary unionist-versus-nationalist political or cultural identity. She has spoken of her fear that Northern Ireland's hard-won peace could recede back into the dark days of the city that she experienced as a child. Morrissey comes from a mixed background, her mother born in England and her father a native of Belfast's Falls Road. In her iconic poem 'Thoughts in a Black Taxi', Morrissey expresses her fear as a child of being defined as either a Catholic or a Protestant when she identified with neither but could be identified as either through her Catholic name or her Protestant school uniform.[32] Morrissey gave voice in this poem to the fear that many people from Belfast had growing up during the Troubles, that they would be marked out or discovered as belonging to the hated other community due to the names they bore, the streets they lived in or the schools they attended. Michael Parker quotes Morrissey's recollection that going daily along the Grosvenor Road in the Belfast High School uniform was 'like having Protestant slapped across your back'.[33]

Much of Morrissey's work engages with themes of distance, belonging and in-betweenness, the meat and drink of the Irish who have travelled or are still travelling within the hybrid diasporic space, neither completely away when they are beyond Ireland nor completely at home when they return. This in-betweenness goes beyond the physical acts of moving away from Belfast and moving back there and in Morrissey's poetry intersects with her perspectives on history, politics and culture. Borders here, both physical and existential, are malleable rather than fixed, a flexibility that the peace process and the Good Friday Agreement has sought to accommodate since 1998. Morrissey's second collection, *Between Here and There*, published in 2002, focuses in on this diasporic condition and ruminates on the challenges facing her relocation back to Belfast after a decade of living away in New Zealand and Japan.

Morrissey's interrogation of identity and belonging connects her to a rich tradition of other Irish writers, including Heaney, Hewitt, Carson and

MacNeice. Hers is a naturally more contemporary and perhaps more optimistic voice than those of her predecessors, which coincides with her work paralleling the peace process itself. So her critique focuses less on the horrors of violence and more on the dysfunctionality of the political system and the persistent sectarianism and social conservatism that remains in Belfast. Morrissey brings a healthy scepticism towards capitalism and neo-liberal economics to her work. Her poem 'Tourism' from her 2002 *Between Here and There* collection is an example of how her critical lens focuses less on the violence of the past than on the exploitation and profiteering of the present. Her focus here concerns the way in which Belfast and its heritage has become packaged by the tourist industry as a commodity for consumption and profit, rather than being grasped as a peacebuilding opportunity with the capacity to reconcile the persistent divisions within the city. She laments the rush to sanitise the sectarian past of the city, overlaying it with neutral narratives more palatable to Belfast's post-Agreement, post-conflict status. Rather than an authentic exercise in turning swords into ploughshares, this presents a mythologised and false impression of the suffering that took place. Morrissey's use of the launch of the *Titanic* becomes a metaphor for the doomed project of peacebuilding in the post-Agreement era. The ship becomes an allegory for the manufacture of peace as an imperfect vessel, built to transport a city fractured as much by class as it is by religion.

Clearly, Morrissey does not shy away from using her poetic voice as a vehicle to engage with debates about how Belfast has been evolving in the post-conflict space since the 1990s. She made the point in an interview that the process of remembering our lived experience is an interpretive and contextual act rather than simply an objective or neutral recording of significant events:

> I'm inspired not just by 'what happened', however that may be made known to us, but primarily by those imaginative acts of historical recreation by which we enter the past. To know the past is a doomed enterprise; creative reimagining is all we've got. Objects in museums only 'reek of meaning' once we've done the work of slotting them back in their original contexts, an idiosyncratic and profoundly artistic process on our part.[34]

Morrissey went on to suggest that she engaged with historical, political and cultural themes through her poetry because that was her chosen specialism and mode of communication, rather than because the medium of poetry itself was particularly suited to engaging with such issues.

On Balance won the European Poet of Freedom Literary Award in 2020, and maintains Morrissey's interest in Belfast with poems such as 'The Millihelen' about the launch of the *Titanic* in Harland and Wolff shipyard.[35] Following the Forward Award in 2017, journalist Kate Kellaway summed up Morrissey's ability to write in a way that opened rather than closed the themes that she engaged with – a fitting metaphor, perhaps, for the state of Belfast itself: 'Even the poems that cross the finishing line with a flourish are open-ended, leaving one with the sense that there will always be more to say, and this is because Morrissey is possessed of her own invigorating brand of Irish fluency and an imagination that never closes.'[36]

Like Sinéad Morrissey, Dr Leontia Flynn is another Belfast-based poet of the post-conflict generation whose work engages not so much with the violence of the Troubles era but rather with the mundane realities and everyday disappointments of what came after. Born in Newcastle, County Down in 1974, Flynn completed her PhD on the work of Medbh McGuckian and has been celebrated as one of the leading poets of her generation with an enviable list of literary awards to her name, including the Forward Prize for Best First Collection. While she studied McGuckian's work, Flynn has been compared to Paul Muldoon in terms of her imaginative and whimsically humorous style. She pokes fun in all directions, not least at the poetic fraternity itself. Unlike that of McGuckian, her poetry is disarmingly accessible, the intention being as much to communicate with the reader as to challenge their powers of deduction. Her work is thematically broad, some poems mapping the challenges of growing up, finding work and worrying about the future, others focusing on physical and existential journeys, many of them rooted in the awkward backdrop of post-Troubles Belfast. Her poem 'Leaving Belfast' from her 2008 *Drives* collection illustrates the ways in which the city sits between conflict and peace; it could go either way and is in transition, but to an unclear destination.

Flynn gives voice in this poem to the wider critique, explored in the previous chapter on tourism, that the post-conflict economy was changing

Belfast for the benefit of outsiders and entrepreneurs, rather than serving the needs of those who live in the city – a glossy but surface-level rebranding of Belfast that masked the embedded and enduring sectarian divisions that remained riddled through its political, cultural and social fabric. There is a frustration in much of Flynn's poetry at a city that, despite its movement out of the Troubles era, is still not quite succeeding in getting its act together, which maps onto the on-again-off-again nature of the political institutions in the wake of the Good Friday Agreement of 1998. Belfast and its people have moved beyond war – but they have not quite made it to peace, either. The city is under construction and looks like it will be nice when it's finished. However, like anyone who has spent years with builders in their house, at the moment there is a first-fix ugliness that has become rather wearing given that the project was supposed to have been finished years ago. Flynn's work stresses the fluidity and fragility of progress in Belfast and the fact that, although the city is moving forwards, it could also go backwards, and what has been gained since the end of the Troubles in the 1990s could just as easily be lost. In fact, her poems allude to the fact that notions of winning and losing are highly contextual, and while entrepreneurs were making money and the middle classes had more opportunities to purchase luxury flats, many others were finding themselves left behind by the gentrification of the city. Like Ciaran Carson's poetry, though perhaps more subliminally and less directly, Flynn's work asks questions about belonging and identity and highlights the contextual nature of how we define ourselves and our relationships with the rest of the community – and the wider world.

There is little doubt that Belfast has produced a remarkable range of talented poets over the last fifty years who could hold their own in any international company. Those discussed here represent a far from exhaustive list, and while some poets, like Heaney and Carson, were obvious inclusions, there are a legion of other poets either born or educated and domiciled in Belfast who merit at least a citation. Alan Gillis is a poet and academic at the University of Edinburgh who is indicative of the more recent wave of talented Belfast poets whose work can stand alongside the more established names. His poem 'Progress' from the 2004 *Somebody Somewhere* collection is a clever and poignant flight of fancy that imagines the Troubles being put into reverse. Here, time rewinds, and lives and events that were destroyed by violence are magically restored, coffins are taken out of the ground and those buried in them are restored to life by the explosions that killed them.

Gillis is a native of Belfast and an exciting poetic talent. Similarly, Ruth Carr, Adrian Rice, Maureen Boyle, Stephen Connolly, Paula Cunningham and many more besides have proven themselves to be officer class in Kavanagh's 'standing army of 10,000 poets'.

A CANTERBURY TALE

I cannot finish this chapter without mentioning a poet who I came to know while working at the University of Kent. Poet and singer-songwriter Steafán Hanvey came to celebrate National Poetry Day at the University of Kent in September 2019 and did readings from his recent book *Reconstructions: The Troubles in Photographs and Words.*[37] The event was organised by the Conflict Analysis Research Centre (CARC), of which I was Director at the time, which has a tradition of connecting academic research with community-level activism. The connection between our academic work on political conflict and artistic reflections of political violence through poetry seemed an ideal combination.

Reconstructions is a book of Hanvey's poems with photographs taken by his father Bobbie, one of Northern Ireland's best-known photojournalists. The majority of the poems and photos relate to the years of violent conflict in the 1970s and 1980s – but there is also work that hints at peace around the corner in the 1990s. I grew up in Belfast during the period that most of the book relates to and lived through many of the events depicted in it when they were classified as news and current affairs rather than history and were conveyed to us by political and security journalists rather than poets.

'Carson-Parson' is a stand-out poem of the book for me, written in response to a well-known photograph taken by Bobbie Hanvey in 1985. It features Rev. Ian Paisley and was taken when Paisley was leading unionist opposition to the Anglo-Irish Agreement, an international treaty signed in November of that year by the British and Irish governments. The agreement gave the government of the Irish Republic a formal role in the internal affairs of Northern Ireland for the first time and was fiercely contested by the unionist community in a campaign of resistance that ultimately failed. Paisley was attempting to invoke the memory of Sir Edward Carson, whose statue stands imposingly at the bottom of Parliament Buildings at Stormont. The poem takes us on Paisley's own political journey, from firebrand preacher and dissenter against all things progressive, to First Minister of a power-sharing government with the late Martin McGuinness in 2008, to outcast within his own party, having done what needed to be done and made peace with his enemy. Hanvey's political analysis is as deft here as his poetic voice when assessing Paisley's character and his impact as a leader within the unionist community:

A bellicose blunder-bussing scattergun of a man,
you seemed to claim that the word defiance
was of your own minting.
I wrack my brain trying to think
of a word for defeated, yet defiant,
and 'Ulster', was all I could muster.[38]

Reconstructions is intelligent, empathetic, razor-sharp (often razor-funny) and, for anyone committed to the concept of conflict transformation and peacebuilding, inspiring, too. Like the peace process itself, there is a constructive ambiguity within the images and words presented. We are pointed in the right direction, but not given the 'answers'.

It was a great talk, and as Director of CARC I was delighted to take Steafán out for dinner with my colleague Dr Nadine Ansorg, who had done most of the work in getting him to Kent in the first place. Before dinner I took him into a local pub in the centre of Canterbury for some liquid refreshment, and as we chatted while waiting to be served, an older man sitting at the bar looked us both up and down and, when he heard our accents, made a remark about hoping neither of us had a belt strapped to us. The inference was obvious: he was alluding to us wearing a suicide belt of explosives with an intent to blow up the bar. This reference struck both Steafán and myself as odd, given that this was not a favoured technique of Irish republicans, though it may have been asking too much of the 'local' to appreciate the nuances of the Irish republican 'armed struggle'. Given that I had just met Steafán and was hoping that he would have a pleasant evening at our invitation, I was mortified at the inference that two people with accents like ours might be there to kill my sedentary inquisitor and his fellow drinkers. I didn't want things to deteriorate any further, so I settled for some thinly veiled sarcasm in response, politely informing him that he was suffering from acutely ingrained xenophobia, but that if he wanted to enrol in my Peace Studies MA module up the hill at the university I could have it out of him in two to three weeks – with adequate reading and study of course. I half smiled at him – but not too warmly.

If I was a poet I would write a poem about that tale in Canterbury, but, as I am not, this book seems an appropriate place to record the episode.

8

THE FUTURE

Belfast, like all cities, is in transition, though its journey has perhaps been more tumultuous than many. As we have seen, it owes its existence to the peculiarities of political geography, its proximity to the sea and a network of rivers including the Lagan, Blackstaff and Farset. These environmental advantages facilitated trade and commerce over several centuries, during which time a small settlement grew into a town before expanding into the city we know today. Its story is one of changing circumstances, not least in political context, as it evolved from being a developed regional city on the island of Ireland within the UK, to the capital of a new political unit after partition and the establishment of Northern Ireland in 1921. The years ahead may witness yet another epoch, where Belfast becomes politically integrated once again with other cities on the island of Ireland but within a context where the whole country is unified and politically independent from the UK. If this type of constitutional change takes place, Belfast and its citizens will be at the centre of the debate and continue the tradition of mobilising over the region's political future just as the Presbyterian radicals and United Irish movement did in the late eighteenth century and Ulster unionists did over the two centuries that followed.

THE NUMBERS GAME

Whether or not this change happens, it will be up to the people of the city and across Northern Ireland to decide their constitutional future as set out in the Good Friday Agreement in 1998. The benchmarks that could be used by a British Secretary of State to trigger a border poll might include opinion poll evidence that shows convincing levels of support for Irish reunification. Alternatively, census data showing a rise in the Catholic population might also provide a trigger point, though religious affiliation is a less reliable measure for political or cultural preference than it was in the past. The 2021 census data was released in September 2022, and by any yardstick it represents a historic moment.[1] The big story was that, for the first time ever, those who identify themselves as Catholic outnumber those who define themselves as Protestant (45.7 per cent to 43.5 per cent). In reality, the fact that Catholics now outnumber the Protestant population does not mean in itself that there is *likely* to be a majority in Northern Ireland in favour of Irish unity, but it certainly adds to the other indicators, all of which are pointing in that direction. The pro-Union majority in Northern Ireland and in its capital city Belfast is no longer certain and seems to be shifting in the direction of a majority being in favour of constitutional change. The census finding therefore has huge symbolic significance, as the whole raison d'être of Northern Ireland was to create a political and administrative region with a stable Protestant majority. Northern Ireland was carved from six of Ulster's nine counties for a reason. Including the other three, Donegal, Cavan and Monaghan, would have been a more obvious political unit, keeping all of Ulster within the UK. However, that would have bolstered the Catholic population to the point that a Protestant majority in Northern Ireland could not have been guaranteed and the region would have been divided and politically unstable. Despite this exercise in Machiavellian political geography, the 2021 census demonstrated that a century after partition the Protestant majority has now evaporated, and with it there must be questions about the consent that remains for the current constitutional arrangements.

The significance of the 2021 census was not limited to the religious headcount, as results relating to ethnic identity also demonstrated a reduction in those expressing a British identity and an increase in people who defined themselves as Irish only. In terms of the key national identity question, 32 per cent said they had a 'British only' identity, with 29 per cent defining themselves as 'Irish only' and 20 per cent categorising themselves as 'Northern Irish only'. This shows that the British identity remains larger than the Irish identity, but the margin is narrow and the large group of those opting for

Northern Ireland would be decisive in determining the result of a future border poll on political reunification.

More significant than the figures themselves is the trend since the previous census ten years earlier. This shows a dramatic decline in the number of people in Northern Ireland who define themselves as British since 2011 and a significant growth in those who identify as Irish. The former has dropped from 40 per cent to 32 per cent, while the latter has risen from 25 per cent to 29 per cent.[2]

Another obvious benchmark would be a majority of nationalist representatives elected to the Northern Ireland Assembly, though again it could be argued that some of those who vote for the SDLP might not necessarily vote for Irish reunification in a border poll. The SDLP has always been more comfortable within the UK political system than Sinn Féin, their nationalism tempered by social democratic impulses that might persuade them to remain within the UK if the case for the status quo was made convincingly by unionists in a referendum campaign.

Notwithstanding the ambiguity of the mechanism, the debate is already in motion and the pressure for a border poll on Irish reunification at some point in the next two decades looks unstoppable, though its outcome is far from certain. The UK Shadow Secretary of State for Northern Ireland, Peter Kyle, indicated in September 2022 that if Labour were in power he would be prepared to set out the criteria required more explicitly and set the wheels in motion: 'I am saying I am not going to be a barrier if the circumstances emerge.'[3]

For those of a unionist persuasion the key statistics are alarming. Northern Ireland is now majority Catholic; nationalists now outnumber unionists in the Northern Ireland Assembly in terms of community designation; and for the first time in history, a nationalist party, Sinn Féin, became the largest party in the Assembly in the May 2022 election, relegating the DUP to second position and thus gaining the right to nominate for the First Minister position in the Executive Office.

Belfast itself, the capital city of Northern Ireland, reflected all of these trends in the 2021 census. Nationalist political strength has been growing on Belfast City Council over the last thirty years and Sinn Féin and the SDLP now hold three of the four Westminster seats in the city, the DUP now restricted to its East Belfast stronghold. Sinn Féin's Tina Black was elected Lord Mayor of Belfast in June 2022, following in the footsteps of several other Sinn Féin holders as the city's 'first citizen'. To put the significance of this in context, the *first ever* nationalist Lord Mayor of Belfast was elected in 1997 when the SDLP's Alban McGuinness was elected to the role.

Beyond the statistics of the 2021 census, political change is surely coming, and those who prepare for it most diligently are likely to influence the political future most effectively. This could result in Belfast and Northern Ireland entering a whole new political paradigm – where the ghosts of the McCrackens, McTiers, Neilsens and Russells will raise ethereal toasts to a future in which Belfast finally achieves political independence from Britain.

Whatever happens in the decades ahead, the political complexion of Belfast has already changed dramatically over the last generation, and while the city was once dominated by unionism, this is no longer the case, and the trend is unlikely to be reversed in the conceivable future. Belfast City Council was a bastion of local political control for unionists for many generations, but its changing profile is reflective of a broader shift across Northern Ireland. The council is now under no overall control, with Sinn Féin being the largest party, having eighteen councillors out of a total of sixty, while the DUP is second, with fifteen. In effect, centrist parties (such as the Alliance Party, with nine seats) hold the balance of power, and responsibility tends to be shared in ways that would have been unheard of in previous generations.

Beyond what looks likely to be a perennial constitutional question hanging over Belfast, Northern Ireland and the rest of the island in the decades ahead, a number of other issues are likely to define the city over the next twenty years. These reflect the fact that the peace process and broader post-conflict institutions have breathed new life into the city, making things possible that would have been improbable in previous generations. There are, of course, enduring problems in the city, not least the structural segregation of those who live there, who still, for the most part, are educated apart, live apart, worship apart and are even buried in religiously segregated graveyards.

There is some evidence that traditional identities are becoming more nuanced and less aligned to the binary choices of British/unionist versus

Irish/nationalist. In addition to the 2021 census, polling data has consistently shown that young people especially are increasingly defining their identities as neither British nor Irish. This trend is also reflected in voting behaviour over recent years, with the non-aligned Alliance Party now the third-largest party following the 2022 Assembly election, more than doubling its number of seats at Stormont.[4] The election outcome provided additional evidence that there are now three dominant blocs in the electorate, with the non-aligned being the largest among younger voters.

MARCHING TO THE BEAT OF THE PAST

Despite signs of change, it is clear that there are still many within the older generation who have nurtured their children on a diet of fear, hatred and intolerance of difference. This bubbles to the surface periodically, and regularly enough to debilitate the political, economic and cultural health as well as the everyday lives of people who live in the city. There are numerous reasons for this. Enduring structural divisions in the city's political geography, its segregated primary and post-primary education provision, its largely binary religious affiliation and participation in different civic and cultural groups all play a large part. However, the city is also blighted by the fact that it has still not come to terms with its past or begun to address the legacy of the 1968–98 Troubles. Belfast's history has not yet retreated to the point that it can be absorbed into its cultural heritage, because its past is still coupled with the politics of the present. So, despite a quarter of a century of ostensible peace, every year in Belfast the calendar is pock-marked with events that are lauded by one community and disparaged by the other. Historical and political commemorations translate seamlessly into cultural and religious demarcations of community identity and exclusion, headlined by what is known as the loyalist Marching Season, which extends over most of the summer. The Twelfth of July parades and the Eleventh Night bonfires that precede them are seen by unionists as a celebration of their civil and religious liberty and a social and cultural high point for their community. For many nationalists, they are regarded as bigoted hate-fests, as the Irish flag and effigies of nationalist politicians 'decorate' many of these bonfires and are burned to cheering crowds.

In turn, unionists have complained about the West Belfast community arts festival Féile an Phobail, where concerts from republican bands such as the Wolfe Tones and the more recent hip-hop band Kneecap have led to audiences chanting in support of the Provisional IRA. In 2022 Kneecap were criticised by unionist politicians for unveiling a new street mural in Belfast featuring a police Land Rover burning and an image that conflated the current Police Service of Northern Ireland (PSNI) with the old Royal Ulster Constabulary (RUC). Kneecap are a working-class trio from West Belfast who rap almost exclusively in the Irish language, and their mural contained the slogan '*nil fáilte roimh an RUC*' ('the RUC aren't welcome'). After the Féile they did an interview with the *Guardian* newspaper claiming that the suggestion that they were fostering hatred or violence was misplaced: 'We didn't burn a police Land Rover, we painted one. Some people are more worried about a piece of art than the effigies of real politicians hanging off bonfires. We don't want to be fighting or advocating violence. We want people to be thinking.'[5] While Féile an Phobail distanced itself from the mural, saying that it was not organised by the festival, Tourism NI made a public statement inferring that its funding offer to events such as the Féile was based on 'due regard' for good community relations.[6]

Today, Belfast remains a culturally vibrant but divided city, and while the 2021 census and recent voting patterns show some change taking place in the binary relationship between Catholics and Protestants, Irish and British, nationalist and unionist, it has not yet changed appreciably for those who live there. There is no commonly accepted narrative on the past, and issues of cultural identity are still perceived by many people as a zero-sum equation, a never ending tug of war between winning and losing. In a conflict mindset (which has been dominant in Belfast for most of the last century and arguably before that), the assertion of cultural rights over parity of esteem for the Irish language, or the construction of bonfires in particular urban areas, can easily become a litmus test for community survival.

Commemoration of the past is literally written on the walls of the city, where anniversaries of historical events reinforce community identity in pursuit of political goals that are as relevant in 2022 as they were in 1922. So kerbstones are painted red, white and blue, and flags of various types adorn houses as if two rival teams are playing in a never-ending football match. In interface areas of the city, where unionist and nationalist communities meet, lurid murals can be found on many gable walls, acting as political and cultural message boards that define community identity.

As an example, issues relating to bonfires on 11 July – what is referred to in Northern Ireland as Bonfire Night, or simply 'the Eleventh' – connect historical events from over 300 years ago with religious organisations such as the Orange institutions, which are themselves linked to political unionism today. Some bonfires in Belfast have raised concerns due to their proximity to houses and the property of local residents. Critics have claimed that they are a danger to life and the local environment, while those who support them see such opposition as part of a culture war being waged by nationalists against the unionist tradition in the city.

Bonfire Night has nothing to do with its equivalent in Britain, which celebrates the thwarting of the Gunpowder Plot masterminded by Catholics Guy Fawkes and Robert Catesby in their conspiracy to burn down the Palace of Westminster in 1605 and assassinate Protestant King James I. The bonfires that take place in unionist areas of Belfast combine a historical tradition with a particular form of cultural heritage for those who take part. Many of the bonfires take several months to build, and some are controlled and policed by loyalist paramilitary organisations or community activists who act as gate-keepers for their design and construction. Looked at positively, these are examples of community cohesion and bonding social capital, bringing the local community together in demonstrations of solidarity and celebration. The bonfires themselves are, for the most part, large, convivial occasions, street parties where people socialise and enjoy themselves.

However, they also function to allow those who attend to vent their frustration and anger at those they deem to be hostile towards the unionist cause and to their British identity. Although from time to time this can include unionists, the overwhelming target for those involved in Bonfire Night on 11 July tends to be the Catholic nationalist community in Northern Ireland, as well as a wider range of hate figures, including members of the Irish government. Since the Brexit referendum in 2016, and especially since the arrival of the Northern Ireland Protocol in January 2020, the EU has also become a favourite source for loyalist enmity on Bonfire Night. The bonfires reflect this resentment by placing symbols of Irish nationalism on them to be burned, usually featuring the Irish flag and effigies of nationalist politicians or their election placards at their summit. In recent years, some of the bonfires in Belfast have seen the acronym KAT (Kill All Taigs) festooned on these multi-storey constructions, despite regular condemnation from unionist politicians. This provides annual and alarming evidence of the visceral hatred that remains endemic in Belfast despite twenty-five years of post-conflict institution-building. The fact that in 2022 cultural celebrations in Belfast were laced with unreconstructed hatred and genocidal tendencies that have not been dulled by the last two and a half decades of relative peace is a sobering reality about the health of the city today.

The Orange Marching Season is when Belfast's sectarian divisions are most cruelly exposed, one side claiming parades to be vibrant cultural expressions of civil and religious liberty and loyalty to the British Crown, the other condemning them as triumphalist and aggressive exhibitions of cultural and political domination. Incidents of sectarian intimidation linked to Orange parades or provocative behaviour by members of the Loyal Orders are often cited by nationalists as evidence of the fact that the heritage being incubated by the Orange Institution is one of bigotry and hatred of the Catholic community.

A particularly egregious example was provided in June 2022 at a dinner hosted by an Orange hall to celebrate Northern Ireland's centenary in Dundonald on the outskirts of Belfast. Shortly after this event, video footage was widely circulated on social media of a group of young men enthusiastically singing a sectarian song celebrating the killing of a young Catholic teacher, Michaela McAreavey, who had been murdered in Mauritius just days after getting married in 2011. While three of those responsible subsequently resigned from the Orange Order, and the Grand Orange Lodge of Ireland condemned the incident as 'utterly abhorrent', many saw it as being indicative of a wider issue, beyond simply the toxic masculinity of the individuals involved.[7] Sports journalist and Orangeman Richard Mulligan was quick to condemn the video as 'shameful' and felt that it had brought ignominy and disgrace to the door of the Orange Order but pointed out that the sentiments expressed were not shared by others: 'Given the Orange Order's links to the video, the organisation came in for criticism, some of it merited. But some suggested that everyone [within the] association was bigoted. It is not the case that every member of the order hates Catholics.'[8] However, others saw this unpleasant incident as part of a more widespread systemic problem within the culture of Orangeism, suggesting that it was built upon anti-Catholicism. The New York-based journalist Niall O'Dowd made the point that, beyond the individuals concerned, it was clear from the video that the song had been sung before, and no one else at the gathering seemed to intervene to stop them or appear surprised by what they heard:

> The words are hideous beyond belief, but what is left unanswered is who wrote them, and when and where they were first sung. It is quite clear from the video the lyrics were well-known. . . . It seems perfectly plausible the 'song' has been sung for years by Orangemen sitting in their citadels, burnishing their hatred for Catholics. It shows the depth of ignorance and bigotry that still courses through hard-line unionism.[9]

Inevitably, those supportive of the Loyal Orders saw this incident as three rotten apples in an otherwise healthy barrel, while those critical of the Orange institutions felt that it demonstrated that the rot was in the barrel itself. The point at issue here is that, irrespective of the particular incidents and who is to blame for the way identities can become weaponised and fused with political disagreements, it is clear that human relationships in Belfast today take place within a tinder box that can be very easily ignited.

TWO OBSTACLES TO PROGRESS

Belfast still has huge potential as a hub of cultural excellence, political innovation and economic progress, but the city is being held back for two reasons. The first is internal, in that Belfast has not successfully addressed the legacy of its own conflict – either during the Troubles era or in relation to partition itself. The society remains chronically divided in political and cultural terms which can be seen in the social segregation of education and housing, as well as through its endemically unstable political institutions.

The government at Stormont has been suspended for almost as long as it has been in operation since the institutions were set up in the wake of the Good Friday Agreement in 1998. Devolution was suspended from 2002 to 2007 when unionists withdrew from the institutions and again from 2017 to 2020 when Sinn Féin's Martin McGuinness resigned as deputy First Minister. After the May 2022 Assembly election, Sinn Féin became the largest party for the first time in history, and the DUP had to confront the fact that it would have to settle for the deputy First Minister position. However, the DUP's refusal to nominate a Speaker after the election in May has meant that neither the Assembly nor the governing Executive has been able to take office, and a caretaker administration has had to keep things going. This has led to a form of zombie government, where decisions have not been taken and money has not been spent, despite Belfast and the rest of Northern Ireland experiencing the worst energy crisis in several generations and numerous other challenges. At the time of writing (March 2023), the DUP's continued refusal to restore the devolved institutions has further degraded political stability and raises broader questions about the actual viability of power-sharing itself.

The second reason why Belfast (and Northern Ireland more generally) is being held back is due to external events over which it has little or no control. In the past these have related to British policies going back to the plantation of Ulster, the implementation of the Penal Laws and eventually to partition itself. More recently, British government ambivalence towards the people who live in Belfast and Northern Ireland as a whole was seen during the UK-wide referendum on membership of the EU in June 2016. During the debate and in the aftermath of the decision to leave the EU, the people in the capital of Northern Ireland were largely ignored.

Brexit hit Northern Ireland like a meteor from outer space. No one really saw it coming – or understood its implications. Seven years after the UK voted to leave the EU, it still represents the most significant political and economic challenge since the foundation of Northern Ireland in 1921. At the time of writing, Britain has churned its way through four different Prime

Ministers since David Cameron resigned on the steps of Downing Street on 24 June 2016, the day after the referendum vote. Despite this, we remain mired in the political and economic quagmire of Brexit, in part because of the British inability to understand that it would have altogether different implications for Belfast than for Birmingham or any other town or city in Great Britain.

Brexit sits as a counterpoint to partition, separated by nearly a century but bookending generations of political strife, cultural division and economic instability. Brexit was delivered by a British government against the wishes of a majority of people in Northern Ireland, who voted to remain within the EU, not to leave (by 56 per cent to 44 per cent) – though ultimately their wishes have been sublimated under those of the whole UK. This is the incendiary aspect of Brexit, in that it confronts us with the reality that the Good Friday Agreement, its devolved institutions and our democratic right to self-determination are subservient to the will of the British government, parliament and even the courts in London.

Like many other themes examined in this book, Brexit connects the present and future of Belfast to its past in a number of ways, many of them not appreciated by the government that still exercises sovereign responsibility for the region. The Irish border – to take one of the most immediate issues relating to the UK's departure from the EU – is not just a territorial demarcator, or even just a political one. It is, of course, both, but it is also a historical, cultural and psychological phenomenon with a resonance in Ireland that was not appreciated when viewed through a British lens. The rise of the border as a political issue after the referendum forced people in Belfast and across Northern Ireland to confront what the Good Friday Agreement had managed to de-escalate. In blunt terms: Which side of the binary line do you live on – the British part of Ireland or the Irish part of Ireland? In this sense, Brexit reweaponised partition and the 'constitutional question' which had been skilfully parked by the terms of the Good Friday Agreement since 1998.

As Britain has chewed through a series of prime ministers since 2016, so Belfast has seen a rapidly changing cast of characters in the Northern Ireland Office, with a procession of different politicians coming and going. While some incumbents have been more able than others, the ministerial churn has further disrupted and degraded the already fractious relationships between the parties at Stormont.

None of this has helped Belfast deal with other issues, such as endemic sectarianism; the persistence of paramilitary groups and growth of racketeering and other criminal activity; economic deprivation and urban decay; as well as the day-to-day struggle everyone in the city is facing over energy prices and the biggest cost of living crisis in a generation. The fact that the Stormont Assembly and Executive has been incapacitated so regularly in recent years has exacerbated many of these problems and diminished the opportunities to mitigate them. As there is no effective government at Stormont with power to set a budget or agree on new strategic initiatives, money given to the Executive that could be spent on health care, education or simply to deal with the growing number of derelict buildings in the city centre has been left unspent.

At the time of writing, politics remains in suspended animation, with the DUP refusing to nominate a Speaker of the Assembly since the May 2022 Assembly election. While a caretaker government kept things going during 2022, it remains to be seen if devolved government at Stormont based on power-sharing between unionists and nationalists actually has a viable future. Without it, the political divisions within Belfast and across Northern Ireland more broadly will only deepen, and the task of coming to terms with our divided past will become harder.

PRIDE IN BELFAST

All of this might seem a rather downbeat assessment of Belfast's future – pessimistic even. However, there is light as well as shade and plenty of room for optimism that the city is transitioning out of its violent past into a more stable and comfortable future. As previous chapters have demonstrated, Belfast is a city of huge potential with a rich heritage and vibrant cultural tradition. While problems remain, the city is changing and embracing opportunities to demonstrate that it wants to get past its one-dimensional image as a binary society demarcated by religious and political division. One very clear example of this change is in the way Belfast has embraced the

LGBTQ+ community and in particular the Pride festival. During the 1970s and 1980s, the city was defined by a civic homophobia, with unionist parties, especially the Democratic Unionists led by Free Presbyterian Moderator Rev. Ian Paisley, condemning non-heterosexual identities as sinful, ungodly or a sickness that needed to be cured. In 1977 Paisley formed 'Save Ulster from Sodomy', which campaigned against the decriminalisation of homosexuality in Northern Ireland. Ironically, the arch-unionist Paisley and his Free Presbyterian colleagues did not want British laws legalising homosexuality extended to the UK as a whole, and they campaigned vigorously against liberalising legislation.[10]

From this unpromising context, Belfast now has a thriving annual Pride festival, embraced by the city and by many of its political leaders and civic associations. The 2022 Pride festival in Belfast shows that the city is now light years ahead of its intolerant past, defining its civic identity today as inclusive, progressive and liberal. With over 130 events over the 10-day festival in July 2022, Belfast positioned itself as a modern and welcoming city, with the official programme showcasing one 'community, united in diversity'.[11] In her introductory remarks to the official guide for the Pride festival, Belfast's recently elected Lord Mayor Tina Black made a deliberate connection between the LGBTQ+ community and the city's ambition to be a diverse and equal society:

> Pride celebrates so much of what makes Belfast the city we all love – and is a resounding demonstration of the diversity and strength of the LGBTQ+ community and the people of Belfast. . . . As a Council, we are keen to promote Belfast as a city of equals, where everyone feels welcome, respected and most importantly safe. Belfast Pride plays a pivotal role in making this vision a reality.[12]

While there are many religiously conservative people in Belfast who remain intolerant of the LGBTQ+ community, it is clear that today this private position has been decoupled from public policymaking. It also shows that political parties and civic organisations can create dominant narratives that set the mood for what is deemed socially acceptable in terms of public debate. So while homophobia was once endemic within public policy in Belfast, it now occupies the territory of fly-tipping and spitting – while people still do it and think about doing it, they are much less enthusiastic about advertising it in public than perhaps used to be the case.

The 2022 Belfast Pride festival was estimated to have been the biggest ever in the city, having been cancelled for the previous two years due to the Covid pandemic, with somewhere in excess of the 60,000 people who took part in 2019. At the political level, there was a welcome demonstration of common cause by the main political parties, with enthusiastic and visible support from politicians such as Sinn Féin First Minister designate Michelle O'Neill and Sinn Féin MP for North Belfast John Finucane, who both took part in the Pride Parade on 30 July. O'Neill reiterated the importance of Pride as a symbol of inclusivity and equality for every community in Northern Ireland: 'This is also about standing up for people's rights and what is right – an equal society and a fair society. As a First Minister for all, I am going to stand up for everybody's rights and make sure that I bring that right to the centre of government.'[13]

Leading members of the SDLP and Alliance party were also enthusiastic participants in Pride, as they had been in previous years. Unionist leaders were also visible in support of Belfast Pride in 2022, including senior figures within the UUP, and there were even signs that the DUP's stance was beginning to change, as South Antrim MLA Pam Cameron took part in an LGBTQ+ event organised by PinkNews. While her remarks were rather oblique in support of the Pride festival, the fact the DUP participated at all should be seen as progress: 'I think no matter where you are on this, language is really important and it's really important that the language used is respectful and that applies to all sides of a debate.'[14] At the same event the previous year, Paula Bradley, then Deputy Leader of the DUP, apologised for the hurt caused to members of the LGBTQ+ community by comments made by party colleagues in the past, which she condemned as being 'absolutely atrocious'.

As well as policing the parade itself, the PSNI also sent a delegation to participate in it as a signal of its commitment towards the values and legal principles that it was dedicated to upholding. Gerard Pollock from the PSNI issued a statement during the festival about why the police were taking part and why Pride was important for the city: 'Pride is an important series of events for those who identify as being LGBT+ and we see this not just as an opportunity to highlight that hate crime, in whatever form, is wrong and the importance of reporting it but also to engage with and show our support for members of the LGBT+ community.'[15] This is a further example of the way Belfast has changed over the last generation, as the thought of the old RUC taking part in Belfast Pride during the 1970s would stretch credulity somewhat. The city is in the process of opening up, and despite the imperfections and inadequacies that remain, it is a place that has changed utterly since the 1970s and 1980s.

Equally importantly, 2022 saw major sporting organisations such as Ulster Rugby and the Gaelic Athletic Association (GAA) send official delegations to the Belfast Pride parade, demonstrating a progressive outlook and the commitment of both organisations towards equality for everyone in the city. While Ulster Rugby deserves recognition for the efforts it has made to promote inclusion and equality through outreach initiatives over the last number of years, East Belfast GAA stands out as a flagship civic organisation that connects sport with the post-conflict era. Kimberley Robertson, Chair of East Belfast GAA (and a native of Boston, Massachusetts), suggested that the ethos and values of Pride reinforced those of her own group, with its emphasis on inclusion and equality: 'We are welcoming to everybody, all walks of life, all communities. Everyone is welcome to find a home in East Belfast GAA and we really wanted to represent ourselves at Pride today.'[16]

BEYOND CULTURAL BINARIES

East Belfast GAA started as an idea on social media in the summer of 2020 and led to the establishment of a GAA team in a part of the city that it would have been inconceivable for them to have been based in during the height of the Troubles. It had been fifty years since a GAA team had existed in East Belfast, St Colmcille's having closed down in 1971 when political violence took hold in the city.[17] After East Belfast GAA was established in 2020, it faced occasional sectarian attacks, with a pipe bomb planted in a bin at the pitch where the players were training and a crude explosive device placed under a player's car shortly after they were formed.[18] Dave McGreevy, co-founder of the club, recalled that there was a low level of sectarian intimidation aimed at players and coaching staff in an attempt to force them out of the area: 'Someone was coming up and putting glass all over the pitches that our kids were using. There was spray-painted crosshair targets on the walls.'[19] However, the fact that it exists at all and is bringing Gaelic games to those in the community who want to play without any accompanying political agenda is a signifier of how Belfast is changing and that there is hope for a non-sectarian future in the city.

East Belfast GAA had their first full season in 2021 and have over 1,000 members from a wide array of religious, political and geographical backgrounds who came together through their love of the game. Their existence and non-partisan profile challenges the traditional unionist view of the GAA as being the sporting wing of Irish nationalism. Their logo contains the Harland and Wolff cranes in homage to East Belfast's industrial heritage, and the first President of the club was Linda Ervine, a Protestant, unionist, Irish-language activist. Ervine was the sister-in-law of former UVF member turned loyalist politician David Ervine, who was a high-profile member of the Progressive Unionist Party (PUP) negotiating team in the talks leading to the Good Friday Agreement in 1998. Linda Ervine remarked on the significance of the club and how there were now possibilities in Belfast to get beyond the binary identities of the past: 'I think it is a symbol of a shared space. It shows that, if you're one thing, it doesn't mean that you can't engage with something else. Coming from the background that I did, I never heard of GAA, I didn't know anything about GAA, but that has changed.'[20] The club reflects diversity and inclusivity in its identity, being careful to avoid orange and green in its kit choices, with a more neutral black with yellow stripes featuring on the team strip. In addition to the shipyard cranes, the club crest includes the red hand of Ulster, the shamrock and the thistle, while the motto 'Together' is included in English, Irish and Ulster Scots.[21] Dr Paul Mullan, Director of the National Lottery Heritage Fund in Northern Ireland, cited Ervine's work and the presence of East Belfast GAA as an example of the way in which spaces are opening for less binary and caricatured representations of identity and more nuanced and complex reflections of cultural practice: 'It is creating this kind of plural space where everybody is comfortable with being different but everyone is proud of where they're from. It is not about making Protestants more nationalist or anything like that. It is about recognising the complexity of your own story.'[22]

Despite such efforts at inclusivity, the existence of a GAA team in the predominantly unionist/loyalist community of East Belfast remains an affront to some who continue to define their identity in binary terms. For them, any sign of incursion by activities traditionally associated with the Irish nationalist community is deemed to be a threat to their British unionist identity. So, when Belfast City Council began to mark out a GAA pitch in Victoria Park with a view to the site becoming a permanent home for the club's training and matches, there was uproar from some loyalists on social media. Following the backlash, the council halted work and erased the pitch markings while it announced a rethink of its plans.[23] This incident demonstrates that, while the existence of East Belfast GAA shows that Belfast is changing and that identities are becoming more fluid, the journey is not a smooth one.

Another example of the way that the peace process is slowly allowing less binary identities to emerge in Belfast has been the growing interest in the Irish language within the Protestant unionist community. Irish-speaking has traditionally been identified with the nationalist and republican community and, for many unionists, with the political agenda of Sinn Féin. The welding together of the Irish language as a cultural practice and support for political reunification of Ireland and independence from Britain has certainly been apparent over the last fifty years. Irish republicans have used the Gaelic language as one of the indicators of the island's distinct cultural identity that defined the nation. This distinctiveness thus justified the exercise of political self-determination without the interference from 'foreign' countries such as the UK. For the last century, unionists, who define themselves as British, have struggled to engage with the Irish language in the zero-sum world where it might appear to lessen their British identity and thus Northern Ireland's constitutional position within the Union. However, the peace process of the 1990s helped to provide some space between these binary identities and allowed us to define our citizenship as Irish, or as British, or as both Irish and

British. This has been a bumpy journey over the last twenty-five years, not least because British governments have tried to renege on their Good Friday Agreement commitments when it has suited them to do so. After the Brexit referendum in 2016, the UK claimed that while this international treaty allows people in Northern Ireland to be both British and Irish, British law actually defines *everyone* as being British, not Irish, and that this domestic legislation trumps its treaty obligations.[24]

While there have been many setbacks in the implementation of the Good Friday Agreement since 1998, it has nevertheless opened up space for political and cultural identities to expand beyond the binary confines so evident in previous generations. Unionists have felt more able to explore their Irishness without feeling that it compromises their Britishness, while nationalists have been able to connect with aspects of their Britishness in a similar way. According to Mullan: 'You should be allowed to express your own sense of identity, otherwise you are forgetting it, or it's being denied to you. For me it's a fight against forgetting. It is about remembering better.'[25]

Linda Ervine had become active as an Irish language activist, content that love of the language was just as compatible with a Protestant unionist identity as it was with a Catholic nationalist outlook. Ervine said that she had a dual identity, both Irish and British, and that as people with complex backgrounds shared the island, the language should also be accessible to both traditions.[26] Ervine's story demonstrates once again the structural divisions within Belfast and how those can often act as a barrier to cultural diffusion and growth. While she wanted to learn Irish, there were no classes in her area because of its predominantly Protestant unionist population, so she was forced to look elsewhere:

In Northern Ireland we often see comments on social media saying that the Irish language is divisive, and that Protestants should not learn it. It is supposed to be the language of the enemy, the language of republicanism. As a working-class Protestant from East Belfast that has not been my experience. There was no opportunity to learn Irish in my part of the city back in 2011. So, the course I attended was in a centre in a nationalist area in South Belfast.[27]

Ervine started the Turas organisation to promote Irish language teaching among working-class unionists in East Belfast and found an appetite among people happy to embrace Irish as part of their culture without fearing that it undermines their political identity. From one class in 2012, Turas now runs over fourteen classes a week, with over three hundred people enrolled. Ervine sees Turas and its promotion of the Irish language as going beyond the language itself and helping to transform divisions within the city at a wider level: 'The work of Turas shows that the Irish language is not divisive. It is something that everyone can enjoy, and it can heal the results of decades of conflict and the legacy of division and fear.'[28] Predictably, this journey has not been a smooth one, and some within the Protestant loyalist community fear that the promotion of the Irish language within the Protestant community is undermining their British identity.

A plan to open an Irish language children's playgroup in East Belfast to provide bilingual early years education was affected by an online hate campaign within the Protestant loyalist community in 2021. Naíscoil na Seolta (meaning 'nursery of the sails', in homage to East Belfast's heritage of shipbuilding) was originally planned as the first Irish language school for children in East Belfast, to be hosted within the grounds of Braniel Primary School. However, following an online campaign by some sections of the loyalist community, Naíscoil na Seolta announced that it was withdrawing from Braniel due to concerns over the children's wellbeing and would seek a location in another part of East Belfast. The headteacher of Braniel Primary School, Diane Dawson, made her disappointment that the initiative would not go ahead at her school clear: 'I am saddened, I am sickened, I am angry, I am in despair about how we move Northern Ireland forward. What upsets me most is that my heart is for children. Why any child would be a threat on any school site is beyond me.'[29]

This provides another example of the complicated and difficult nature of Belfast's transition out of political division and the legacy of the past. Naíscoil na Seolta eventually found a new site in a church hall on the Belmont Road in the east of the city and opened its doors in October 2021.[30] However, the episode demonstrates the sensitivities surrounding efforts to build cultural initiatives that go beyond the parallel lines of binary identities a generation after the peace process was supposed to have made that a reality. The city is changing, but is not changed. It is certainly moving forwards, but the pace is sporadic, uncertain and easily reversed.

END OF AN ERA AND NEW BEGINNINGS

The response in Belfast to the death of Queen Elizabeth II in September 2022 provided another example of the way in which the city has changed over recent years. One of the most symbolic moments in the peace process had come during the Queen's visit to Belfast in 2012, which followed a state visit to the Irish Republic the previous year. Both visits were highly symbolic and had helped to cement improving political relationships between Britain and Ireland and normalise what had been politically abnormal for at least a generation.

Queen Elizabeth's reign spanned most people's living memory in Belfast and across the rest of Ireland and the UK. Her role, while constitutional and ceremonial, has also been political and cultural, as she was formally Head of State of the UK, Defender of the Protestant faith and titular head of the British Army. She was thus joined at the hip with the political and military establishment, and policies delivered in Belfast have been carried out in her name.

The Queen's four-day state visit to the Republic of Ireland in May 2011 was a hugely symbolic event for both countries. It marked the first time a British monarch had visited independent Ireland; when George V made the previous state visit a century earlier in 1911 there was no Irish border, and there was no Northern Ireland. The Queen's 2011 visit would never have taken place without the Good Friday Agreement in 1998 and political stability at Stormont.

Queen Elizabeth laid a wreath and bowed her head at the Garden of Remembrance in Dublin, at the graves of the Old IRA men and women who had fought against Britain for Irish independence in the early twentieth century. She also visited the Gaelic football stadium Croke Park, where British soldiers had shot and killed fourteen people in 1920, during the Irish War of Independence, in reprisal for an earlier IRA attack. At a state banquet, she gave a keynote speech that attempted to draw a line under the past and to mark out a new beginning for the two countries. While references to the British role in conflict in Ireland were oblique, they were there nonetheless, and were easily picked up by the ultra-sensitive hearing of everyone in the audience.

Building on this success, the Queen was back on the island of Ireland the following June – this time in the northern part – during her Diamond Jubilee tour, when she met with then Deputy First Minister Martin McGuinness at Belfast's Lyric Theatre. The chosen venue was a relatively neutral space, and Sinn Féin had also made it very clear that the event was to be understood as a celebration of the contribution of the arts to reconciliation in Northern Ireland, and certainly not connected to the Queen's Jubilee. As the former Chief of Staff of the Provisional IRA shook the delicate white-gloved hand of the titular head of the British Army on 27 June 2012, it was difficult to imagine a more emblematic moment in the peace process or in the journey Belfast itself had taken since partition in 1921 or the arrival of British troops in the summer of 1969.

In 2012, both Queen Elizabeth and Martin McGuinness were making peace rather than war, and although the British media focused on the Queen's magnanimity in meeting McGuinness, it was the Deputy First Minister who was taking the greater political risk. Shaking the hand of the Queen while holding office in an institution that recognised the political legitimacy of Northern Ireland was too much for some on the Irish republican side. But while militants attacked McGuinness for metaphorically 'bending the knee', they were few in number, and everyone else saw it as evidence of a growing political confidence within Irish nationalism.

This is important context to the announcement on 9 September 2022 that Queen Elizabeth II had died, triggering a lengthy period of national mourning, culminating with her state funeral ten days later. The response to the Queen's death in Belfast demonstrated once again how much the city has changed since the Troubles era. In past decades, it would have divided Belfast, but in September 2022 the city was united in paying its respects. There were, of course, sensitivities that those well attuned to politics in Northern Ireland could detect, but protocol was observed and there was little acrimony between unionists and nationalists across the city during the various civic events that took place. Inconceivable forty or even thirty years earlier, Sinn Féin and Irish nationalism more broadly paid its respects to the monarch to whom republicans were unwilling to swear allegiance while she was on the British throne, and who used to be referred to disparagingly by former Sinn Féin President Gerry Adams as 'Mrs Windsor'.

One of the striking things that became apparent from the protocol surrounding the Queen's funeral was how politically dominant republicans and nationalists had become in Belfast compared with their powerless minority status in 1952 when the Queen ascended the throne. In the 1951 British general election, Irish nationalists won none of the Belfast seats, with the Unionist Party returning MPs for three out of the four constituencies and an Irish Labour candidate winning in West Belfast. Fast-forward to the last general election before the Queen's death, in 2019, Irish nationalists now held three of the same four constituencies, Sinn Féin winning West and North Belfast and the SDLP returning Claire Hanna in South Belfast. Unionist representation in the city had been reduced to the one seat in East Belfast which has been held by Gavin Robinson of the DUP since 2015. Beyond Westminster, Sinn Féin had become the largest party in Northern Ireland in the 2022 Assembly election (the first time in Northern Ireland's 101-year history that a nationalist party had outpolled a unionist one).

As Sinn Féin has become more electorally successful and participated fully in political institutions within Northern Ireland, it has also matured and become more strategically astute. This was evident following the Queen's death but was also on show months earlier when Sinn Féin became the largest party in Northern Ireland and Michelle O'Neill became First Minister designate following the May 2022 Assembly election. Sinn Féin had focused its election campaign on getting the devolved institutions working for the *whole* community and on social and economic problems linked to the cost of living crisis. Sinn Féin's ambitions for Irish political reunification or for other objectives linked to its Irish cultural agenda, such as action on the long-awaited Irish Language Act, were sublimated under a relatively quiet campaign where it sought transfer votes (under Northern Ireland's proportional representation system) from people who might not define themselves as republicans. Since the election, O'Neill has repeatedly voiced her desire to get to work to address the issues and problems facing everyone in the community, and her ambition to be a First Minister for everyone in Northern Ireland.

This political context shaped Sinn Féin's response to the Queen's death and its participation in subsequent events to mark her passing, up to and including attending the state funeral in Westminster Abbey on 19 September. President of Sinn Féin Mary Lou McDonald (a possible future Taoiseach of the Republic of Ireland) issued a statement of condolence that was remarkable for its warmth and for the way it cast Queen Elizabeth as a peacemaker in Northern Ireland:

> I wish to extend deepest sympathy to the British Royal Family on the death of Queen Elizabeth II. Her passing marks the end of an era.
>
> ... I salute her contribution to the huge change that has evolved in recent years.
>
> Her death is a moment of heartbreak and pride for the British people. To them, and especially to Irish unionists, I extend on behalf of Sinn Féin and Irish Republicans sincere condolences.
>
> *Ar dheis Dé go raibh a hanam dilis.*[31]

This was carefully crafted wording which was both warm and effusive, while also making clear that this was a moment of heartbreak for *British* people rather than *Irish* people, and that republicans recognised and sympathised with the pain, rather than sharing in it themselves. Sinn Féin Vice President and First Minister designate Michelle O'Neill's remarks were similar in tone, emphasising that she deeply regretted the death of the Queen and offering her sincere sympathies and condolences to the family. She singled out the unionist community in Northern Ireland and acknowledged the profound sorrow that *they* would feel, and went on to pay tribute to the positive role that the Queen had played in the peace process: 'Personally, I am grateful for Queen Elizabeth's significant contribution and determined efforts to advancing peace and reconciliation between our two islands. Throughout the peace process she led by example in building relationships with those of us who are Irish, and who share a different political allegiance and aspirations to herself and her Government.'[32]

One of the most notable events during the period came with the arrival of the newly minted King Charles III to Belfast for a memorial service at St Anne's Cathedral. The previous day, the outgoing Speaker of the Assembly, Sinn Féin's Alex Maskey, had led tributes to the Queen in advance of the new King's visit, with a book of condolence opened at Stormont. Unusually for the Assembly (which had been recalled for the occasion), none of the rancour that was usually in plentiful supply was in evidence, as the politicians all found common cause with each other.

The following day King Charles III met politicians and other civic leaders at Hillsborough Castle. He and First Minister designate Michelle O'Neill seemed at ease in one another's company, and, to the amusement of many, the new King seemed more familiar with the Sinn Féin Vice President than with the leader of the DUP. He appeared not to know Sir Jeffrey Donaldson, and when he quipped to O'Neill that her party was now the largest in Northern Ireland, Maskey joked back, 'Don't tell Jeffrey'.[33]

The royal party then travelled on to the service at St Anne's, where 'an assembly of unionists, republicans, nationalists and those for whom the Constitution is not a main focus united to pay tribute to the late Queen. When she first came to the throne,' said the BBC report, 'no one would have anticipated an assembly so diverse and inclusive.'[34] Alex Maskey delivered a message of condolence to King Charles on behalf of the people of Northern Ireland. His remarks recognised Queen Elizabeth's interest in the peace process but also contained a message to those who remained stuck in a zero-sum mentality over political and cultural diversity:

> She showed that a small and insignificant gesture – a visit, a handshake, crossing the street or speaking a few words of Irish – can make a huge difference in changing attitudes and building relationships. The Queen's recognition of both British and Irish traditions, as well as the wider diversity of the community was 'exceptionally significant'. . . . In all of this she personally underlined that one tradition is not diminished by reaching out to show respect to another.[35]

If anyone had suggested during the 1970s when Maskey was interned, or in the 1980s when he was shot and injured by loyalist paramilitaries, that a few decades later he would be leading tributes to the recently deceased British Head of State and joking with her successor, few would have believed them. The ease and generosity of spirit evident between the King and republicans responsible for the assassination of Charles' uncle Lord Mountbatten in 1979 and Sinn Féin veterans like Maskey, who had accused the British armed forces of repeated attempts to have him assassinated during the 1980s, was something to behold in 2022.

The visit of King Charles to Hillsborough and Belfast and the unproblematic attendance of Sinn Féin leaders and Irish nationalist politicians at the Queen's state funeral at Westminster Abbey built on previous visits and meetings. It would be difficult to think of a more symbolic example of the transition of Belfast as a city since the bleak days of the Troubles a generation before.

TO 2024 AND BEYOND

The city of Belfast is slowly casting off its reputation as a centre of religious intolerance, political division and violence. Mistrust and insecurity over rival cultural and political identities certainly remains within the DNA of the city, and this is likely to endure so long as the structural divisions within society persist. However, this is gradually being overlaid with a more progressive and inclusive quality as Belfast opens up to its own citizens as well as external visitors. Key to this has been the peace process and much-maligned political institutions that despite their inadequacy have helped to bring a measure of stability to Belfast and Northern Ireland as a whole. However, to paraphrase Winston Churchill's often-cited remark about the inadequacy of democracy, 'power-sharing is the worst form of government – except for all the others'. The devolved institutions that were established at Stormont the year after the Good Friday Agreement was concluded have undoubtedly been dysfunctional, but they have nonetheless provided a stability that has allowed other things to happen. The violence that tore the city apart during the 1970s and 1980s has reduced hugely, and while sectarianism remains, today Belfast is a relatively safe place, certainly when measured against cities of comparable size in the rest of the UK or Ireland.

The city has undergone a demographic revolution, and the cultural, economic and political dominance of the Protestant/unionist/British community has been counterbalanced by the growth of those who identify more closely with the Catholic/nationalist/Irish tradition. There are, of course, nuances behind the numbers, but the fundamental message from all the data is that Belfast has changed and majority community no longer means what it used to. Notions of community have become more fractured, diverse and complex, and the city is changing to reflect that reality.

Dr Paul Mullan reflected on the changes that have taken place in the city's civic spaces over the last decade. He suggested that both demographic shifts and the Good Friday Agreement have been fundamental to the way in which the city is being reimagined. He noted that, as a result, there was a new receptiveness to compromise within political parties on the council when he devised the 'principles for remembering' in 2010:

> Unionism at this point in time is realising, 'We're not in the majority anymore. We are going to have to hold on. How do we hold on to what we have here?' But also nationalism is going, 'Well, if we could make a few wins here that doesn't necessarily mean that unionism has to lose and some form of compromise could actually help us all.' The party leaders all were able to agree. . . . They were able to agree a reimagined city hall and that is what you see now. And that also happened during the time of the flags protest. Compromises were made.[36]

Belfast now has a vibrant night-time economy, a burgeoning tourist industry and a hotel sector that has grown exponentially since the peace process of the 1990s. Despite its flaws and inadequacies, twenty-five years since the Good Friday Agreement was concluded, Belfast now has a level of political stability, economic regeneration and infrastructural capacity that has led to a new-found civic confidence. 'The Belfast Agenda',[37] published in 2017 by Belfast City Council, was the culmination of two years of consultation with other stakeholder groups to construct a shared vision for the city and a set of practical steps to achieve it. 'The Belfast Agenda' developed a vision to 2035 which did not fall short in ambition: 'Belfast will be a city re-imagined and resurgent. A great place to live and work for everyone. Beautiful, well connected and culturally vibrant, it will be a sustainable city shared and loved by all its citizens, free from the legacy of conflict.'[38] Despite the rather breathless advertising agency feel of the language, the fact that such ideas could even be written down in 2017 says something positive about Belfast's direction of travel. To be fair to it, the vision was accompanied by a series of more tangible benchmarks linked to investment, productivity, employment, external tourism and deprivation, which can be measured over the next decade to assess how close the strategy is to accomplishing its objectives.

The ambition inherent within 'The Belfast Agenda' was displayed in 2017 when Belfast City Council joined forces with Derry and Strabane councils to launch a bid to become European Capital of Culture in 2023. Belfast had applied unsuccessfully in 2008 so it was thought that a joint bid would be more competitive and cost-effective this time around. Despite the Brexit referendum the previous year, it was believed that the UK's decision to leave the EU would not affect the eligibility of a UK city in 2023, as non-EU cities such as Istanbul had previously been successful in the competition. However, these hopes were dashed in November 2017 when the European Commission announced that it was removing the UK from eligibility. Talks took place the following year with the Commission to get the decision reversed, but it was confirmed in 2018 that the application to become the European Capital of Culture in 2023 was 'no longer viable'.[39]

Despite the obvious disappointment at this decision, Belfast City Council decided to proceed with aspects of its application and have a twelve-month programme of cultural events in the city in 2023 that would showcase a number of aspects of its original bid. This was crystallised into Belfast City Council's cultural strategy published in 2019 and entitled 'A City Imagining', which built on the vision of cultural diversity and inclusivity evident in 'The Belfast Agenda'. 'A City Imagining' was careful not to be too prescriptive about how it defined culture or sought to operationalise it, the emphasis being on the council and its partners acting as facilitators for community-driven initiatives during a year of cultural celebration in 2023.

'A City Imagining' was an ambitious prospectus that announced the intention to press ahead with a year of 'immersive cultural activity' in 2023 despite no longer being in the running to badge Belfast as a European Capital of Culture. This was to include securing the designation of Belfast as a UNESCO City of Music, which was achieved in November 2021 when the United Nations granted the award in recognition of the city's 'rich musical heritage'.

Unfortunately, some of the activities planned for Belfast's year of culture in 2023 were impacted by the Covid pandemic, and as a result Belfast City Council has put the initiative back to 2024. Whatever cultural programme is delivered across the city in 2024 and beyond, there can be little debate that it has been facilitated by the generation of relative stability since the peace process of the late 1990s. Belfast has always been culturally vibrant, but the emergence of the post-conflict economy and the opening up of the city to external tourists has helped to provide the economic infrastructure to harness and foster the talent that exists.

Belfast's revitalisation has been reflected in its recent status as a centre for film and television production, and by the fact that the city was given the Hollywood treatment in Sir Kenneth Branagh's film loosely based on his childhood. *Belfast* was nominated for a number of Oscars at the 94th Academy Awards ceremony, and won an Oscar for Best Original Screenplay. In an emotional acceptance speech, Branagh said that the film was the search for hope and joy in the face of violence and loss: 'we will never forget all of those lost in the heartbreaking, heartwarming, human story of that amazing city of Belfast on the fabulous island of Ireland'.[40] While not everyone liked its sepia-toned, slightly folksy reflection on the past, the fact that his nostalgic love letter to the city was made at all is a tribute to where the city finds itself today. We can always quibble over and critique how we look back at the past – but the 1968–98 era does at least feel like it is receding into history now, in terms of the politically motivated violence that defined it.

I go back to Belfast three or four times a year, sometimes more frequently, if I have an excuse. I have been doing so for twenty-five years since I first 'immigrated' to Britain for an academic job in 1998. Luckily my partner is second-generation Irish so has indulged my salmon-like impulse to return home on a regular basis. The journey has become something of a family ritual, especially when we drive up to Scotland to get the ferry, and the feeling of excited anticipation when sailing up Belfast Lough has never dimmed. If Stena Line ferries knew how much business I have given them over the last twenty-five years, I like to think they would have given me a lifetime service award by now.

Thankfully, my eleven-year-old son also now regards Belfast as his second home, as he has been there so often and has learned that when he's asked to name the best city in the world, if he says 'Belfast', an ice cream will come his way within minutes.

The last time we were home, I was struck by two things that for me epitomise Belfast today. Firstly, the level of urban decay in the city is palpable, even in parts of South Belfast that are relatively affluent. Botanic Avenue and Great Victoria Street cover an area that stretches from Queen's University down into the centre of the city and used to be known as the 'golden mile' because of the preponderance of bars, restaurants and night life, as well as its vibrant day-time economy. In the old days, it was where students spent their maintenance grants, when such luxuries existed, and latterly where they spent their student loans. Walking around it when I was back for the New Year in 2023, I was struck by the number of derelict buildings and by just how dilapidated the area has become. Some beautiful Victorian houses have been abandoned for so long that vegetation is growing out of their broken windows and rusting guttering. Some of this is a result of the area becoming dominated by student housing, avaricious private landlords and the migration of local communities out of the area because of falling house prices and anti-social behaviour. Some landlords are notoriously slow to repair student houses because the expansion of Queen's and Ulster Universities has produced an abundant supply of students and an under-supply of accommodation. As a result, landlords know that they can maximise profit by cramming students into overcrowded and poorly maintained properties, and if the tenant cannot put up with the conditions, there will always be another who can.

I know from personal experience how bad some of the housing is in the university area, as I wrote my first book in the early 1990s as a postdoctoral student with a family of rats for company, a collapsed ceiling in the toilet and no hot water. The landlord kept promising to do repairs but never got around to doing them, and the noise of rats gnawing through skirting boards at night has stayed with me to this day. Thankfully, I was saved from the rat horde by getting a job at Ulster University and moving up to the beautiful north coast.[41]

However, that was thirty years ago, and not all of today's decay in the city centre can be blamed on students or greedy landlords. Disinvestment, property developers buying buildings and waiting for nature to destroy them so they don't have to and a lack of long-term urban planning are equally if not more to blame for the fact that buildings are being abandoned and left to disintegrate in the commercial heart of the city.

This rather depressing thought was tempered by the second thing that struck me as I walked around the city, which was that, despite the dilapidation and decay, a huge amount of new investment was plain to see, as was the sheer volume of tourists walking around. It seems as if every time I go back another gleaming glass hotel or office block has been erected, while Belfast City Hall illuminated in blue at night-time looks like a beautiful sapphire right in the heart of the city centre.

The Belfast Region City Deal worth around £1 billion was announced in December 2021, and looks set to bring a fresh wave of jobs and investment into the city. This partnership of public and private sector money was hailed as 'transformative' by parties and business groups across the political spectrum and suggests that up to 20,000 new jobs will be created in the digital and creative industries, as well as in manufacturing, over the next decade. The final phase of Ulster University's enhanced Belfast campus opened at the start of the 2022–23 academic year, bringing an additional 15,000 students and staff into the city. This 75,000-square-metre campus on the edge of the Cathedral Quarter area is an unmissable addition to the city's building stock and provides yet another example of the transformation of the built environment in Belfast.

Even Harland and Wolff shipyard is preparing itself for an unlikely relaunch, having recently won a contract worth £1.6 billion to build three new ships for the Royal Navy. Harland and Wolff has not built a new ship since 2003 and was reduced to oil rig refurbishment and building offshore wind turbines in recent years. However, it was bought out of receivership in 2020 by London-based company InfraStrata and anticipates its skeleton crew of just over 200 to expand to over 1,000 and work to commence on the ships in 2025. This contract could, if the shipyard delivers on its side of the bargain over the next decade, provide a new lease of life for the most famous manufacturing name in the city. In fact, Harland and Wolff coming back from the dead provides a perfect metaphor for the rise of Belfast itself in the twenty-first century.

Aesthetically, this new investment in the centre of Belfast seems at odds with the dilapidation and decay that surrounds it, but it is to be welcomed nonetheless. The new wave of public art in the city, especially around the Cathedral Quarter, is a tourist attraction in its own right. Belfast used to showcase contested identities and its divided history on wall murals in the east and west of the city, and many of these still remain and have a legitimacy in their own right, but they have been supplemented now with more abstract artworks that have nothing to do with the Troubles era. These are not only interesting and evocative in themselves, but they also highlight a new wave of cultural energy in the city and provide a hopeful vision for the future.

Everywhere you look in the centre of town you can see small gaggles of people, pessimistically dressed in rainwear, listening intently to tour guides telling them about the history of the city. I found this quite inspiring, as I could see first-hand that people are coming to visit the city, are learning more about its history and, if Tripadvisor reviews are to be believed, are going away for the most part with a positive impression. This can only result in reputational benefits for Belfast and will give it a real chance to showcase its history and culture, and the greatest asset of all – its people.

Belfast still has significant political and cultural divisions and economic challenges, but it has surely never been better placed to face them over the last hundred years than it is today.

ENDNOTES

PREFACE

1. Use of the word 'murder' here is provocative and political, and it is deliberately so. The Parachute Regiment shot dead fourteen unarmed people intentionally – several of whom were children shot in the back and none of whom posed a threat. 'Murder' (rather than the more neutral 'killing') would seem to be appropriate but is still likely to be seen by some readers as provocative. But the fact that it is so relates to the denial of responsibility for this celebrated case of injustice for a generation by the UK, until the Saville Inquiry and former Prime Minister David Cameron's unequivocal apology in 2010.
2. The Royal Military Police were nicknamed the 'red caps' because of their scarlet berets, but they were effectively a branch of the British military rather than the local police force.

INTRODUCTION

1. Graham Spencer, *Disturbing the Peace?* (London: Ashgate, 2000). See also Roy Greenslade, 'The Belfast Blindspot: How Britain Still Doesn't Get Northern Ireland, *New Statesman*, 23 October 2019, https://www.newstatesman.com/politics/northern-ireland/2019/10/belfast-blindspot-how-britain-still-doesn-t-get-northern-ireland.
2. BBC 24 Hours, 'Bernadette Devlin Attacks British Home Secretary', 31 January 1972, https://www.bbc.co.uk/programmes/p00nm166.
3. Ed Pearce, 'One Long Piece of Perplexity', *Fortnight*, issue 296 (June 1991), p. 15.
4. This was before risk assessment forms (as distinct from research ethics forms) became pervasive within the higher education sector in the UK. The point being made here is not that risk assessment is not needed, merely that Belfast was singled out for it by my institution when research in London, for instance, was not deemed to need such risk management.
5. Jack Boulton, 'Frontier Wars: Violence and Space in Belfast, Northern Ireland', *Totem: The University of Western Ontario Journal of Anthropology*, vol. 22, issue 1 (2014).
6. Martin Dillon, *The Shankill Butchers: A Case Study of Mass Murder* (London: Cornerstone, 1990).
7. Frank Wright, *Northern Ireland: A Comparative Analysis* (London: Rowman & Littlefield, 1988).
8. See Feargal Cochrane, *Ending Wars* (Cambridge: Polity, 2008); John Paul Lederarch, *Building Peace* (Washington: United States Institute for Peace, 1999).
9. François Molle, 'Water, Politics, and River Basin Governance: Repoliticizing Approaches to River Basin Management', *Water International*, vol. 34, issue 1 (2009), pp. 62–70.

10. Fergus Whelan, *May Tyrants Tremble: The Life of William Drennan, 1754–1820* (Dublin: Irish Academic Press, 2020).

11. Jim Smyth, 'Wolfe Tone's Library: The United Irishmen and "Enlightenment"', *Eighteenth-Century Studies*, vol. 45, issue 3 (2012).

12. Mary McNeill, *The Life and Times of Mary Ann McCracken, 1770–1866: A Belfast Panorama* (Dublin: Irish Academic Press, 2019).

13. Dr Paul Mullan, Director, National Lottery Heritage Fund for Northern Ireland. Interviewed by author, 21 February 2022.

14. Dr Paul Mullan. Interviewed by author.

CHAPTER 1: THE LAGAN AND THE LINEN

1. Marianne Elliott, *Hearthlands* (Belfast: Blackstaff Press, 2017), p. 5.

2. Elliott, *Hearthlands*, p. 8.

3. Molle, 'Water, Politics, and River Basin Governance'.

4. Jonathan Bardon, *Belfast: An Illustrated History* (Belfast: Blackstaff Press, 1982), p. 8.

5. Bardon, *Belfast*, pp. 9–10.

6. Bardon, *Belfast*, p. 10.

7. Cathal O'Byrne, *As I Roved Out*, reprinted edn (Belfast: Blackstaff Press, 1982), p. 34. (First edn Belfast: Irish News, 1946).

8. O'Byrne, *As I Roved Out*, p. 34.

9. As a result of English government policies, Catholic land ownership fell from around 60 per cent in 1641 to 14 per cent by 1703, following William's victory over James II and the subsequent 'Act of Settlement'. By the 1750s, the figure is estimated to have fallen to around 5 per cent.

10. BBC News, 'Belfast's Secret Rivers Revealed', 29 April 2010, http://news.bbc.co.uk/1/hi/northern_ireland/8651644.stm.

11. 4NI.co.uk, 'Belfast's Hidden Rivers "Uncovered"', 29 April 2010, https://www.4ni.co.uk/northern-ireland-news/110735/belfast-s-hidden-rivers-uncovered.

12. Creative Belfast Uncovered, 'Creative Belfast Uncovered – The River Farset', 23 May 2016, https://www.youtube.com/watch?v=D_lwebv5An0.

13. Rebecca Black, 'Poll: £100k for Belfast's Giant Tulip in Middle of Nowhere – Is It Worth It?', *Belfast Telegraph*, 16 September 2016, https://www.belfasttelegraph.co.uk/news/northern-ireland/poll-100k-for-belfasts-giant-tulip-in-middle-of-nowhere-is-it-worth-it-35052529.html.

14. BBC News, 'Belfast's *Origin* Wins Spectator "Worst Public Art" Award', 27 March 2017, https://www.bbc.co.uk/news/uk-northern-ireland-39403983.

15. For more detail see Raymond Gillespie, *Early Belfast: The Origins and Growth of an Ulster Town to 1750* (Belfast: Ulster Historical Foundation, 2007).

16. Ciaran Carson, *The Star Factory* (London: Head of Zeus, 1997), p. 46.

17. Carson, *The Star Factory*, p. 48.

18. Gerry Adams, *Falls Memories* (Dublin: Brandon Books, 1982), p. 142.

19. Carson, *The Star Factory*, p. 48.

20. Bardon, *Belfast*, p. 2.

21. William Maguire, *Belfast: A History* (Lancaster: Carnegie Books, 2009), p. 55.

22. W.A. McCutcheon, *The Canals of the North of Ireland* (Newton Abbot: David & Charles, 1965), pp. 40–1.

23. McCutcheon, *The Canals of the North of Ireland*, pp. 44–5.

24. Bardon, *Belfast*, p. 71.

25. Bardon, *Belfast*, p. 71.

26. S.J. Connolly (ed.), *Belfast 400: People, Place and History* (Liverpool: Liverpool University Press, 2012), p. 196.

27. Bardon, *Belfast*, pp. 90–1.

28. Bardon, *Belfast*, p. 34.

29. Linde Lunney, 'Joy, Robert', *Dictionary of Irish Biography*, October 2009, https://www.dib.ie/biography/joy-robert-a4358.

30. Bardon, *Belfast*, p. 44.

31. Bardon, *Belfast*, p. 66.

32. Bardon, *Belfast*, p. 68.

33. Stephen Royale, 'Workshop of the Empire, 1820–1914', in S.J. Connolly (ed.), *Belfast 400: People, Place and History* (Liverpool: Liverpool University Press, 2012), p. 214.

34. Rosemary Cullen Owens, *A Social History of Women in Ireland, 1870–1970* (Dublin: Gill & Macmillan, 2005), p. 194.

35. Frank Frankfort Moore, *In Belfast by the Sea* (Dublin: University of Dublin Press, 2007), pp. 56–7.

36. Royale, 'Workshop of the Empire', p. 209.

37. Maguire, *Belfast*, p. 81 (though the census that year operated within an expanded map of Belfast, thus covering a greater area than previous surveys).

38. Clifton House, 'The Cholera Pandemic of 1832: Preparations Begin', https://cliftonbelfast.com/the-cholera-pandemic-of-1832-preparations-begin/.

39. Maguire, *Belfast*, p. 82.

40. Maguire, *Belfast*, p. 83.

CHAPTER 2: THE RADICALISM

1. John Ranelagh, *Ireland: An Illustrated History* (London: HarperCollins, 1981), p. 116.

2. Edmund Curtis, *A History of Ireland* (London: Methuen, 1936), p. 287.

3. Daniel Defoe, 'The paralel: or, persecution of Protestants the shortest way to prevent the growth of popery in Ireland' (originally published 1704, reprinted Gale ECCO print edition, 2010).

4. Ulster-Scots Society of America, 'Ulster Scots and the Birth of America', http://www.ulsterscotssociety.com/about_ulster-scots.html.

5. Bardon, *Belfast*, p. 47.

6. Roger Courtney, *Dissenting Voices: Rediscovering the Irish Progressive Presbyterian Tradition* (Belfast: Ulster Historical Foundation, 2013).

7. Roy Foster, *Modern Ireland, 1600–1972* (London: Penguin, 1988), p. 265.

8. Bill Rolston, 'A Lying Old Scoundrel', *History Ireland*, vol. 11, issue 1 (2003).

9. O'Byrne, *As I Roved Out*, p. 47.

10. O'Byrne, *As I Roved Out*, p. 47.

11. C.J. Woods, 'Cunningham, Waddell', *Dictionary of Irish Biography*, October 2009, https://www.dib.ie/biography/cunningham-waddell-a2312.

12. O'Byrne, *As I Roved Out*, p. 12.

13. Rolston, 'A Lying Old Scoundrel'.

14. For more on the life and significance of Mary Ann McCracken, see McNeill, *The Life and Times of Mary Ann McCracken*.

15. Clifton House was opened in 1774 as Belfast's first poorhouse. It then became a nursing home for over 100 years and is now an events and meeting space.

16. Clifton House, https://cliftonbelfast.com/event/iwd-2022-mary-ann-mccracken-1770-1866-mary-alice-mcneill-1897-1984-their-lives-legacies/; Belfast Charitable Society, https://belfastcharitablesociety.org/mary-ann-mccracken-foundation/.

17. Some put his appointment to the Belfast Society later, at 1793; see James Quinn, 'Thomas Russell, United Irishman', *History Ireland*, vol. 10, issue 1 (2002),

https://www.historyireland.com/18th-19th-century-history/thomas-russell-united-irishman/.

18. R.B. McDowell, 'The Personnel of the Dublin Society of United Irishmen, 1791–4', *Irish Historical Studies*, vol. 2, issue 5 (1940), p. 12.

19. Whelan, *May Tyrants Tremble*.

20. Extract from a letter from Dr William Drennan to Samuel McTier, 21 May 1791. Jean Agnew (ed.), *Drennan–McTier Letters, Volume 1* (Dublin: Women's History Project, 1998), p. 357, quoted in C.M. Barry, 'Benevolent conspiracy', *Irish Philosophy*, 5 February 2015, https://www.irishphilosophy.com/category/person/long-18th-century/william-drennan/.

21. Quoted in Bardon, *A History of Ulster*, pp. 222–3.

22. For more on the life and political significance of Wolfe Tone, read Marianne Elliott, *Partners in Revolution: The United Irishmen and France* (New Haven and London: Yale University Press, 1990).

23. Richard Madden, *The United Irishmen, Their Lives and Times* (Dublin: Martin Lester, 1843), p. 223, https://archive.org/stream/s1unitedirishmen01madduoft/s1unitedirishmen01madduoft_djvu.txt.

24. Kenneth Dawson, *The Belfast Jacobin: Samuel Neilson and the United Irishmen* (Dublin: Irish Academic Press, 2017).

25. A.T.Q. Stewart, 'The Transformation of Presbyterian Radicalism in the North of Ireland 1792–1825', unpublished MA thesis, Queen's University Belfast, 1956, pp. 7–8.

26. Bardon, *A History of Ulster*, p. 221.

27. Foster, *Modern Ireland*, p. 266.

28. Bardon, *A History of Ulster*, p. 230.

29. James Quinn, 'Lake, Gerard', *Dictionary of Irish Biography*, October 2009, https://www.dib.ie/biography/lake-gerard-a4643.

30. Quinn, 'Lake, Gerard'.

31. Maguire, *Belfast*, p. 63.

32. Bardon, *Belfast* p. 64.

33. Maguire, *Belfast*, p. 63.

34. Daniel Grahan, 'The Scullabogue Massacre', *History Ireland*, vol. 4, issue 3 (1996), https://www.historyireland.com/18th-19th-century-history/the-scullabogue-massacre-1798/.

35. Letter from William Drennan to Mrs McTier, June 1801, quoted in Feargal Cochrane, 'The Unionist Response to the Anglo-Irish Agreement', unpublished PhD thesis, Queen's University Belfast, December 1992, p. 91.

36. Peter Froggatt, 'MacDonnell, James', *Dictionary of Irish Biography*, May 2012, https://www.dib.ie/biography/macdonnell-james-a5184.

37. Froggatt, 'MacDonnell, James'.

38. Guy Beiner, *Forgetful Remembrance: Social Forgetting and Vernacular Historiography of a Rebellion in Ulster* (Oxford: Oxford University Press, 2018).

CHAPTER 3: THE SHIPS

1. Samson was built in 1974 and Goliath in 1969.

2. Connor Lynch, 'East Belfast GAA Unveil New Club Crest Ahead of First Matches This Weekend', *Belfast Live*, 16 July 2020, https://www.belfastlive.co.uk/news/belfast-news/east-belfast-gaa-unveil-new-18609335.

3. Carnduff's portable typewriter is now held in the Ulster Museum in Belfast.

4. 'Wee Yard' was the colloquial name for Harland and Wolff's rival shipyard Workman Clark and Company.

5. Laurence Kirkpatrick, 'The "Eagle Wing" 1636', *Presbyterian Historical Society of Ireland*, https://www.presbyterianhistoryireland.com/history/the-eagle-wing-1636/.
6. Bardon, *Belfast*, p. 110.
7. Kevin Johnson, 'Sectarianism and the Shipyard', *Irish Times*, 29 November 2008, https://www.irishtimes.com/news/sectarianism-and-the-shipyard-1.916936.
8. Bardon, *Belfast*, p. 128.
9. Jonathan Bardon, *A History of Ulster* (Belfast: Blackstaff Press, 1992), p. 335.
10. Johnson, 'Sectarianism and the Shipyard'.
11. Bardon, *A History of Ulster*, pp. 335–6.
12. Stephen Cameron, *Titanic: Belfast's Own* (Newtownards: Colourpoint, 2011), pp. 11–12.
13. Johnson, 'Sectarianism and the Shipyard'.
14. Bardon, *Belfast*, p. 114.
15. John Dorney, 'In the Hands of an Armed Mob – The Belfast Riots of 1864', *Irish Story*, 9 April 2020, https://www.theirishstory.com/2020/04/09/in-the-hands-of-an-armed-mob-the-belfast-riots-of-1864/#.YbdIAZHP02x.
16. Andrew Boyd, *Holy War in Belfast* (Tralee: Anvil Books, 1969), pp. 12–13.
17. Boyd, *Holy War in Belfast*, p. 21.
18. Fergus O'Ferrell, 'Daniel O'Connell and Henry Cooke: The Battle for Civil and Religious Liberty in Modern Ireland', *Irish Review*, issue 1 (1986), p. 23.
19. Janice Holmes, 'Hanna, Hugh', *Dictionary of Irish Biography*, October 2009, https://www.dib.ie/biography/hanna-hugh-a3787.
20. Boyd, *Holy War in Belfast*, p. 39.
21. Holmes, 'Hanna, Hugh'.
22. Wyn Craig Wade, *The Titanic: End of a Dream* (1979), quoted in Ciaran Carson, *The Star Factory* (London: Head of Zeus, 1997), p. 55.
23. Bardon, *Belfast*, p. 130.
24. David Hammond, *Steelchest, Nail in the Boot & the Barking Dog: The Belfast Shipyard – A Story of the People by the People* (Belfast: Flying Fox Films, 1986), pp. 107–8.
25. Bardon, *Belfast*, p. 175.
26. Pirrie's legacy lives on today in the Titanic Hotel in Belfast; his original office has been restored and the William Pirrie Room can now be hired out for large corporate meetings.
27. Cameron, *Titanic*, p. 19.
28. Hammond, *Steelchest, Nail in the Boot & the Barking Dog*, p. 85.
29. Cameron, *Titanic*, p. 24.
30. Michael McCaughan, 'The Ultimate Disaster Symbol', *Causeway* (Winter 1996), p. 22, https://www.dividedsociety.org/journals/causeway-cultural-traditions-journal/vol-3-no-4/ultimate-disaster-symbol.
31. McCaughan, 'The Ultimate Disaster Symbol'.
32. Connal Parr, 'Expelled from Yard and Tribe: The "Rotten Prods" of 1920 and Their Political Legacies', *Studi Irlandesi*, vol. 11, issue 11 (2021), p. 301.
33. Parr, 'Expelled from Yard and Tribe', pp. 299–321.
34. Henry Patterson, 'The Belfast Shipyard Expulsions', *Creative Centenaries*, 29 March 2021, https://www.creativecentenaries.org/blog/the-belfast-shipyard-expulsions.
35. Patterson, 'The Belfast Shipyard Expulsions'.
36. While six counties of Ulster were incorporated into Northern Ireland, the other three counties in Ulster, Monaghan, Cavan and Donegal, were not, and they joined the rest of what became known as the Free State in independent Ireland. This is one of the reasons why Irish nationalists object to Northern Ireland and Ulster being

used co-terminously by politicians and in the media, as they claim it is an artificial and illegitimate entity.

37. Maguire, *Belfast: A History*, p. 195.

CHAPTER 4: THE BUILDINGS

1. The selection of buildings is intended to be indicative, not exhaustive, and it is recognised that many other buildings not listed here also have strong cases for inclusion. The Europa Hotel, for instance, known locally as the most bombed hotel in Europe, as it withstood over thirty bomb attacks during the Troubles, could easily have been included in the chapter. The Europa hosted President Bill Clinton and Hillary Clinton during his 1995 visit to Belfast and on subsequent occasions, letting out over 100 of the hotel rooms to his presidential entourage. The Europa also played a role in the peace process when, during the referendum campaign on the Belfast/ Good Friday Agreement, it allowed the Independent Yes Campaign to unfurl a huge YES sign from the roof halfway down the building. However, the objective here is not to provide a complete listing of important buildings in Belfast but rather to use a selection of them to illustrate their significance across different periods in the city's history.
2. John Killen, *A History of the Linen Hall Library 1788–1988* (Belfast: Linen Hall Library, 1990), p. ix.
3. Killen, *A History of the Linen Hall Library*, pp. 5–6.
4. Killen, *A History of the Linen Hall Library*, p. 117.
5. Connolly, *Belfast 400*, p. 162.
6. Bardon, *Belfast*, p. 56.
7. Personal comment to author and to the participants on the 1798 Walking Tour of Belfast, 20 February 2022.
8. Officially known as the Civil Authorities (Special Powers) Act (Northern Ireland) 1922, this was emergency legislation renewed annually to maintain public order and was passed by the Northern Ireland Parliament in 1922. See Conflict Archive on the Internet (CAIN) website, https://cain.ulster.ac.uk/hmso/spa1922.htm.
9. Officially known as the Flags and Emblems (Display) Act (Northern Ireland) 1954. See CAIN website, https://cain.ulster.ac.uk/hmso/fea1954.htm.
10. The website of Tribeca Belfast is predictably professional and slick, with the sort of straplines that manage to convey the impression of being inspirational and vacuous simultaneously, such as 'Tribeca Belfast is a new area focused on bringing together the old, the young, the brave and the curious.' See https://www.tribeca-belfast.co.uk/.
11. Ulster Architectural Heritage Society, https://www.ulsterarchitecturalheritage.org. uk/case-studies/assembly-rooms/.
12. Michael Jackson, 'Calls for Assembly Rooms to Be Turned into United Irishmen Visitor Centre', BelfastMedia.com, 24 December 2021, https://belfastmedia.com/ assembly-rooms.
13. Bardon, *Belfast*, p. 147.
14. A.T.Q. Stewart, *The Ulster Crisis* (London: Faber, 1968), p. 21.
15. Stewart, *The Ulster Crisis*, p. 22.
16. Alan Wright, 'Hoping for the Best but Preparing for the Worst', *Fortnight*, issue 233, 10–23 February 1986, p. 5.
17. Feargal Cochrane, *Unionist Politics and the Politics of Unionism since the Anglo-Irish Agreement* (Cork: Cork University Press, 2001), p. 159.
18. Bardon, *Belfast*, p. 225.
19. David Trimble, Nobel Lecture, 10 December 1998, https://www.nobelprize.org/ prizes/peace/1998/trimble/lecture/.

20. Brian Barton, *The Blitz: Belfast in the War Years* (Belfast: Blackstaff Press, 1989), p. 30.
21. The Belfast Blitz in April and May 1941 led to over 1,000 deaths and destroyed half the housing stock in the city, displacing over 200,000 people.
22. Barton, *The Blitz*, p. 38.
23. Mark Simpson, 'Republican Leaders Featured in New Stormont Exhibition', BBC News, 24 March 2022, https://www.bbc.co.uk/news/uk-northern-ireland-60856442.
24. Dean Ruxton, '"Belfast Let Itself Go with a Vengeance": Reporting the King's Speech, 1921', *Irish Times*, 22 June 2021, https://www.irishtimes.com/news/ireland/irish-news/belfast-let-itself-go-with-a-vengeance-reporting-the-king-s-speech-1921-1.4600618.
25. Marie Anderson, *Police Ombudsman Statutory Report*, 13 January 2022, https://www.policeombudsman.org/PONI/files/e0/e0cb934a-760f-4885-b423-b4fa40375aa4.pdf, pp. 95–110.
26. https://www.belfastcity.gov.uk/things-to-do/city-hall/stained-glass-windows.
27. BBC News, 'Archive: Tom King Faces Protest at Belfast City Hall in 1985', https://www.bbc.co.uk/news/av/uk-northern-ireland-31067705.
28. Lily Johnson, 'Crumlin Road Gaol', *HistoryHit*, 12 April 2021, https://www.historyhit.com/locations/crumlin-road-gaol/.
29. Patrick Greg, *The Crum: Inside the Crumlin Road Prison* (Belfast: Glen Publishing, 2013), p. 24.
30. Greg, *The Crum*, p. 24.
31. Greg, *The Crum*, p. 36.
32. See 'Maze and Long Kesh' by the Prisons Memory Archive (PMA), available at https://www.prisonsmemoryarchive.com/the-prisons/maze-and-long-kesh/.
33. Laura McAtackney, *An Archaeology of the Troubles: The Dark Heritage of Long Kesh/Maze Prison* (Oxford: Oxford University Press, 2014).

CHAPTER 5: THE TROUBLES

1. The bulk of the chapter focuses on the impact of the Troubles on those who lived in Northern Ireland and beyond it. In order to convey this effectively, a small number of iconic moments during the period are highlighted as being emblematic of the wider social and political impact that the violence has had on a society that remains scarred by its past a generation later. These cases have been chosen in part because of their impact both at the time and on the political and security environment that followed. These moments illustrate that the violence came from all directions, republican and loyalist paramilitaries as well as the British security forces, and that some violent events stimulated new forms of civic activism aimed at trying to bring it to an end.
2. Elliott, *Hearthlands*, p. 164.
3. Rita Canavan, *Eyewitness: The Burning of Bombay Street*, Clonard Residents Association Belfast, https://www.youtube.com/watch?v=j5_qn19h3WM.
4. For the Scarman Report from the tribunal, see CAIN website, https://cain.ulster.ac.uk/hmso/scarman.htm.
5. British Pathé News Historical Collection, 18 August 1969, https://www.britishpathe.com/video/VLVACASBPC5WNS4FCTI894PBI5D12-NORTHERN-IRELAND-ARMY-CHIEF-SEES-HONEYMOON-NEARING-END/query/politician.
6. Tony Macaulay, *Paperboy* (London: HarperCollins, 2011), pp. 184–5.
7. *Sunday Times* Insight Team, *Ulster* (London: Penguin, 1972), p. 209.
8. *Sunday Times* Insight Team, *Ulster*, p. 209.
9. *Sunday Times* Insight Team, *Ulster*, p. 213.

10. Patrick Bishop & Eamonn Mallie, *The Provisional IRA* (London: Corgi, 1988), p. 160.

11. Malachi O'Doherty, *The Year of Chaos: Northern Ireland on the Brink of Civil War, 1971–72* (London: Atlantic Books, 2021), p. 100.

12. Connla Young, '50th Anniversary of the Falls Curfew Remembered', *Irish News*, 6 July 2020, https://www.irishnews.com/news/northernirelandnews/2020/07/06/news/50th-anniversary-of-falls-curfew-remembered-1996012/.

13. *Sunday Times* Insight Team, *Ulster*, p. 220.

14. Young, '50th Anniversary of the Falls Curfew Remembered'.

15. *Sunday Times* Insight Team, *Ulster*, p. 221.

16. Brendan O'Leary & John McGarry, *The Politics of Antagonism* (Dublin: Athlone Press, 1993), p. 127.

17. Fionnuala Ní Aoláin, *The Politics of Force* (Belfast: Blackstaff Press, 2000), p. 14.

18. Frank Kitson, *Low Intensity Operations: Subversion, Insurgency and Peacekeeping* (London: Faber, 1971), https://files.libcom.org/files/low-intensity%20operations.pdf.

19. John McGuffin, *The Guineapigs* (London: Penguin, 1974), p. 65.

20. Danny Kennally & Eric Preston, *Belfast, August 1971: A Case to Be Answered* (London: Independent Labour Party, 1971), p. 39.

21. O'Doherty, *The Year of Chaos*, p. 50.

22. Feargal Cochrane, *Northern Ireland: The Fragile Peace* (New Haven and London: Yale University Press, 2021), p. 59.

23. Jonathan Tonge, *Northern Ireland: Conflict and Change* (London: Pearson, 2002), p. 44.

24. Kenneth Bloomfield, *Stormont in Crisis: A Memoir* (Belfast: Blackstaff Press, 1994), p. 165.

25. O'Doherty, *The Year of Chaos*, p. 329.

26. Peter Taylor, *Loyalists* (London: Bloomsbury, 1999), p. 108.

27. BBC News, 'Shankill Bomb: Paramedics Recall Horror of Finding Victims', 21 October 2018, https://www.bbc.co.uk/news/uk-northern-ireland-45890446.

28. Brian Rowan, 'Shankill Bomb: A Dark Day amid Talks of Peace', BBC News, 23 October 2018, https://www.bbc.co.uk/news/uk-northern-ireland-45943874.

29. Maeve Connolly, 'Remembering a Black Week in Our History', *Irish News*, 21 October 2003, cited in Cochrane, *Northern Ireland: The Fragile Peace*, p. 130.

30. Cochrane, *Unionist Politics and the Politics of Unionism since the Anglo-Irish Agreement*, p. 306.

31. Rowan, 'Shankill Bomb'.

CHAPTER 6: THE TOURISM

1. Bill Rolston, 'Changing the Political Landscape: Murals and Transition in Northern Ireland', *Irish Studies Review*, vol. 11, issue 1 (2003).

2. 'The Agreement: Agreement Reached in the Multi-Party Negotiations' (Belfast: HMSO, 1998), p. 13.

3. Stephen Boyd, 'Heritage Tourism in Northern Ireland: Opportunity under Peace', *Current Issues in Tourism*, vol. 3, issue 2 (2000), p. 153.

4. Caroline Anson, 'Planning for Peace: The Role of Tourism in the Aftermath of Violence', *Journal of Travel Research*, vol. 38 (1999), p. 58; Boyd, 'Heritage Tourism in Northern Ireland', p. 151.

5. See Tourism NI website, 'Northern Ireland Tourism Performance and Statistics Dashboard', https://www.tourismni.com/industry-insights/ni-tourism-performance-dashboard/, slide 8 of 16.

6. Amanda Ferguson, 'Tourism Is Booming as Belfast Leaves Behind the Shadow of the Troubles', *Irish Times*, 4 August 2018, https://www.irishtimes.com/business/transport-and-tourism/tourism-is-booming-as-belfast-leaves-behind-the-shadow-of-the-troubles-1.3585449.

7. Malcolm Foley & J. John Lennon, 'JFK and Dark Tourism: Heart of Darkness', *Journal of International Heritage Studies*, vol. 2, issue 4 (1996), p. 198.

8. Debbie Lisle, *Holidays in the Danger Zone: Entanglements of War and Tourism* (Minneapolis: University of Minnesota Press, 2016).

9. Coiste, 'Coiste Irish Political Tours', https://coiste.ie/.

10. Aaron Tinney, 'Victims Slam Belfast Terror Tour for "Profiting from Misery and Death"', *Belfast Telegraph*, 12 August 2017, https://www.belfasttelegraph.co.uk/news/northern-ireland/victims-slam-belfast-terror-tour-for-profiting-from-misery-and-death-36024550.html.

11. Tinney, 'Victims Slam Belfast Terror Tour for "Profiting from Misery and Death"'.

12. Chris Jenkins, 'Belfast's Immoral Conflict Tourism', *Guardian*, 7 May 2012, https://www.theguardian.com/commentisfree/2012/may/07/belfast-immoral-conflict-tourism.

13. Sara McDowell, 'Selling Conflict Heritage through Tourism in Peacetime Northern Ireland: Transforming Conflict or Exacerbating Difference?', *International Journal of Heritage Studies*, vol. 14, issue 5 (2008), p. 419.

14. Feargal Cochrane, *Northern Ireland: The Reluctant Peace* (New Haven and London: Yale University Press, 2013), p. 296.

15. BBC News, 'Robinson Hails Maze Conflict Resolution Centre', 29 April 2012, https://www.bbc.co.uk/news/uk-northern-ireland-17886134.

16. Jim Allister, 'DUP Are Sinn Fein's New Maze Prisoners', 25 June 2013, http://www.jimallister.org/2013/06/492/.

17. Crumlin Road Gaol, 'Crumlin Road Gaol Launches New Troubles Tour', https://www.crumlinroadgaol.com/latest-news/crumlin-road-gaol-launches-new-troubles-tour/.

18. Licensed & Catering News, 'Bright Future for Iconic Troubles Prison', https://lcnonline.co.uk/bright-future-for-iconic-troubles-prison/.

19. American readers will better understand this as a trash can lid.

20. McDowell, 'Selling Conflict Heritage through Tourism in Peacetime Northern Ireland', pp. 405–21.

21. See http://www.culturenorthernireland.org/features/visual-arts/video-art-troubles-ulster-museum.

22. More detail on artist representation of the Troubles can be seen at the Troubles Archive supported by the Northern Ireland Arts Council, http://www.troublesarchive.com/.

23. Paul Mullan, 'Decade of Centenaries Closing Conference', 12 April 2022, https://www.youtube.com/watch?v=PFIKyxmMz7k.

24. Stephen Litvin, 'Tourism: The World's Peace Industry?', *Journal of Travel Research*, vol. 37, issue 1 (1998), pp. 63–6.

25. Richard Sharpley & Philip Stone (eds), *The Darker Side of Travel: The Theory and Practice of Dark Tourism* (Bristol: Channel View Publications, 2009).

26. Mark Wylie, DC Tours. Interviewed by author, 24 February 2022.

27. Mark Wylie, DC Tours.

28. Mark Wylie, DC Tours.

29. Paul Donnelly, DC Tours. Interviewed by author, 24 February 2022.

30. Mark Wylie and Paul Donnelly, DC Tours. Interviewed by author, 24 February 2022.

31. Mark Wylie and Paul Donnelly, DC Tours.

32. Paul Donnelly, DC Tours.
33. Dr Paul Mullan, Director, Northern Ireland National Lottery Heritage Fund. Interviewed by author, 21 February 2022.
34. Patrick Geoghegan, 'Kane, Richard Rutledge', *Dictionary of Irish Biography*, October 2009, https://www.dib.ie/index.php/biography/kane-richard-rutledge-a4379.
35. Beiner, *Forgetful Remembrance*.
36. I took the tour as part of my research for the book on 20 February 2022. It was led by Seán Napier, and we all met up at St George's Church on High Street. For old times' sake I parked my car in the same car park I had been impounded in due to a bomb scare in the early 1990s, referred to at the beginning of the chapter. In 2022 the most frightening part of the experience was the cost of parking in the centre of Belfast today compared to thirty years ago.
37. BBC News, 'City History Captured on Walls', 1 October 2008, http://news.bbc.co.uk/1/hi/northern_ireland/7646268.stm.
38. 1798 Walking Tour Twitter Feed, https://twitter.com/1798walkingtour/status/1492910680546197505.
39. BBC News, 'City History Captured on Walls'.
40. Mullan, 'Decade of Centenaries Closing Conference'.
41. Mullan, 'Decade of Centenaries Closing Conference'.
42. Belfast City Council, 'A City Imagining', 2019, https://www.belfastcity.gov.uk/documents/a-city-imagining#chapter1thestorysofar.
43. Mullan, 'Decade of Centenaries Closing Conference'.
44. Belfast City Council, 'A City Imagining'.
45. Belfast City Council, 'A City Imagining'.
46. Phil Harrison, 'What's Wrong with his Face?', *Fortnight*, issue 486 (July 2022), pp. 46–7.
47. Henry McDonald, '"Film Valentine to Belfast" Hailed as a Tourism Booster', *Sunday Times*, 28 November 2021, https://www.thetimes.co.uk/article/film-valentine-to-belfast-hailed-as-a-tourism-booster-3nc7hg8br.
48. Dr Paul Mullan. Interviewed by author, 21 February 2022.

CHAPTER 7: THE POETRY

1. The cultural canon that has emerged from Belfast over the last fifty years is vast, and a single chapter is incapable of doing justice to all its disciplines, as art, literature, theatre, film and television can all stake a legitimate claim as the city's cultural heartbeat. As a result, this chapter mostly restricts itself to looking at how Belfast poets and their poetry reflect and refract the city, its history, its politics and its people. To help the clarity of the narrative, the poets are discussed in broad chronological order, which is why more recent women poets appear towards the end of the chapter rather than at the beginning.
2. There are, of course, hundreds of plays that deserve inclusion, and the two playwrights whose work is covered here are used simply to represent the role that theatre and television has played in the wider political and cultural life of Belfast. Their inclusion is emblematic of the vast catalogue of other work that has been produced and is not intended to be read as representative of or pre-eminent within that genre.
3. The other play in the trilogy was *Coming to Terms with Billy* (1984).
4. The Billy Plays became so iconic that Graham Reid wrote a catch-up piece twenty-five years later, *Love Billy*, which managed to attract the now Sir Kenneth Branagh back to reprise his first acting role.
5. Appropriately, this chapter takes some poetic licence on the precise geographical boundaries of Belfast in laying claim to Seamus Heaney and some other cultural

figures listed here. With apologies to Bellaghy in County Derry, although Heaney was born in Bellaghy, he was educated at Queen's University Belfast, which is where his writing first flourished, and he is therefore included on this basis.

6. 'Escaped from the Massacre?', *Honest Ulsterman*, vol. 50 (Winter 1975), pp.183–5. Cited in Neal Alexander, *Ciaran Carson: Space, Place, Writing* (Liverpool: Liverpool University Press, 2010; online edn, Liverpool Scholarship Online, 20 June 2013).
7. Michael Longley, in Frank Ormsby, *A Rage for Order* (Belfast: Blackstaff Press, 1992), p. xvii.
8. Dennis O'Driscoll, 'To Set the Darkness Echoing', *Guardian*, 8 November 2008, https://www.theguardian.com/books/2008/nov/08/seamus-heaney-interview.
9. Chloe Foussaines, 'Joe Biden's Love of Irish Poet Seamus Heaney Dates Back to His Teenage Years', *Town and Country*, 19 January 2021, https://www.townandcountrymag.com/society/politics/a35253095/joe-biden-seamus-heaney-irish-poet/.
10. Sameer Rahim, 'Interview with Seamus Heaney', *Telegraph*, 11 April 2009, https://www.telegraph.co.uk/culture/books/5132022/Interview-with-Seamus-Heaney.html.
11. O'Driscoll, 'To Set the Darkness Echoing'.
12. Mark Simpson, 'Seamus Heaney Centre "Did Not Give Permission" to Use Poet's Image', BBC News, 20 December 2020, https://www.bbc.co.uk/news/uk-northern-ireland-55427002.
13. Brendan Hughes, 'Queen's University Breaks Three-Month Silence on NI Centenary Seamus Heaney Portrait Row', Belfast Live, 17 March 2021, https://www.belfastlive.co.uk/news/queens-university-breaks-three-month-20194262.
14. Simpson, 'Seamus Heaney Centre "Did Not Give Permission" to Use Poet's Image'.
15. 'Michael Longley', The Poetry Foundation, https://www.poetryfoundation.org/poets/michael-longley.
16. Michael Longley, *The Slain Birds* (London: Jonathan Cape, 2022).
17. Martin Doyle, 'Michael Longley: "Brexit Is a Monumental Disaster Promoted by Bare-Faced Lies"', *Irish Times*, 12 September 2022, https://www.irishtimes.com/culture/books/2022/09/12/michael-longley-brexit-is-a-monumental-disaster-promoted-by-bare-faced-lies/.
18. BBC News, 'Longley New Professor of Poetry', 23 September 2007, http://news.bbc.co.uk/1/hi/northern_ireland/6982117.stm.
19. Nicholas Wroe, 'Literature's Loose Cannon', *Guardian*, 23 March 2002, https://www.theguardian.com/books/2002/mar/23/poetry.academicexperts.
20. Wroe, 'Literature's Loose Cannon'.
21. Jonathan Hufstader, *Tongue of Water, Teeth of Stones* (Lexington, KY: University Press of Kentucky, 1999), p. 191.
22. Catriona Crowe, 'Testimony to a Flowering', *Dublin Review* (Spring 2003), https://thedublinreview.com/article/testimony-to-a-flowering/.
23. Crowe, 'Testimony to a Flowering'.
24. Crowe, 'Testimony to a Flowering'.
25. The *Sunday Independent* was traditionally antagonistic to the political project of Irish reunification in general and to parties such as Sinn Féin in particular. Lampooned as 'the Sindo', its critics have frequently identified the paper with a narrow vision of Irish nationalism that tends to overlook Northern Ireland as being part of the imagined community.
26. Colm Tóibín, quoted in Edna Longley, 'In Belfast', *London Review of Books*, vol. 14, issue 1, 9 January 1992, https://www.lrb.co.uk/the-paper/v14/n01/edna-longley/belfast-diary.
27. https://fieldday.ie/about/.

28. Frank Ormsby, 'The Honest Ulsterman Revisited: A Lecture by Professor Frank Ormsby', in association with the Seamus Heaney Centre, Queen's University Belfast, 2022, https://qft.vhx.tv/seamus-heaney-centre/videos/the-honest-ulsterman-revisited.

29. Frank Ormsby, in Mark Carruthers & Stephen Douds, *Stepping Stones: The Arts in Ulster, 1971–2001* (Belfast: Blackstaff Press, 2001), p. 54.

30. Ormsby, in Carruthers & Douds, *Stepping Stones*, p. 74.

31. Judith Cole, 'Sinéad Morrissey: "We Had a Very Different Upbringing and I'm Grateful to My Parents for That . . . It Was Very Liberating Not to Be on Either Side Here"', *Belfast Telegraph*, 23 September 2017, https://www.belfasttelegraph.co.uk/life/features/sinead-morrissey-we-had-a-very-different-upbringing-and-im-grateful-to-my-parents-for-that-it-was-very-liberating-not-to-be-on-either-side-here-36159548.html.

32. Morrissey attended Belfast High School, a state school which, due to the religiously segregated education system in Northern Ireland, had a de facto Protestant intake.

33. Scott Brewster & Michael Parker, 'Falling into Light: New Generation Northern Irish Poets', in Scott Brewster & Michael Parker (eds), *Irish Literature since 1990: Diverse Voices* (Manchester: Manchester University Press, 2009), p. 180.

34. Ian Duhig, 'Sinéad Morrissey: A Maker of Intricate Poem Machines', *Irish Times*, 21 October 2017, https://www.irishtimes.com/culture/books/sinead-morrissey-a-maker-of-intricate-poem-machines-1.3260694.

35. BBC News, 'Sinéad Morrissey Recites 'The Millihelen on The Arts Show', 22 September 2017, https://www.bbc.co.uk/news/av/uk-northern-ireland-41359991.

36. Kate Kellaway, '*On Balance* Poetry Review – An Imagination That Never Closes', *Guardian*, 24 October 2017, https://www.theguardian.com/books/2017/oct/24/on-balance-sinead-morrissey-poetry-review.

37. Steafán Hanvey, *Reconstructions: The Troubles in Photographs and Words* (Dublin: Merrion Press, 2018).

38. Steafán Hanvey, 'Carson-Parson', in *Reconstructions*, p. 75.

CHAPTER 8: THE FUTURE

1. NISRA, 'Census 2021 Main Statistics: Population More Diverse than Ever Before', 22 September 2022, https://www.nisra.gov.uk/system/files/statistics/census-2021-main-statistics-for-northern-ireland-phase-1-press-release.pdf.

2. NISRA, 'Census 2021: Main Statistics for Northern Ireland Statistical Bulletin – National Identity', 22 September 2022, https://www.nisra.gov.uk/system/files/statistics/census-2021-main-statistics-for-northern-ireland-phase-1-statistical-bulletin-national-identity.pdf.

3. Darren Marshall, 'Labour Would Set Out Border Poll Criteria – Peter Kyle', BBC News, 25 September 2022, https://www.bbc.co.uk/news/uk-northern-ireland-63024056.amp.

4. Feargal Cochrane, 'Why You Really Need to Keep an Eye on the Northern Ireland Election', *Big Issue*, 2 May 2022, https://www.bigissue.com/opinion/why-you-really-need-to-keep-an-eye-on-the-northern-ireland-election/.

5. Brian Coney, ' "We're Not An Army – We're Three Boys from Belfast": Rap Crew Kneecap Laugh Off Their Week of Controversy', *Guardian*, 19 August 2022, https://www.theguardian.com/music/2022/aug/19/rap-kneecap-belfast-interview.

6. Suzanne McGonagle, 'Wolfe Tones Singer Says "People Are Allowed to Have Their Heroes" amid Continuing Féile Controversy', *Irish News*, 18 August 2022, https://www.irishnews.com/news/northernirelandnews/2022/08/18/news/wolfe_tones_singer_says_people_are_allowed_to_have_their_heroes_amid_continuing_fe_ile_controversy-2801975/.

7. Suzanne McGonagle, 'Sectarian Song "Besmirching" Memory of Michaela McAreavey Was "Disgusting", Orangeman and Journalist Says', *Irish News*, 13 June 2022, https://www.irishnews.com/news/northernirelandnews/2022/06/13/news/sectarian-song-besmirching-memory-of-michael-mcareavey-was-disgusting-orange-man-and-journalist-says-2740810/.

8. McGonagle, 'Sectarian Song "Besmirching" Memory of Michaela McAreavey Was "Disgusting"'.

9. Niall O'Dowd, 'Hideous Michaela McAreavey Song Proves Orange Hatred Hasn't Gone Away', *Irish Central*, 8 June 2022, https://www.irishcentral.com/opinion/niallodowd/michaela-mcareavey-orange-hatred.

10. It took a case from academic Jeffrey Dudgeon in the European Court of Human Rights in 1981 that found the UK government to be in breach of the European Convention on Human Rights before legislation was finally introduced into Northern Ireland in 1982 that decriminalised homosexuality.

11. Belfast Pride Festival, *Official Festival Guide: Community: United in Diversity*, 30 June 2022, https://issuu.com/belfastpride/docs/bp_2022_guide.

12. Belfast Pride Festival, *Official Festival Guide*, pp. 2–3.

13. Michelle O'Neill, 'First Minister Designate Michelle O'Neill at Belfast Pride 2022', YouTube, https://www.youtube.com/watch?v=BmEOfIXd7-Y.

14. Patrick Kelleher, 'Sinn Féin's Michelle O'Neill Calls on DUP to Help Advance LGBTQ+ Rights in Northern Ireland', PinkNews, 6 July 2022, https://www.pinknews.co.uk/2022/07/06/michelle-oneill-sinn-fein-dup-lgbtq-pinknews-pride-reception/.

15. BBC News, 'Belfast Pride 2022 Parade "Biggest Ever" Police Say', 30 July 2022, https://www.bbc.co.uk/news/uk-northern-ireland-62337799.

16. BBC News, 'Belfast Pride 2022 Parade "Biggest Ever" Police Say'.

17. Kevin Magee, 'St Colmcille's Gaelic Football Club, East Belfast: The Team That Disappeared', BBC News, 9 March 2015, https://www.bbc.co.uk/news/uk-northern-ireland-31770367.

18. Seanín Graham, 'Even Putting GAA and East Belfast Together in the Same Sentence – What It Spoke to Me Was a Future of Hope and Change', *Irish Times*, 3 September 2022, https://www.irishtimes.com/ireland/social-affairs/2022/09/03/a-gaa-club-in-east-belfast-even-putting-gaa-and-east-belfast-together-in-the-same-sentence-what-it-spoke-to-me-was-a-future-of-hope-and-change/.

19. Graham, 'Even Putting GAA and East Belfast Together'.

20. BelfastMedia.com, 'A Year in the Life of East Belfast GAA', 30 May 2022, https://belfastmedia.com/a-year-in-the-life-of-east-belfast-gaa.

21. Anna Caffola, '"I've Never Had So Much Craic": Gaelic Games Come to Loyalist East Belfast', *Observer*, 18 October 2020, https://www.theguardian.com/uk-news/2020/oct/18/ive-never-had-so-much-craic-gaelic-games-come-to-loyalist-east-belfast.

22. Dr Paul Mullan, Director, National Lottery Heritage Fund Northern Ireland. Interviewed by author, 21 February 2022.

23. Graham, 'Even Putting GAA and East Belfast Together'.

24. Irish human rights activist Emma De Souza and her American husband had to fight a lengthy legal battle with the Home Office before it reluctantly conceded in 2020 that all Irish and British people born in Northern Ireland would be treated as EU citizens for immigration purposes in the UK. The outcome remains a legal and political fudge rather than an acceptance by the UK that people in Northern Ireland can be defined as Irish rather than British in accordance with the terms of the Good Friday Agreement.

25. Dr Paul Mullan. Interviewed by author, 21 February 2022.

26. John Downing, 'Protestants, Loyalists and Unionists in Belfast Learning Irish is Very Much Their Language', *Irish Independent*, 3 March 2022, https://www.independent.ie/irish-news/protestants-loyalists-and-unionists-in-belfast-learning-irish-is-very-much-their-language-41408498.html.

27. Linda Ervine, 'Northern Protestants like Me Are Embracing the Irish Language', *Irish Independent*, 4 September 2021, https://www.independent.ie/life/northern-protestants-like-me-are-embracing-the-irish-language-40815135.html.

28. Ervine, 'Northern Protestants Like Me Are Embracing the Irish Language'.

29. Jonathan McCambridge, 'Principal "Sickened" after Hate Campaign Forces Irish Language Nursery Naiscoil Na Seolta to Move', *Irish News*, 28 July 2021, https://www.irishnews.com/news/northernirelandnews/2021/07/28/news/principal-sickened-after-hate-campaign-forces-irish-language-nursery-naiscoil-na-seolta-to-move-2402460/.

30. Naíscoil na Seolta, https://www.scoilnaseolta.org/about-us.

31. Irish World, 'President of Sinn Féin Mary Lou McDonald Pays Tribute to Queen', 8 September 2022, https://www.theirishworld.com/president-of-sinn-fein-mary-lou-mcdonald-pays-tribute-to-queen/.

32. Irish World, 'Michelle O'Neill Leads SF Tributes to Queen', 8 September 2022, https://www.theirishworld.com/michelle-oneill-leads-sf-tributes-to-queen/.

33. Enda McClafferty, 'King Charles III: A Condolence Speech Laced with Political Undertones', BBC News, 13 September 2022, https://www.bbc.co.uk/news/uk-northern-ireland-62894438.

34. BBC News, 'King Charles III Says Queen Prayed for Northern Ireland', 13 September 2022, https://www.bbc.co.uk/news/uk-northern-ireland-62878272.

35. Cate McCurry & Jonathan McCambridge, 'King Charles III Asks DUP Leader about Northern Ireland Protocol', *Belfast Telegraph*, 13 September 20222, https://www.belfasttelegraph.co.uk/news/northern-ireland/king-charles-iii-asks-dup-leader-about-northern-ireland-protocol-41986235.html.

36. Dr Paul Mullan. Interviewed by author, 21 February 2022.

37. Belfast City Council, 'The Belfast Agenda', 2017, https://www.belfastcity.gov.uk/documents/the-belfast-agenda#developed.

38. Belfast City Council, 'The Belfast Agenda'.

39. Robbie Meredith, 'NI Cities' Capital of Culture 2023 Bid "No Longer Viable"', BBC News, 7 April 2018, https://www.bbc.co.uk/news/uk-northern-ireland-43675093.

40. Catherine Shoard, 'Kenneth Branagh Wins First Oscar as *Belfast* Takes Best Original Screenplay', *Guardian*, 28 March 2022, https://www.theguardian.com/film/2022/mar/28/kenneth-branagh-wins-first-oscar-as-belfast-takes-best-original-screenplay.

41. I was fortunate to get a job in the fabulous (though now closed) Centre for the Study of Conflict at what was then called the University of Ulster and to be mentored by Professor Seamus Dunn, who was its Director. It was full of amazingly bright researchers, several of whom became lifelong friends, and was without doubt the happiest period in my academic career.

BIBLIOGRAPHY

4NI.co.uk. 'Belfast's Hidden Rivers "Uncovered"', 29 April 2010, https://www.4ni. co.uk/northern-ireland-news/110735/belfast-s-hidden-rivers-uncovered.

Adams, Gerry. *Falls Memories* (Dublin: Brandon Books, 1982).

Agnew, Jean (ed.). *Drennan–McTier Letters, Volume 1* (Dublin: Women's History Project, 1998), quoted in C.M. Barry, 'Benevolent Conspiracy', *Irish Philosophy*, 5 February 2015, https://www.irishphilosophy.com/category/person/long-18th-century/william-drennan/.

Alexander, Neal. *Ciaran Carson: Space, Place, Writing* (Liverpool: Liverpool University Press, 2010; online edn, Liverpool Scholarship Online, 20 June 2013).

Allister, Jim. 'DUP Are Sinn Fein's New Maze Prisoners', 25 June 2013, http://www.jimallister.org/2013/06/492/.

Anderson, Marie. *Police Ombudsman Statutory Report*, 13 January 2022, https://www.policeombudsman.org/PONI/files/e0/e0cb934a-760f-4885-b423-b4fa40375aa4.pdf, pp. 95–110.

Anson, Caroline. 'Planning for Peace: The Role of Tourism in the Aftermath of Violence', *Journal of Travel Research*, vol. 38 (1999), pp. 57–61.

Bardon, Jonathan. *A History of Ulster* (Belfast: Blackstaff Press, 1992; 2nd edn 1996).

Bardon, Jonathan. *Belfast: An Illustrated History* (Belfast: Blackstaff Press, 1982).

Barton, Brian. *The Blitz: Belfast in the War Years* (Belfast: Blackstaff Press, 1989).

BBC 24 Hours. 'Bernadette Devlin Attacks British Home Secretary', 31 January 1972, https://www.bbc.co.uk/programmes/p00nm166.

BBC News. 'Archive: Tom King Faces Protest at Belfast City Hall in 1985', https://www.bbc.co.uk/news/av/uk-northern-ireland-31067705.

BBC News. 'Belfast Pride 2022 Parade "Biggest Ever" Police Say', 30 July 2022, https://www.bbc.co.uk/news/uk-northern-ireland-62337799.

BBC News. 'Belfast's *Origin* Wins Spectator "Worst Public Art" Award', 27 March 2017, https://www.bbc.co.uk/news/uk-northern-ireland-39403983.

BBC News. 'Belfast's Secret Rivers Revealed', 29 April 2010, http://news.bbc.co.uk/1/hi/northern_ireland/8651644.stm.

BBC News. 'Census 2021: Politicians React to Latest Northern Ireland Results', 22 September 2022, https://www.bbc.co.uk/news/uk-northern-ireland-62991618.

BBC News. 'City History Captured on Walls', 1 October 2008, http://news.bbc.co.uk/1/hi/northern_ireland/7646268.stm.

BBC News. 'King Charles III Says Queen Prayed for Northern Ireland', 13 September 2022, https://www.bbc.co.uk/news/uk-northern-ireland-62878272.

BBC News. 'Longley New Professor of Poetry', 23 September 2007, http://news.bbc.co.uk/1/hi/northern_ireland/6982117.stm.

BBC News. 'Robinson Hails Maze Conflict Resolution Centre', 29 April 2012, https://www.bbc.co.uk/news/uk-northern-ireland-17886134.

BBC News. 'Shankill Bomb: Paramedics Recall Horror of Finding Victims', 21 October 2018, https://www.bbc.co.uk/news/uk-northern-ireland-45890446.

BBC News. 'Sinéad Morrissey Recites The Millihelen on The Arts Show', 22 September 2017, https://www.bbc.co.uk/news/av/uk-northern-ireland-41359991.

Beiner, Guy. *Forgetful Remembrance: Social Forgetting and Vernacular Historiography of a Rebellion in Ulster* (Oxford: Oxford University Press, 2018).

Belfast City Council. 'A City Imagining', 2019, https://www.belfastcity.gov.uk/documents/a-city-imagining#chapter1thestorysofar.

Belfast Pride Festival. *Official Festival Guide: Community: United in Diversity*, 30 June 2022, https://issuu.com/belfastpride/docs/bp_2022_guide.

BelfastMedia.com. 'A Year in the Life of East Belfast GAA', 30 May 2022, https://belfastmedia.com/a-year-in-the-life-of-east-belfast-gaa.

Bishop, Patrick & Eamonn Mallie. *The Provisional IRA* (London: Corgi, 1988).

Black, Rebecca. 'Poll: £100k for Belfast's Giant Tulip in Middle of Nowhere – Is It Worth It?', *Belfast Telegraph*, 16 September 2016, https://www.belfasttelegraph.co.uk/news/northern-ireland/poll-100k-for-belfasts-giant-tulip-in-middle-of-nowhere-is-it-worth-it-35052529.html.

Bloomfield, Kenneth. *Stormont in Crisis: A Memoir* (Belfast: Blackstaff Press, 1994).

Boulton, Jack. 'Frontier Wars: Violence and Space in Belfast, Northern Ireland', *Totem: The University of Western Ontario Journal of Anthropology*, vol. 22, issue 1 (2014).

Boyd, Andrew. *Holy War in Belfast* (Tralee: Anvil Books, 1969).

Boyd, Stephen. 'Heritage Tourism in Northern Ireland: Opportunity under Peace', *Current Issues in Tourism*, vol. 3, issue 2 (2000), pp. 150–74.

Brewster, Scott & Michael Parker. 'Falling into Light: New Generation Northern Irish Poets', in Scott Brewster & Michael Parker (eds), *Irish Literature since 1990: Diverse Voices* (Manchester: Manchester University Press, 2009), pp. 177–98.

British Pathé News Historical Collection. 18 August 1969, https://www.britishpathe.com/video/VLVACASBPC5WNS4FCTI894PBI5D12-NORTHERN-IRELAND-ARMY-CHIEF-SEES-HONEYMOON-NEARING-END/query/politician.

Bryan, Dominic. 'Titanic Town: Living in a Landscape of Conflict', in S.J. Connolly (ed.), *Belfast 400: People, Place and History* (Liverpool: Liverpool University Press, 2012), pp. 317–55.

Buckland, Patrick. *James Craig* (Dublin: Gill & Macmillan, 1980).

Caffola, Anna. '"I've Never Had So Much Craic": Gaelic Games Come to Loyalist East Belfast', *Observer*, 18 October 2020, https://www.theguardian.com/uk-news/2020/oct/18/ive-never-had-so-much-craic-gaelic-games-come-to-loyalist-east-belfast.

Cameron, Stephen. *Titanic: Belfast's Own* (Newtownards: Colourpoint, 2011).

Carruthers, Mark & Stephen Douds. *Stepping Stones: The Arts in Ulster, 1971–2001* (Belfast: Blackstaff Press, 2001).

Carson, Ciaran. *The Star Factory* (London: Head of Zeus, 1997).

Carty, Ed & David Young. 'Martin and Peter Go Back to Crumlin Gaol at Her Majesty's Pleasure', *Irish Independent*, 24 June 2014, https://www.independent.ie/irish-news/news/martin-and-peter-go-back-to-crumlin-gaol-at-her-majestys-pleasure-30381981.html.

Clifton House. 'The Cholera Pandemic of 1832: Preparations Begin', https://cliftonbelfast.com/the-cholera-pandemic-of-1832-preparations-begin/.

Cobain, Ian. 'Troubled Past: The Paramilitary Connection That Still Haunts the DUP', *Guardian*, 27 June 2017, https://www.theguardian.com/politics/2017/jun/27/troubled-past-the-paramilitary-connection-that-still-haunts-the-dup.

Cochrane, Feargal. 'Any Takers? The Isolation of Northern Ireland', *Political Studies*, vol. 42, issue 3 (1994).

Cochrane, Feargal. *Ending Wars* (Cambridge: Polity, 2008).

Cochrane, Feargal. *Northern Ireland: The Fragile Peace* (New Haven and London: Yale University Press, 2021).

Cochrane, Feargal. *Northern Ireland: The Reluctant Peace* (New Haven and London: Yale University Press, 2013), paperback.

Cochrane, Feargal. 'The Unionist Response to the Anglo-Irish Agreement', unpublished PhD thesis, Queen's University Belfast, December 1992.

Cochrane, Feargal. *Unionist Politics and the Politics of Unionism since the Anglo-Irish Agreement* (Cork: Cork University Press, 2001).

Cochrane, Feargal. 'Why You Really Need to Keep an Eye on the Northern Ireland Election', *Big Issue*, 2 May 2022, https://www.bigissue.com/opinion/why-you-really-need-to-keep-an-eye-on-the-northern-ireland-election/.

Cole, Judith. 'Sinéad Morrissey: "We Had a Very Different Upbringing and I'm Grateful to My Parents for That . . . It Was Very Liberating Not to Be on Either Side Here"', *Belfast Telegraph*, 23 September 2017, https://www.belfasttelegraph.co.uk/life/features/sinead-morrissey-we-had-a-very-different-upbringing-and-im-grateful-to-my-parents-for-that-it-was-very-liberating-not-to-be-on-either-side-here-36159548.html.

Coney, Brian. '"We're Not an Army – We're Three Boys from Belfast": Rap Crew Kneecap Laugh Off Their Week of Controversy', *Guardian*, 19 August 2022, https://www.theguardian.com/music/2022/aug/19/rap-kneecap-belfast-interview.

Connolly, S.J. (ed.). *Belfast 400: People, Place and History* (Liverpool: Liverpool University Press, 2012).

Courtney, Roger. *Dissenting Voices: Rediscovering the Irish Progressive Presbyterian Tradition* (Belfast: Ulster Historical Foundation, 2013).

Creative Belfast Uncovered. 'Creative Belfast Uncovered – The River Farset', 23 May 2016, https://www.youtube.com/watch?v=D_lwebv5An0.

Crowe, Catriona. 'Testimony to a Flowering', *Dublin Review* (Spring 2003), https://thedublinreview.com/article/testimony-to-a-flowering/.

Cullen Owens, Rosemary. *A Social History of Women in Ireland, 1870–1970* (Dublin: Gill & Macmillan, 2005).

Curtis, Edmund. *A History of Ireland* (London: Methuen, 1936).

Dawson, Kenneth. *The Belfast Jacobin: Samuel Neilson and the United Irishmen* (Dublin: Irish Academic Press, 2017).

Defoe, Daniel. 'The paralel: or, persecution of Protestants the shortest way to prevent the growth of popery in Ireland' (originally published 1704, reprinted Gale ECCO print edition, 2010).

Dillon, Martin. *The Shankill Butchers: A Case Study of Mass Murder* (London: Cornerstone, 1990).

Dorney, John. 'In the Hands of an Armed Mob – The Belfast Riots of 1864', *Irish Story*, 9 April 2020, https://www.theirishstory.com/2020/04/09/in-the-hands-of-an-armed-mob-the-belfast-riots-of-1864/#.YbdIAZHP02x.

Downing, John. 'Protestants, Loyalists and Unionists in Belfast Learning Irish Is Very Much Their Language', *Irish Independent*, 3 March 2022, https://www.independent.ie/irish-news/protestants-loyalists-and-unionists-in-belfast-learning-irish-is-very-much-their-language-41408498.html.

Doyle, Martin. 'Michael Longley: "Brexit Is a Monumental Disaster Promoted by Bare-Faced Lies"', *Irish Times*, 12 September 2022, https://www.irishtimes.com/culture/books/2022/09/12/michael-longley-brexit-is-a-monumental-disaster-promoted-by-bare-faced-lies/.

Duhig, Ian. 'Sinéad Morrissey: A Maker of Intricate Poem Machines', *Irish Times*, 21 October 2017, https://www.irishtimes.com/culture/books/sinead-morrissey-a-maker-of-intricate-poem-machines-1.3260694.

Elliott, Marianne. *Hearthlands* (Belfast: Blackstaff Press, 2017).

Elliott, Marianne. *Partners in Revolution: The United Irishmen and France* (New Haven and London: Yale University Press, 1990).

Ervine, Linda. 'Northern Protestants like Me Are Embracing the Irish Language', *Irish Independent*, 4 September 2021, https://www.independent.ie/life/northern-protestants-like-me-are-embracing-the-irish-language-40815135.html.

Ferguson, Amanda. 'Tourism Is Booming as Belfast Leaves Behind the Shadow of the Troubles', *Irish Times*, 4 August 2018, https://www.irishtimes.com/business/transport-and-tourism/tourism-is-booming-as-belfast-leaves-behind-the-shadow-of-the-troubles-1.3585449.

Foley, Malcolm & J. John Lennon. 'JFK and Dark Tourism: Heart of Darkness', *Journal of International Heritage Studies*, vol. 2, issue 4 (1996).

Foster, Roy. *Modern Ireland, 1600–1972* (London: Penguin, 1988).

Foussaines, Chloe. 'Joe Biden's Love of Irish Poet Seamus Heaney Dates Back to His Teenage Years', *Town and Country*, 19 January 2021, https://www.townandcountrymag.com/society/politics/a35253095/joe-biden-seamus-heaney-irish-poet/.

Froggatt, Peter. 'MacDonnell, James', *Dictionary of Irish Biography*, May 2012, https://www.dib.ie/biography/macdonnell-james-a5184.

Geoghegan, Patrick. 'Kane, Richard Rutledge', *Dictionary of Irish Biography*, October 2009, https://www.dib.ie/index.php/biography/kane-richard-rutledge-a4379.

Gillespie, Raymond. *Early Belfast: The Origins and Growth of an Ulster Town to 1750* (Belfast: Ulster Historical Foundation, 2007).

Graham, Seanín. 'Even Putting GAA and East Belfast Together in the Same Sentence – What It Spoke to Me Was a Future of Hope and Change', *Irish Times*, 3 September 2022, https://www.irishtimes.com/ireland/social-affairs/2022/09/03/a-gaa-club-in-east-belfast-even-putting-gaa-and-east-belfast-together-in-the-same-sentence-what-it-spoke-to-me-was-a-future-of-hope-and-change/.

Grahan, Daniel. 'The Scullabogue Massacre', *History Ireland*, vol. 4, issue 3 (1996), https://www.historyireland.com/18th-19th-century-history/the-scullabogue-massacre-1798/.

Greenslade, Roy. 'The Belfast Blindspot: How Britain Still Doesn't Get Northern Ireland', *New Statesman*, 23 October 2019, https://www.newstatesman.com/politics/northern-ireland/2019/10/belfast-blindspot-how-britain-still-doesn-t-get-northern-ireland.

Greg, Patrick. *The Crum: Inside the Crumlin Road Prison* (Belfast: Glen Publishing, 2013).

Hammond, David. *Steelchest, Nail in the Boot & the Barking Dog: The Belfast Shipyard – A Story of the People by the People* (Belfast: Flying Fox Films, 1986).

Hanvey, Steafán. *Reconstructions: The Troubles in Photographs and Words* (Dublin: Merrion Press, 2018).

Harrison, Phil. 'What's Wrong with his Face?', *Fortnight*, issue 486 (July 2022).

Holmes, Janice. 'Hanna, Hugh', *Dictionary of Irish Biography*, October 2009, https://www.dib.ie/biography/hanna-hugh-a3787.

Hufstader, Jonathan. *Tongue of Water, Teeth of Stones* (Lexington, KY: University Press of Kentucky, 1999).

Hughes, Brendan. 'Queen's University Breaks Three-Month Silence on NI Centenary Seamus Heaney Portrait Row', *Belfast Live*, 17 March 2021, https://www.belfastlive.co.uk/news/queens-university-breaks-three-month-20194262.

Irish World, 'Michelle O'Neill Leads SF Tributes to Queen', 8 September 2022, https://www.theirishworld.com/michelle-oneill-leads-sf-tributes-to-queen/.

Irish World, 'President of Sinn Féin Mary Lou McDonald Pays Tribute to Queen', 8 September 2022, https://www.theirishworld.com/president-of-sinn-fein-mary-lou-mcdonald-pays-tribute-to-queen/.

Jackson, Michael. 'Calls for Assembly Rooms to Be Turned into United Irishmen Visitor Centre', BelfastMedia.com, 24 December 2021, https://belfastmedia.com/assembly-rooms.

Jenkins, Chris. 'Belfast's Immoral Conflict Tourism', *Guardian*, 7 May 2012, https://www.theguardian.com/commentisfree/2012/may/07/belfast-immoral-conflict-tourism.

Johnson, Kevin. 'Sectarianism and the Shipyard', *Irish Times*, 29 November 2008, https://www.irishtimes.com/news/sectarianism-and-the-shipyard-1.916936.

Johnson, Lily. 'Crumlin Road Gaol', *HistoryHit*, 12 April 2021, https://www.historyhit.com/locations/crumlin-road-gaol/.

Kellaway, Kate. '*On Balance* Poetry Review – An Imagination That Never Closes', *Guardian*, 24 October 2017, https://www.theguardian.com/books/2017/oct/24/on-balance-sinead-morrissey-poetry-review.

Kelleher, Patrick. 'Sinn Féin's Michelle O'Neill Calls on DUP to Help Advance LGBTQ+ Rights in Northern Ireland', PinkNews, 6 July 2022, https://www.pinknews.co.uk/2022/07/06/michelle-oneill-sinn-fein-dup-lgbtq-pinknews-pride-reception/.

Kennally, Danny & Eric Preston. *Belfast, August 1971: A Case to Be Answered* (London: Independent Labour Party, 1971).

Killen, John. *A History of the Linen Hall Library 1788–1988* (Belfast: Linen Hall Library, 1990).

Kirkpatrick, Laurence. 'The "Eagle Wing" 1636', *Presbyterian Historical Society of Ireland*, https://www.presbyterianhistoryireland.com/history/the-eagle-wing-1636/.

Kitson, Frank. *Low Intensity Operations: Subversion, Insurgency and Peacekeeping* (London: Faber, 1971).

Lederarch, John Paul. *Building Peace* (Washington: United States Institute for Peace, 1999)

Lisle, Debbie. *Holidays in the Danger Zone: Entanglements of War and Tourism* (Minneapolis: University of Minnesota Press, 2016).

Litvin, Stephen. 'Tourism: The World's Peace Industry?', *Journal of Travel Research*, vol. 37, issue 1 (1998).

Longley, Edna. 'In Belfast', *London Review of Books*, vol. 14, issue 1, 9 January 1992, https://www.lrb.co.uk/the-paper/v14/n01/edna-longley/belfast-diary.

Longley, Michael. *The Slain Birds* (London: Jonathan Cape, 2022).

Lunney, Linde. 'Joy, Robert', *Dictionary of Irish Biography*, October 2009, https://www.dib.ie/biography/joy-robert-a4358.

Lynch, Connor. 'East Belfast GAA Unveil New Club Crest Ahead of First Matches This Weekend', *Belfast Live*, 16 July 2020, https://www.belfastlive.co.uk/news/belfast-news/east-belfast-gaa-unveil-new-18609335.

McAtackney, Laura. *An Archaeology of the Troubles: The Dark Heritage of Long Kesh/Maze Prison* (Oxford: Oxford University Press, 2014).

Macaulay, Tony. *Paperboy* (London: HarperCollins, 2011).

McCambridge, Jonathan. 'Principal "Sickened" after Hate Campaign Forces Irish Language Nursery Naíscoil Na Seolta to Move', *Irish News*, 28 July 2021, https://www.irishnews.com/news/northernirelandnews/2021/07/28/news/principal-sickened-after-hate-campaign-forces-irish-language-nursery-naiscoil-na-seolta-to-move-2402460/.

McCaughan, Michael. 'The Ultimate Disaster Symbol', *Causeway* (Winter 1996), https://www.dividedsociety.org/journals/causeway-cultural-traditions-journal/vol-3-no-4/ultimate-disaster-symbol.

McClafferty, Enda. 'King Charles III: A Condolence Speech Laced with Political Undertones', BBC News, 13 September 2022, https://www.bbc.co.uk/news/uk-northern-ireland-62894438.

McCurry, Cate & Jonathan McCambridge. 'King Charles III Asks DUP Leader about Northern Ireland Protocol', *Belfast Telegraph*, 13 September 2022, https://www.

belfasttelegraph.co.uk/news/northern-ireland/king-charles-iii-asks-dup-leader-about-northern-ireland-protocol-41986235.html.

McCutcheon, W.A. *The Canals of the North of Ireland* (Newton Abbot: David & Charles, 1965).

McDonald, Henry. '"Film Valentine to Belfast" Hailed as a Tourism Booster', *Sunday Times*, 28 November 2021, https://www.thetimes.co.uk/article/film-valentine-to-belfast-hailed-as-a-tourism-booster-3nc7hg8br.

McDowell, R.B. 'The Personnel of the Dublin Society of United Irishmen, 1791–4', *Irish Historical Studies*, vol. 2, issue 5 (1940).

McDowell, Sara. 'Selling Conflict Heritage through Tourism in Peacetime Northern Ireland: Transforming Conflict or Exacerbating Difference?', *International Journal of Heritage Studies*, vol. 14, issue 5 (2008).

McGonagle, Suzanne. 'Sectarian Song "Besmirching" Memory of Michaela McAreavey Was "Disgusting", Orangeman and Journalist Says', *Irish News*, 13 June 2022, https://www.irishnews.com/news/northernirelandnews/2022/06/13/news/sectarian-song-besmirching-memory-of-michael-mcareavey-was-disgusting-orange-man-and-journalist-says-2740810/.

MacGonagle, Suzanne. 'Wolfe Tones Singer Says "People Are Allowed to Have Their Heroes" amid Continuing Féile Controversy', *Irish News*, 18 August 2022, https://www.irishnews.com/news/northernirelandnews/2022/08/18/news/wolfe_tones_singer_says_people_are_allowed_to_have_their_heroes_amid_continuing_fe_ile_controversy-2801975/.

McGuffin, John. *The Guineapigs* (London: Penguin, 1974).

McNeill, Mary. *The Life and Times of Mary Ann McCracken, 1770–1866: A Belfast Panorama* (Dublin: Irish Academic Press, 2019).

Madden, Richard. *The United Irishmen, Their Lives and Times* (Dublin: Martin Lester, 1843), https://archive.org/stream/s1unitedirishmen01madduoft/s1unitedirishmen-01madduoft_djvu.txt.

Magee, Kevin. 'St Colmcille's Gaelic Football Club, East Belfast: The Team That Disappeared', BBC News, 9 March 2015, https://www.bbc.co.uk/news/uk-northern-ireland-31770367.

Maguire, William. *Belfast: A History* (Lancaster: Carnegie Books, 2009).

Marshall, Darren. 'Labour Would Set Out Border Poll Criteria – Peter Kyle', BBC News, 25 September 2022, https://www.bbc.co.uk/news/uk-northern-ireland-63024056.amp.

Maume, Patrick (ed.). *In Belfast by the Sea* (Dublin: University of Dublin Press, 2007).

Meredith, Robbie. 'NI Cities' Capital of Culture 2023 Bid "No Longer Viable"', BBC News, 7 April 2018, https://www.bbc.co.uk/news/uk-northern-ireland-43675093.

Molle, François. 'Water, Politics, and River Basin Governance: Repoliticizing Approaches to River Basin Management', *Water International*, vol. 34, issue 1 (2009), pp. 62–70.

Moore, Frank Frankfort. *In Belfast by the Sea* (Dublin: University of Dublin Press, 2007).

Mullan, Paul. 'Decade of Centenaries Closing Conference', 12 April 2022, https://www.youtube.com/watch?v=PFIKyxmMz7k.

Ní Aoláin, Fionnuala. *The Politics of Force* (Belfast: Blackstaff Press, 2000).

NISRA. 'Census 2021: Main Statistics for Northern Ireland Statistical Bulletin – National Identity', 22 September 2022, https://www.nisra.gov.uk/system/files/statistics/census-2021-main-statistics-for-northern-ireland-phase-1-statistical-bulletin-national-identity.pdf.

NISRA. 'Census 2021 Main Statistics: Population More Diverse than Ever Before', 22 September 2022, https://www.nisra.gov.uk/system/files/statistics/census-2021-main-statistics-for-northern-ireland-phase-1-press-release.pdf.

O'Byrne, Cathal. *As I Roved Out*, reprinted edn (Belfast: Blackstaff Press, 1982).

O'Doherty, Malachi. *The Year of Chaos: Northern Ireland on the Brink of Civil War, 1971–72* (London: Atlantic Books, 2021).

O'Dowd, Niall. 'Hideous Michaela McAreavey Song Proves Orange Hatred Hasn't Gone Away', *Irish Central*, 8 June 2022, https://www.irishcentral.com/opinion/niallodowd/michaela-mcareavey-orange-hatred.

O'Driscoll, Dennis. 'To Set the Darkness Echoing', *Guardian*, 8 November 2008, https://www.theguardian.com/books/2008/nov/08/seamus-heaney-interview.

O'Ferrell, Fergus. 'Daniel O'Connell and Henry Cooke: The Battle for Civil and Religious Liberty in Modern Ireland', *Irish Review*, issue 1 (1986), pp. 20–7.

O'Leary, Brendan & John McGarry. *The Politics of Antagonism* (Dublin: Athlone Press, 1993).

O'Neill, Michelle. 'First Minister Designate Michelle O'Neill at Belfast Pride 2022', YouTube, https://www.youtube.com/watch?v=BmEOfIXd7-Y.

Ormsby, Frank. *A Rage for Order* (Belfast: Blackstaff Press, 1992).

Ormsby, Frank. 'The Honest Ulsterman Revisited: A Lecture by Professor Frank Ormsby', in association with the Seamus Heaney Centre, Queen's University Belfast, 2022, https://qft.vhx.tv/seamus-heaney-centre/videos/the-honest-ulsterman-revisited.

Parr, Connal. 'Expelled from Yard and Tribe: The "Rotten Prods" of 1920 and Their Political Legacies', *Studi Irlandesi*, vol. 11, issue 11 (2021), pp. 299–321.

Patterson, Henry. 'The Belfast Shipyard Expulsions', *Creative Centenaries*, 29 March 2021, https://www.creativecentenaries.org/blog/the-belfast-shipyard-expulsions.

Pearce, Ed. 'One Long Piece of Perplexity', *Fortnight*, issue 296 (June 1991).

Phoenix, Eamon, 'British Concerned over UDR Credibility', *Irish Times*, 2 January 2017, https://www.irishtimes.com/news/politics/british-concerned-over-udr-credibility-1.2913026.

Quinn, James. 'Lake, Gerard', *Dictionary of Irish Biography*, October 2009, https://www.dib.ie/biography/lake-gerard-a4643.

Quinn, James. 'Thomas Russell, United Irishman', *History Ireland*, vol. 10, issue 1 (2002), https://www.historyireland.com/18th-19th-century-history/thomas-russell-united-irishman/.

Rahim, Sameer. 'Interview with Seamus Heaney', *Telegraph*, 11 April 2009, https://www.telegraph.co.uk/culture/books/5132022/Interview-with-Seamus-Heaney.html.

Ranelagh, John. *Ireland: An Illustrated History* (London: HarperCollins, 1981).

Rolston, Bill. 'A Lying Old Scoundrel', *History Ireland*, vol. 11, issue 1 (2003).

Rolston, Bill. 'Changing the Political Landscape: Murals and Transition in Northern Ireland', *Irish Studies Review*, vol. 11, issue 1 (2003).

Rowan, Brian. 'Shankill Bomb: A Dark Day amid Talks of Peace', BBC News, 23 October 2018, https://www.bbc.co.uk/news/uk-northern-ireland-45943874.

Royale, Stephen. 'Workshop of the Empire, 1820–1914', in S.J. Connolly (ed.), *Belfast 400: People, Place and History* (Liverpool: Liverpool University Press, 2012).

Russell, Thomas. *A Letter to the People of Ireland, on the Present Situation of the Country* (Belfast: Northern Star Office, 1796), available in its original format at https://books.google.co.uk/books?id=QYiSM2_4vcwC&newbks=0&printsec=frontcover&dq=&hl=en&redir_esc=y#v=onepage&q&f=false.

Ruxton, Dean. '"Belfast Let Itself Go with a Vengeance": Reporting the King's Speech, 1921', *Irish Times*, 22 June 2021, https://www.irishtimes.com/news/ireland/irish-news/belfast-let-itself-go-with-a-vengeance-reporting-the-king-s-speech-1921-1.4600618.

Sharpley, Richard & Philip Stone (eds). *The Darker Side of Travel: The Theory and Practice of Dark Tourism* (Bristol: Channel View Publications, 2009).

Shoard, Catherine. 'Kenneth Branagh Wins First Oscar as *Belfast* Takes Best Original Screenplay', *Guardian*, 28 March 2022, https://www.theguardian.com/film/2022/mar/28/kenneth-branagh-wins-first-oscar-as-belfast-takes-best-original-screenplay.

Simpson, Mark. 'Republican Leaders Featured in New Stormont Exhibition', BBC News, 24 March 2022, https://www.bbc.co.uk/news/uk-northern-ireland-60856442.

Simpson, Mark. 'Seamus Heaney Centre "Did Not Give Permission" to Use Poet's Image', BBC News, 20 December 2020, https://www.bbc.co.uk/news/uk-northern-ireland-55427002.

Smyth, Jim. 'Wolfe Tone's Library: The United Irishmen and "Enlightenment"', *Eighteenth-Century Studies*, vol. 45, issue 3 (2012).

Spencer, Graham. *Disturbing the Peace?* (London: Ashgate, 2000).

Stewart, A.T.Q. 'The Transformation of Presbyterian Radicalism in the North of Ireland 1792–1825', unpublished MA thesis, Queen's University Belfast, 1956.

Stewart, A.T.Q. *The Ulster Crisis* (London: Faber, 1968).

Sunday Times Insight Team. *Ulster* (London: Penguin, 1972).

Taylor, Peter. *Loyalists* (London: Bloomsbury, 1999).

'The Agreement: Agreement Reached in the Multi-Party Negotiations' (Belfast: HMSO, 1998).

The Poetry Foundation. 'Michael Longley', https://www.poetryfoundation.org/poets/michael-longley.

Tinney, Aaron. 'Victims Slam Belfast Terror Tour for "Profiting from Misery and Death"', *Belfast Telegraph*, 12 August 2017, https://www.belfasttelegraph.co.uk/news/northern-ireland/victims-slam-belfast-terror-tour-for-profiting-from-misery-and-death-36024550.html.

Tonge, Jonathan. *Northern Ireland: Conflict and Change* (London: Pearson, 2002).

Ulster-Scots Society of America. 'Ulster-Scots and the Birth of America', http://www.ulsterscotssociety.com/about_ulster-scots.html.

Wade, Wyn Craig. *The Titanic: End of a Dream* (1979), quoted in Ciaran Carson, *The Star Factory* (London: Head of Zeus, 1997).

Whelan, Fergus. *May Tyrants Tremble: The Life of William Drennan, 1754–1820* (Dublin: Irish Academic Press, 2020).

Wohlmuther, Cordula & Werner Wintersteiner (eds). *International Handbook on Tourism and Peace* (Klagenfurt/Celovec, Austria: Centre for Peace Research and Peace Education, 2014).

Woods, C.J. 'Cunningham, Waddell', *Dictionary of Irish Biography*, October 2009, https://www.dib.ie/biography/cunningham-waddell-a2312.

Wright, Alan. 'Hoping for the Best but Preparing for the Worst', *Fortnight*, issue 233, 10–23 February 1986.

Wright, Frank. *Northern Ireland: A Comparative Analysis* (London: Rowman & Littlefield, 1988).

Wroe, Nicholas. 'Literature's Loose Cannon', *Guardian*, 23 March 2002, https://www.theguardian.com/books/2002/mar/23/poetry.academicexperts.

Young, Connla. '50th Anniversary of the Falls Curfew Remembered', *Irish News*, 6 July 2020, https://www.irishnews.com/news/northernirelandnews/2020/07/06/news/50th-anniversary-of-falls-curfew-remembered-1996012/.

INDEX